Coventr

SACRIFICE for STALIN

SACRIFICE for STALIN

The Cost and Value of the
Arctic Convoys Re-assessed

DAVID WRAGG

First published in Great Britain in 2005 by
Pen & Sword Maritime
an imprint of
Pen & Sword Books Ltd
47 Church Street
Barnsley
South Yorkshire
S70 2AS

ISBN 1 84415 357 6

A CIP catalogue record for this book is
available from the British Library.

Typeset by Kirsten Barber,
Leeds, West Yorkshire

Printed and bound in England by
CPI UK

For a complete list of Pen & Sword titles please contact
PEN & SWORD BOOKS LIMITED
47 Church Street, Barnsley, South Yorkshire, S70 2AS, England
E-mail: enquiries@pen-and-sword.co.uk
Website: www.pen-and-sword.co.uk

Contents

Acknowledgements

In researching and compiling any such book as this, an author is heavily dependent on the help and assistance of many others. In particular, I am indebted for the provision of photographs to the Photographic Archive team at the Imperial War Museum and to the Sound Archive for promptly unearthing first hand accounts by those who sailed with the convoys.

No work on something as vast as our wartime history can cover every inch of ground, and for those whose appetite is whetted by this book, I would draw their attention to the bibliography at the back. There are accounts of the war at sea from every perspective, including the all-important personal accounts, as well as volumes of sheer factual matter.

David Wragg
Edinburgh
27 April 2005

Glossary

AA	anti-aircraft
CAM-ship	catapult-armed merchant vessel
CAP	combat air patrol
DEMS	defensively equipped merchant ship
E-boat	German motor torpedo-boat or motor gunboat
HMS	His Majesty's Ship
HMCS	His Majesty's Canadian Ship
KG	*Kampfgeschwader*, *Luftwaffe* equivalent to an RAF Group
Kriegsmarine	German Navy
Luftwaffe	German Air Force
MAC-ship	merchant aircraft carrier (a merchant vessel with a flight deck)
MOWT	Ministry of War Transport
MRA	Maritime Regiment of Artillery
panzerschiff	armoured ship known to the British press as a 'pocket battleship'
RAF	Royal Air Force
RCAN	Royal Canadian Navy
RN	Royal Navy
RNR	Royal Naval Reserve
RNVR	Royal Naval Volunteer Reserve
SBNONR	Senior British Naval Officer North Russia
SO(E)	senior officer, escort
U-boat	German submarine
USAAF	United States Army Air Force
USN	United States Navy
USS	United States Ship

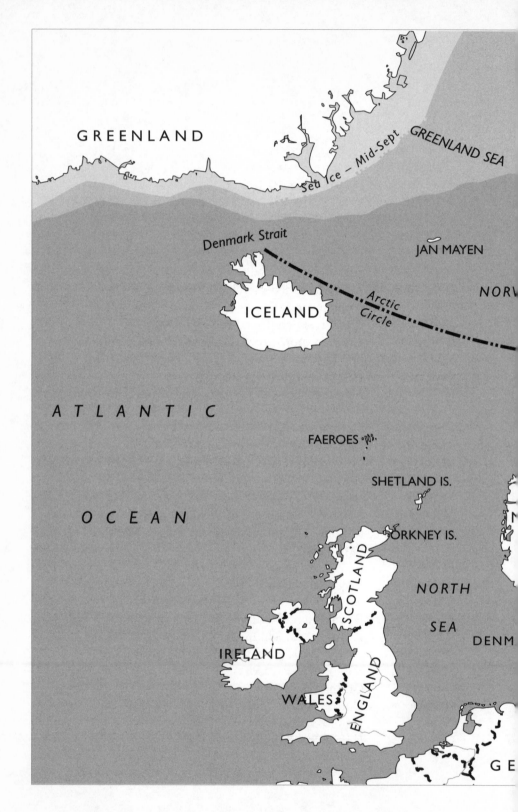

GREENLAND

GREENLAND SEA

Sea Ice – Mid-Sept

Denmark Strait

JAN MAYEN

NORW

Arctic
Circle

ICELAND

NOR

ATLANTIC

FAEROES

SHETLAND IS.

OCEAN

ORKNEY IS.

SCOTLAND

NORTH

SEA

DENM

IRELAND

ENGLAND

WALES

GE

Locations along the Arctic Convoy Route

Introduction

Operation Barbarossa, the German invasion of the Soviet Union in 1941, marked a turning point in the Second World War that was second only to the Japanese attack on Pearl Harbor. Although Stalin had been warned, he had chosen to ignore the warnings, and overnight the Soviet Union was transformed from a country that might not have been an ally of Nazi Germany, but was at the very least a co-conspirator in the occupation of Poland, into an ally of the United Kingdom; but what an ally! This was a country that had already occupied the Baltic States and incorporated them into its own territory, and had been to war with Finland. Comparisons with the Third Reich were not hard to find.

Enemy action apart, the convoys to northern Russia were undoubtedly the grimmest of the convoy routes maintained during the Second World War. On these, sailing past occupied Norway and north of the Arctic Circle, the weather was as much an enemy as the *Kriegsmarine* and the *Luftwaffe*. A total of 811 ships sailed in the Arctic convoys to Russia, of which 720 completed their voyages, another 33 turned back for one reason or another, and 58 were sunk, giving a loss rate of 7.2 per cent. Of the ships that reached Russia, 717 sailed back (some were being delivered to the Soviet Union), and of these, 29 were sunk, a loss rate of 4 per cent. This was the price of delivering to Russia some 4 million tons of war stores, including some 5,000 tanks and more than 8,000 aircraft through the Arctic convoys.

The truth was that the Soviet Union was a demanding ally incapable of seeing the broader picture or of seeing the sacrifices being made by others. Much of the blame for the initial successes of the German thrust eastwards must lie with Stalin, who, pre-war, had purged the Soviet armed forces of many of their best and most experienced senior officers. Although Russian forces had invaded eastern Poland to provide a 'buffer zone' between the Soviet Union and German-occupied territory, Stalin had steadfastly ignored warnings of German intentions and failed to order the appropriate dispositions of his forces.

Soviet demands for help came while the UK was struggling to cope with the demands of war and had seen defeat in Norway and France, Greece and North Africa. The only bright spot was that now Germany was fighting on a new and demanding front, and the first benefit to the British was the ending of the blitz as the *Luftwaffe*'s efforts were redirected to the east.

In London and Washington, the fear was that Stalin might surrender at least part of Soviet territory, allowing the Germans access to much-needed fuel and agricultural produce, and giving them the means of continuing total war against the UK. Stalin desperately needed equipment, and the main route for equipment originating in the UK and the eastern United States was via the treacherous seas around the North Cape to the ports of Archangel and Murmansk.

Here, not only is the operation of the convoys considered, augmented by eye-witness accounts, but for the first time, the whole question of whether or not the sacrifice was worthwhile is examined.

Soviet naval and air force units played little part in the protection of the convoys, leaving this to the Royal Navy and, to a lesser extent, the United States Navy, while the Royal Air Force had to base maritime reconnaissance aircraft in the Soviet Union. Meanwhile, the Royal Air Force had to defend Malaya against Japanese attack using obsolete and at best obsolescent aircraft, including such failures as the American-built Brewster Buffalo, as it was denied the better equipment sent to the Soviet Union.

It was the poor preparation of the German armed forces for the vast distances of the Soviet Union and the harshness of the Russian winter that undid Hitler's plans for conquest. These factors were compounded by the late start due to Hitler having to rescue his Italian ally from the misadventures in the Balkans and by the decision to divide the German advances.

Was British and American equipment really necessary? Few Soviet accounts mention its use, still less its value. In fact, most of the equipment used by the Soviet armed forces was produced in their own factories, although in some areas, such as aircraft, the technology was not state of the art. Could Allied aid have been put to better use elsewhere? Was the sacrifice of so many lives and so many scarce ships on the Arctic convoys worthwhile or a terrible waste at a time when the effective closure of the Mediterranean meant that supplies for the British Eighth Army in North Africa had to be sent via the Cape and the Suez Canal? Would Stalin have surrendered part of his realm?

Here the evidence is examined and argues that without Western help, the Soviet Union could not have moved so quickly in overcoming the German armies, with the result that Soviet occupation of central and Eastern Europe could have been prevented. By helping the Soviet Union, the British and French decision to issue an ultimatum to Germany over the occupation of Poland was a nonsense, because it simply left Poland to exchange one style of jackboot for another.

Chapter 1

Norway and Iceland – the Keys to the Arctic

'The leadership which found the prospect of peace in our time in a small piece of paper was a leadership intensely acceptable to a nation which had made up its mind in 1918 not to fight another war if it could possibly be avoided,' suggested the authors of a Mass Observation report in 1940.

Norway and Iceland figured little, even on the minds of those preoccupied with the prospect of war in Europe. For those who did think about it (and for much of the 1930s they were few in number), the forthcoming war was seen as settling down to a rerun of the previous conflict, with both sides facing each other across a continental battlefield, while at sea the major fleets would engage. In fact, the one difference that was recognized was the threat of air power, for the belief had been nurtured between the two wars that the bomber would always get through.

One reason for ignoring Norway, which had been safely neutral during the Great War, was that the intervention of the Soviet Union was not expected – not, at least, until it occupied the eastern part of Poland in September 1939, after Germany had overrun the west. The Molotov–Ribbentrop Pact was a well-kept secret before the outbreak of war. It was soon to become clear that the agreement between Soviet Russia and Nazi Germany went well beyond the division of Poland, and extended into spheres of influence. Norway was well beyond the reach of the Soviets, and within Norway itself the policy-makers also believed that the country would see the conflict follow similar lines to that of the Great War. Although defence expenditure was reluctantly increased during the two years before the outbreak of war in 1939, it was not enough, and the Norwegian armed forces were too small and still inadequately equipped once war broke out.

1

War was a Nasty Shock

In the UK, the truth was that the first year of war had come as a nasty shock to the British people as pre-war surveys had found an exaggerated belief in the country's strength, and especially in its armaments and defences. The public had been blissfully unaware of the impact of the defence cuts between the wars, and of the impact of the 'Ten Year Rule', which stipulated that the country would have ten years in which to prepare for war, when in fact it had taken just six years from Hitler taking absolute power in Germany to the outbreak of war in Europe, and the first three or four years of this period had been wasted. The British armed forces during the late 1930s were not only weak in numbers, they lacked too much of the latest technology. True, the British Army's 25-pounder field gun was regarded as very good, but on the other hand, its Matilda tank lacked a gun capable of engaging German forces at a worthwhile range. Nazi Germany rearmed and reoccupied the Rhineland, but it was only when Hitler started to make territorial demands that the alarm bells started ringing. Even so, for the mass of people on both sides of the Atlantic Ocean, the major preoccupation for most of the period between the two world wars was the state of the economy. Earlier, in 1932, a British parliamentary by-election saw one candidate fight on a rearmament platform; he lost.

When, during the Munich Crisis of 1938, Chamberlain, the British Prime Minister, waved a piece of paper and announced 'Peace in our time', it was as music to the ears of the man in the street.

There were those who had seen war as inevitable, both in the UK and in the United States. One of these was Winston Churchill, destined to become the British wartime leader. Nevertheless, the threat was to some extent seen differently depending on whether one was in the UK or the United States. Those Britons who saw war coming, viewed Germany as the danger. Their American counterparts often saw the real threat as emerging from Japan. American interest in auxiliary, or escort, aircraft carriers initially arose from the perceived need to transport aircraft across the vast stretches of the Pacific, for the United States Army Air Force, or Air Corps as it was in the 1930s, as much as for the United States Navy. Few foresaw a war in Europe at the same time as one in the Pacific. Between the wars, British governments had even given assurances to the peoples of the dominions of Australia and New Zealand that in the event of a threat emerging

2

in the Far East, a strong British fleet would be sent eastwards to the fortress of Singapore. It was acknowledged that Singapore could only be a strong fortress if occupied by a large fleet.

Germany was not the only threat to peace in Europe. When Italy invaded Abyssinia, present day Ethiopia, in 1935, many believed that the UK and France would go to war with Italy, but the French cavilled and the League of Nations did nothing. So convinced that war would come was the Commander-in-Chief of the British Mediterranean Fleet, that he even had his officers draw up plans for an aerial attack on the Italian Navy's base at Taranto, in the instep of the foot of Italy. His foresight was not wasted as these plans later formed the basis for the successful raid by the Fleet Air Arm in November 1940, but in the meantime nothing was done. The Royal Navy was ordered to keep an eye on Italian shipping movements through the Suez Canal supplying their forces in Abyssinia, but it was not to interfere with shipping, even though it could have closed the Suez Canal to the Italians. In the United States at the time, isolationism was the official policy, and the country was not a member of the League of Nations, even though this had been one of the features of the peace plan formulated by President Woodrow Wilson during the final stages of the Great War.

Isolationism has been a recurring theme in American foreign policy, but it has never been consistent. American intervention in the 'old' world dated from as early as 1816, when a combined British, American and Dutch naval squadron suppressed the Barbary pirates that had preyed upon shipping, mainly in the Mediterranean, being based in North Africa, but also sometimes beyond. The Munro Doctrine was always a doctrine rather than a convention, and was never given a legal basis. It mainly took the view that European nations should confine themselves to the old world, while the United States should confine its interests to the new world.

On both sides of the Atlantic there was concern about the Bolshevik threat. This was felt more strongly in the European nations, not only because they were closer to it and had seen the hardship that had driven many Russians into exile, but because there had been evidence of revolutionary movements in many European countries, such as Germany and Hungary. The threat was taken most seriously in Germany where there had been attempts to create a Soviet-style society in some areas and this had been one of the factors behind the rise of the National Socialist Party. American attitudes to the Soviet Union were ambivalent. There were many who viewed Communism with distaste, but the overthrow of hereditary monarchies appealed to many Americans because of their own republicanism, and many American businessmen were well to the fore in seeking to establish business links with the Soviet Union.

European fears of revolution gave many an opportunity to excuse some of the worst features of Nazi Germany.

Mussolini's Italy was not taken seriously by many, which proved to be a mistake.

Unready for War

If the British public had an exaggerated belief in the strength of their armed forces and their state of readiness, this was as nothing compared to the lack of realism elsewhere in Europe. Strangely, this inability to face facts also occurred in Germany, where the redevelopment and modernization of the armed forces was patchy and piecemeal. The Germans did much to create a strong air force, but the army lacked mechanized transport and even artillery limbers were horse-drawn, while the navy did not expect a war to break out until 1944 or 1945. The situation was far worse in France, the Netherlands and Belgium.

European politicians did not like thinking about war, since it involved committing money to the armed forces and taking decisions over military manpower, including such difficult questions as conscription. They were helped by the fact that, as already mentioned, their electorates did not like thinking about war either. The Great War had been traumatic. It had been the last straw that had finally tipped Russia into revolution, and while the end of the Austro-Hungarian Empire was unlamented, most of Belgium had been occupied, while France from the English Channel to the border with Switzerland had been a front line of a kind never experienced before and on an unprecedented scale.

There was also a recasting of alliances between the wars. Italy had been an ally of the UK, France and the United States in the Great War, but could now be viewed as a potential opponent. Instead of keeping the Adriatic closed to the enemy, Italy now threatened shipping traffic through the Mediterranean and, most of all, the Maltese islands. Japan was another Great War ally that was no longer conforming to what was expected of her. True, Japanese forces had done little during the earlier conflict, but their potential in a global conflict had been emphasized by Japanese victory in the Russo-Japanese war of 1904–05, and especially the great naval victory at Tsushima, which almost unnoticed by the Western powers marked the start of Japan's territorial ambitions in the east.

Tsarist Russia had been an ally in the Great War, but its position in any future conflict was unclear. It was even unclear just how deep the enmity between the newly formed Soviet Union and Nazi Germany was, since during the period of the Weimar Republic, collaboration between the two countries had existed industrially and militarily, enabling Germany to bypass some of the restrictions placed upon it at Versailles. Soviet Russia also maintained trading links with Nazi Germany.

Something can be gathered about the preparedness of the combatants at the outset of the Second World War from their respective descriptions of the first autumn and winter of the war. To the British, this was the period of the 'phoney war'; to the Germans, it was the 'sitting war', *sitzkrieg*. Yet, for the combatant navies and to some extent the air forces, there had been very little phoney about the early months. There had been war at sea from the first day and bombers, at first eschewing civilian targets or even military targets close to centres of population, had laid mines and attempted the occasional attack on shipping. It was only the opposing armies that had been sitting once the Germans and then the Russians had occupied Poland. British and French forces gathered behind the Maginot Line, constructed to protect France after the trauma of the First World War.

Unfortunately, the Maginot Line did not extend all the way from Switzerland to the English Channel – it stopped short, at the border with Belgium. While British and French war plans recognized the importance of providing support for Belgium, Belgium and the Netherlands were both neutral at the time of their invasion. Belgium had no tanks in its army, and just four anti-tank guns. The equipment belonging to its armed forces was poor, and the belief was that in an attack, British and French forces would come to the country's aid. While this was true, there was no system of joint command and there had been no joint exercises. Belgium did not have a true equivalent to the Maginot Line, but its defence was also based on strongly guarded fixed positions, including the forts by the bridges at Eben Emael, overlooking the junction of the Albert Canal and the River Meuse.

The British Army of the interwar years had been relatively small and based on long-service professionals, with a reserve – the Territorial Army. It was generally considered as lacking the ability to expand rapidly in a crisis, and with insufficiently strong and experienced reserve forces. Before the outbreak of war, conscription had been introduced, with rapid expansion of the reserves as well. The British practice was to devolve considerable decision making to the generals in the field.

Scandinavia – the Focal Point

Little could be done to stop the German invasion of Denmark on 9 April 1940. The country was occupied within hours. Pacifist governments had so reduced the nation's defences that resistance was hopeless, and to obtain Danish surrender all that was needed was for three small German transports to sail into the harbour at Copenhagen, the capital, while the main force crossed the frontier.

Norway was a different matter. Norwegian resistance was aided by the harsh climate and inhospitable terrain, and the fact that resistance was possible encouraged the British and the French to send an expeditionary force, but the campaign ended in disaster. At the time, the failure of the Norwegian campaign was just another setback, a waste of opportunity, manpower and all too scarce resources. Had it been possible to foretell the future and see just how important possession of Norway by Germany would be, Britain might have been better off continuing to fight in Norway rather than in France.

If anything should have warned the Germans of the danger of overreaching themselves at an early stage in the war, it was the invasion of Norway. The invasion of both Denmark and Norway was set by Hitler for a full month before the start of the massive onslaught in the West to occupy France and the Low Countries. Both countries had a long history of neutrality.

While Germany needed to secure both countries to ensure the passage of German warships out of the Baltic, rather than depend entirely on the Kiel Canal, which could be blocked, there was an additional reason for invading Norway. Most of Germany's iron ore came from Sweden, but because shipping was interrupted by the Gulf of Bothnia freezing in winter, the best route for the iron ore was into Norway by railway and down the coast. As Hitler already had an

6

invasion of the Soviet Union in mind, occupying Norway would also make it difficult for the Allies to send material via the North Cape to Russian ports.

A further factor that influenced the invasion was the British seizure of the German transport *Altmark*, supply ship for the ill-fated *panzerschiff Graf Spee*, while in Norwegian waters, which resulted in the freeing of many captured British merchant seamen. British operations in Norwegian territorial waters angered the Norwegian government, which had nevertheless tacitly accepted the use of its territorial waters by German shipping.

Norway

For the invasion of Norway, German troops landed from the sea at the major ports of Oslo, Kristiansand, Bergen, Trondheim and Narvik, and air-landed troops arrived at the airports at Oslo and Stavanger. For the most part, this operation went according to plan, but the loss of the troop transport *Bhicker* at Oslo, which carried the main headquarters' staff, allowed the Norwegian government and the King to flee the city, encouraging resistance.

Even before the invasion, the Norwegian Army had started to mobilize, while the Norwegian government asked the UK and France for help. The UK had already played a part in securing Norwegian independence more than thirty years earlier and it was natural that assistance should be provided. Together with France they sent troops, assembling an initial expeditionary force of 13,000, even though it was estimated at the time that an army of at least 50,000 troops would be needed to liberate the country. The ground forces were supported by the Royal Navy and Royal Air Force, with the British Home Fleet dispatched to the area reinforced by a number of warships from the Mediterranean Fleet including the aircraft carrier *Glorious*. Carriers, initially including the UK's newest, HMS *Ark Royal*, and oldest, *Furious*, were necessary both as aircraft transports and because of the limited number of airfields available ashore. Nevertheless, a weakness in this strategy was that in 1940, the Royal Navy had no aircraft embarked on its carriers capable of fending off German fighters.

Initially, all three countries hoped that Sweden would support Norway, but it soon became clear that Sweden intended to maintain its own strict neutrality. Swedish armed intervention on the side of

Norway, given its relatively strong armed forces and its long border with Norway, would almost certainly have made a difference.

The UK and France saw the key to holding Norway as the recapture of Trondheim, from which a counter-attack southwards could repel the invaders. At the outset, the port of Narvik was seen as being the easiest place to take and hold with the limited forces available, since so much of the available trained strength of both nations' armies and air forces was already stationed in France in anticipation of a German attack.

At sea, the Royal Navy soon established control. A destroyer action in Narvik Fjord on 10 April saw two German destroyers and some merchantmen sunk, although later two British destroyers were sunk. That same day, an attack by Fleet Air Arm aircraft operating from the Royal Naval Air Station at Hatston on the mainland of Orkney, sank the cruiser *Konigsberg*, the first loss of a substantial operational warship to air power. Three days later, the veteran battleship HMS *Warspite* and nine destroyers sank the remaining eight German destroyers left in Norwegian waters.

British forces landed near Narvik on 12 April. These troops, under Major-General Mackesy, were expected to seize the town with the support of naval gunfire, but Mackesy had no immediate intention of taking Narvik, preferring to wait for the snow to melt and for reinforcement by a half brigade of French Chasseurs Alpins, already earmarked for other operations. He was also reluctant to cause heavy civilian casualties through the use of heavy naval gunfire, and nothing the naval commander, Admiral Lord Cork, could say or do would make him change his mind.

This left the Germans free to strengthen their defences at Narvik. Meanwhile, British and French troops were landed near Namsos, further south between Narvik and Trondheim, and at Andalsnes, 150 miles south of Trondheim. The intention was for the troops from Namsos to head 100 miles south to Trondheim, so that those at Andalsnes could move north. Unfortunately, four feet of snow hindered the movement of troops from Namsos, while at the same time they had no protection from German air attack. At Andalsnes, the troops were supposed to cut one of the two railway lines running north to Trondheim, but instead they found themselves fighting off repeated German attacks from the south.

On 17 April 1940, faced with a rapidly deteriorating situation, the British War Cabinet decided that the best way of taking Trondheim would be by an amphibious assault, supported by heavy naval fire from battleships and by carrier-borne aircraft. This was a high-risk strategy since the equipment was not available for such an assault (and was not to be ready for some time), while the troops lacked the necessary training and experience. It was not surprising then that the next day, the chiefs of staff decided that the plan involved too many risks and would endanger too many major units of the Royal Navy. This change of mind angered Winston Churchill, later to become the British wartime Prime Minister, but at the time back in his First World War role as First Lord of the Admiralty. Churchill attempted to instil a sense of urgency, pointing out that once the ice in the Gulf of Bothnia thawed, there was a real risk that the Germans would persuade or even force the Swedes to allow troop movements overland by rail. The Secretary of State for War, Churchill's opposite number with responsibility for the British Army, later pointed out that a revised plan, taking Trondheim in a pincer movement, posed almost as much risk as the amphibious assault favoured by Churchill.

This left British and French troops attempting to fight their way through to Trondheim, while Mackesy remained adamant about not taking Narvik. One British brigade managed to get to within 50 miles of Trondheim by 19 April, before the Germans counter-attacked two days later, forcing them back on Namsos, from where it was evacuated on the night of 3 May.

To the south, British and Norwegian forces had joined up at Andalsnes, and eventually managed to advance as far south as Lillehammer, in an attempt to take the railway. Heavy fighting again resulted in retreat. Typical of the attitude at the time was that of a senior commander, who was happy to withdraw in the mistaken belief that if *his* troops found movement through the heavy snow difficult, the Germans surely could not advance! He was wrong and the Allied force was pushed back to Andalsnes, which was evacuated on the night of 1 May.

During the campaign both Namsos and Andalsnes were subjected to heavy bombing by the *Luftwaffe*, who did not share Mackesy's misgivings about causing civilian casualties! Air cover was provided by fighters operating from the aircraft carriers HMS *Ark Royal* and *Glorious*, and by RAF Gloster Gladiators operating from a frozen lake at Lesjeshogen, 40 miles from Andalsnes. A squadron of Hawker Hurricanes, based at an airfield ashore, arrived too late to make a difference, while the Gladiators, the Royal Air Force's last biplane fighters, were no match for the *Luftwaffe*'s Messerschmitt Bf109s.

Narvik was eventually surrounded by more than 20,000 British, French and Polish troops, facing a garrison of just 6,000 Germans, which was finally subjected to a three hour pounding by heavy gunfire from the battleship HMS *Warspite*, and three cruisers on 24 April. Nevertheless, without a coordinated assault, the garrison was able to hold firm.

Finally, when the German invasion of France and the Low Countries started, the British and French decided on 24 May to withdraw from Norway and defend France. The irony was that to evacuate Narvik successfully they had to take the town, which was occupied on 27 and 28 May, using two French Foreign Legion battalions and a battalion of Norwegian troops, all commanded by the French General, Bethouart. A further irony was that the 24,000 British, French, Polish and Norwegian troops who left by 8 June, were too late to save France. Final evidence of the flawed strategy and the misuse of resources came during the withdrawal. Having saved their high performance Hurricanes by successfully landing these aboard the aircraft carrier HMS *Glorious*, many of the RAF personnel and the aircraft were to be lost as the ship was blown out of the water by the two German battle-cruisers *Scharnhorst* and *Gneisenau*.

The Norwegians continued fighting until 9 June, when the country finally surrendered. The one successful outcome was that the operation did give the King and the government time to escape into exile, where they were joined by many members of the Norwegian armed forces and a substantial part of the country's considerable merchant marine.

Winston Churchill blamed much of the failure of the Norwegian campaign on the commanders involved not having got their staff work correct at such an early stage of the war. The rapid advance of the Germans through France and the Low Countries meant that the evacuation at Dunkirk overlapped with that from Norway, and this, with the fall of France, undoubtedly played some part. Even so, Churchill was critical of Mackesy and disappointed that British forces could be defeated by German forces struggling over difficult terrain in conditions of snow and ice, while our forces could land, almost at will, on the Norwegian coastline. He also felt let down by the chiefs of staff, who reversed his ambitious plan for the taking of

Trondheim and replaced it with a more difficult operation, with almost as high a degree of risk.

Yet, the Royal Navy saw the campaign off to a splendid start with clear successes, showing that even if Germany had mastery of the air, it had still to use this to gain control of the seas. Had Mackesy followed his orders, Narvik could have been taken and secured as a base. Unnecessary civilian casualties were something to be avoided, especially at this early stage of the war, before attitudes had hardened. Even so, elsewhere in Norway, towns were being heavily bombed, doubtless with many civilian casualties! The irony is that Narvik eventually was taken and the Allied forces were evacuated!

British and Polish forces could have remained at Narvik, possibly joined by some of their French comrades. Their presence would have been a thorn in the side of the Germans, keeping substantial numbers of troops tied down, along with *Luftwaffe* and naval units. Reinforced, they could have made headway south. The Norwegians were to prove themselves good resistance fighters, and with friendly forces in the north of their country, doubtless would have been encouraged still further.

The initial mistake was to divide forces between Namsos and Andalsnes when these could have been more useful together at Trondheim. After all, these landings were 100 and 150 miles respectively from the objective, and could only be reached by air. To travel by sea or across difficult terrain in bad weather was not an option for the Allies at this stage of the war. Time was not on their side. Waiting for the weather to improve not only meant the possibility of German reinforcements, possibly coming by rail through Sweden, it also gave the Germans time to reinforce their positions at Trondheim, and elsewhere.

A presence even at Narvik would have been invaluable once Hitler invaded the Soviet Union, making the survival of the convoys easier. A presence at Trondheim would have held the prospect of liberating Norway. Without the benefit of foresight, the struggles to fight convoys through to the Soviet Union could not be predicted, but the tragedy was that whoever held Norway held control of the sea routes to Russia by the North Cape. In the Allies' hands this would have meant preventing the Germans from taking the best route in and out of the Baltic; access to Swedish iron ore, the closest source of imported ore to British factories; and not having to use a special unit of BOAC, the British Overseas Airways Corporation, for Mosquito flights carrying ball bearings from Sweden to the UK.

Taking British and French troops from Norway to defend France when that country's fate was already sealed is comparable to the decision to reduce the British forces in North Africa in order to defend Greece, at a time when there was a real prospect of Italian defeat in North Africa. Greece was lost anyway and the division of forces between two theatres was wrong, giving the Germans time to mount a campaign of their own in North Africa and against the Maltese islands. At one time it looked as if in North Africa as well, the Germans would succeed against the British where the Italians had failed.

Iceland

Politically, the situation with Iceland was completely different from that with Norway. Iceland had complete internal self-government, but foreign affairs and defence were handled by Denmark. After Denmark was invaded by German forces, Iceland declared temporary independence and stated that its foreign policy was one of neutrality. The country, with an area of some 32,000 square miles, had a population of around 250,000 and lacked any armed forces.

Concerned that Iceland might be the next to be invaded, aided by a *coup d'état* by German residents, and that ships and aircraft stationed there would be a further obstacle to the hard-pressed Atlantic convoys, the British government offered protection. The offer was refused as the Icelandic authorities feared German retaliation, and as an island with scant natural resources it was dependent on keeping its shipping routes open. Nevertheless, British concern was such that on 10 May 1940, 'Force Sturges' commanded by Colonel Robert Sturges of the Royal Marines landed with less than 900 men to prevent the Germans attempting to seize the country. Assurances were given that there would be no interference in the country's internal affairs. While the Icelandic government issued a formal protest and German citizens were taken into custody, the Icelandic Prime Minister described the UK as 'a friendly nation' and asked the people to 'consider British soldiers as guests'. Canadian troops were landed later, and in July 1941, before the entry of the United States into the war, the Americans took over the occupation of Iceland. The involvement of the United States was largely a political move, partly because it was deemed to be in the Western Hemisphere, and thus an American responsibility under the Munro Doctrine, but also because the British

12

government wished it, as it released British troops for the North African campaign.

Good intentions or not, the British occupation of Iceland was not welcomed by many of the inhabitants, many of whom went as far as to paint Nazi swastika emblems on their houses to emphasize the point. By the time American troops entered Iceland, the welcome was warmer as the inhabitants were more aware of the dangers of German occupation.

Iceland became a major departure point for convoys to the Arctic and also for their escorts. Convoys would be given a light escort, usually from Scotland, and reform in Iceland, often with additional ships from the United States. The light escort would continue once the convoys left Iceland with the main ocean escort following a day or two later as the ships closed to within range of German air power.

Chapter 2

Russia Shows its True Colours

Although Finland had been part of Tsarist Russia, Finnish nationalism had been a force to be reckoned with long before the Russian Revolution. As with many of the ethnic minorities within Russia, the Finns had little in common with other European Russians.

Finnish is a very different language from Russian, being closely related to Magyar, the language of Hungary. Until the nineteenth century, Finnish territory had been the cause of rivalry between Russia and Sweden, before becoming part of Imperial Russia. The Russian Revolution gave the Finns the opportunity for which they had been waiting. Better still, the confusion and lack of effective organization in Russia which followed, including the Russian Civil War, which lasted from 1918 to 1920, meant that the new regime had to accept the loss of Finland. The leaders of the emerging Union of Soviet Socialist Republics had far more pressing objectives at the outset, including annexation of the Ukraine, a country with rich natural resources including fertile farmlands.

The new Soviet Union was also turned in upon itself, with forced collectivization and then the Stalinist purges. Memories of the Allied intervention on the side of the White Russians were still fresh, so there can be little doubt that the Soviet leadership had been left with at least the suspicion that any attempt to invade Finland would result in British and American support for that country. This view was almost certainly correct, for despite massive defence cuts in the UK and growing support for isolationism in the United States, both countries feared the spread of Bolshevism.

The outbreak of war in Europe in September 1939 changed all of this. The time was right, and Finland, with just 4 million people, appeared relatively small and vulnerable to Soviet military superiority. Even before the outbreak of war, the Soviet Union and Germany had

14

negotiated individual spheres of influence, as Winston Churchill recalled: 'Both sides agreed in particular that Finland belonged to the Russian sphere of influence.' The Soviet Union moved quickly to annex its former territories, the Baltic states of Estonia, Latvia and Lithuania, initially insisting on treaties of friendship and cooperation, and then in June 1940, garrisoning greater numbers of troops there than existed in the armies of the individual nations. Within months, the governments of the three small nations had been replaced and the territories incorporated into the Soviet Union.

Finland was next. Having taken his share of Poland, Stalin next moved to seize Finland. Starting in November 1939, the so-called Winter War saw Finland cede some of its territory, but the numerically inferior Finnish forces prevented outright victory and cost the Soviet Union an estimated 200,000 men, 1,600 tanks and more than 700 aircraft. In his desire to rebuild Russia's empire and dominate the eastern end of the Baltic, Stalin frittered away many assets that would be desperately needed in the years to come.

The Soviets Seize the Opportunity

Finland was poorly prepared for war, with an army of just ten divisions plus some special units. It had only thirty-six pieces of artillery of Great War vintage for each division and was also short of automatic weapons. The saving grace was that the infantry had been trained to make the best use of the terrain. The winter snow was seen as a more likely time of year for an invasion as in the summer months the swampy terrain would make movement by heavy armour difficult. Economically, the country had scant natural resources, and plans for rationing were laid as early as September 1939, not in direct anticipation of being embroiled in the war, but because it was recognized that a European war could mean the interruption of supplies and normal trading patterns.

Put under pressure by the Soviet Union in late 1939, the Finns refused to cede territory or their independence, even though the Soviet Union established a Finnish Peoples' Government-in-Exile. Between 12 October and 9 November 1939, representatives of the Finnish government held talks in Moscow with Stalin and the Soviet foreign minister, Vyacheslav Molotov. The Soviet demands were aimed at providing greater defence in depth so that an attacker moving through Finland could be stopped before reaching Leningrad,

15

which meant moving the frontier more than 40 miles into Finnish territory, and also taking control of a number of islands in the Gulf of Finland. The port of Hanko, to the west of the capital, Helsinki, was to be leased to the Soviet Union for thirty years to become a naval base that could close the Gulf of Finland. Other territorial concessions in the north were intended to provide a buffer zone to protect the port of Murmansk. Concerned that granting such concessions could be the thin end of the Soviet wedge, the Finns refused to cede any territory.

A contrived frontier incident on 26 November 1939, led to war starting four days later as Soviet forces advanced into Finland. Civilians had already been evacuated from the frontier areas in Finnish Karelia, while the period of negotiations had enabled the army to be mobilized. The Finnish commander, Marshal Baron Carl Gustav von Mannerheim had established the Mannerheim Line of defences across the Karelian isthmus, with forty-four strong points based on concrete bunkers, although lacking heavy artillery or anti-tank weapons.

The Soviet view was that the invasion would be welcomed by Finnish industrial workers and peasants, and that the Leningrad military district would have sufficient resources to win the campaign. Little assistance for Finland was expected from the UK and France, and in this respect at least, Soviet rationale was right. It was a good indication of the weakness of the democracies that, despite Soviet participation in the invasion of Poland and clear aggression against its small neighbours, it was not until 14 December 1939, after the Russo-Finnish War, or 'Winter War', had started, that Russia was expelled from the League of Nations, the unsuccessful and toothless interwar predecessor of the United Nations.

Having seen German strategy work in Poland, the Russians were under the impression that blitzkrieg tactics would win the day. It was not just that they had done so for Germany in the invasion of Poland, which had allowed the Soviet Union to invade its agreed portion of that country, once its heroic, but antiquated, armed forces had been crippled by the German onslaught. The truth was that Soviet and German tactics had much in common. Both believed in the concept of blitzkrieg, or lightning war, with the air forces, although not actually part of their armies, tasked with army support as their main function. Both armies believed in the tank and the paratrooper – indeed, the Russians had been the leaders in developing the concept of airborne

16

assault, even if it fell to the Germans to put this into practice a little later.

But Finland was not Poland, and the time of year also meant that the meteorological conditions were not auspicious for attack.

Russia Attacks

The Soviet Union devoted twenty-six divisions of the Red Army to the invasion of Finland, consisting of 1.2 million men, equivalent to more than a quarter of Finland's pre-war population, with 3,000 aircraft and 1,500 tanks initially, and supported by artillery and road transport. Problems of communication, supply, command and control, prevented the entire force being deployed at once, while much of the terrain was impassable for tanks and there were few roads for the lorries. Training had been inadequate and there were no ski-equipped troops, but worse still was the fact that the Soviet armed forces had been purged of many of their best senior officers, and in particular those with the most imagination and decisiveness in command. Much necessary equipment was missing, including white winter camouflage clothing and protection for equipment in sub-zero conditions.

Russian technology at the time was relatively primitive – the result both of the isolation of the country for the first twenty years after the Revolution and the loss of many of the best and most inventive minds such as the pioneer of large flying boats and, later, helicopters, Igor Sikorsky. Yet, given the equipment of the day, it would have been hard to find vehicles suitable for the Arctic conditions encountered by Russian troops. No one dared object, regardless of their rank, for the Stalinist purges had already seen the army lose upwards of half its officers, including many of the most experienced. Military questions were, in any case, subordinate to political ones, with each unit having a political commissar who could overrule its commanding officer. Troops were told that if they became prisoners of war, they would be imprisoned on being released, and that if they failed to achieve their objectives, their families would suffer. The cruelty of the regime was enough for these arguments to be convincing. In battle, many committed suicide rather than surrender.

'I'm so absorbed in the work that I don't even notice the days pass,' wrote Lev Zakharovich Mekhlis, a political commissar with the Red Army to his wife in late 1939. 'I sleep only 2–3 hours. Yesterday it was minus 35 degrees below freezing ... I feel very

17

well ... I have only one dream – to destroy the White Guards of Finland. We'll do it. Victory's not far off.'

The frozen Finnish tundra and forest was not the sun-baked Polish plain. Weapons and vehicles were unusable, including the tanks on which the Russians were to depend so heavily. The tanks skidded on the ice. Motor vehicles became embedded in snowdrifts up to 10 feet deep. Beneath the snow in some areas, the ground was swampy during the day, and men who sank into this mess during the day were frozen in it by night as temperatures plummeted after dark. The transport system could not keep pace with the demand for food – so important in such freezing conditions. Soldiers immobilized by their wounds, froze to death before they could be taken to a medical centre. On the other hand, if they could walk, as reported in the case of a wounded Finn, shot six times in the chest, they survived to receive medical help because, in the low temperatures, wounds bled so slowly.

The Russians had not even made the most elementary preparations, despite the size of the Soviet armed forces and Russia's vast Arctic regions. The troops sent into battle lacked adequate clothing, suitable tents or even any tents at all in many cases. The transport system was not capable of sustaining combat, and no forward reserves of food, fuel or munitions were established. Russian infantry had to march the 200 miles from the railway at Murmansk, and lost a substantial part of its strength as men dropped out through frostbite. By contrast, the heavily outnumbered Finns had mobility – with good quality skis and clothing.

The initial Russian assault on the Mannerheim Line was quickly checked, while further north, two incursions at Salla and Suomussalmi were repulsed. After the initial setbacks, the Russians renewed their assault in February, with an artillery barrage and advance at Summa in the south. Due to their overwhelming force, on 14 February, 1940, Soviet forces overran Finland's forward positions. Despite fierce Finnish resistance, on 26 February, the Finns lost the island fortress of Koivisto. They were also forced to retreat from the port of Petsamo, north of the Arctic Circle. A second assault in the south, across the frozen Gulf of Finland cutting off the town of Viipuri, led the Finnish government to put out peace feelers on 6 March.

Given the closed nature of Soviet society, and the desire to keep bad news away from anyone in authority, reliable statistics did not materialize. Recent and impartial estimates of Soviet losses suggest 200,000 men, some 700 aircraft and 1,600 tanks. However, during the 1950s, Stalin's successor, Nikita Krushchev, claimed that a million Russian soldiers had died in the campaign, against a known 25,000 Finnish troops killed and sixty-one aircraft destroyed. He also claimed that Russia had lost more than 1,000 aeroplanes, more than 2,000 tanks and vast quantities of supplies. Krushchev, of course, had every reason to exaggerate the losses in his campaign to discredit the Stalin regime (if such a campaign was truly necessary), but there can be little doubt that this was a bloody campaign with much waste.

Throughout, the Finns fought a highly mobile war, with well-equipped and well camouflaged troops. Neither side could be pleased with the outcome. The Soviet Union failed in its objective, but when peace came in this short war, on 13 March 1940, Finland had to cede the Karelia isthmus and a major military base in the Hanko Peninsula, as well as the town of Viipuri, to Russia.

As we will see later, coming on top of the losses incurred through the Stalinist purges, these losses also placed the Soviet forces in poor condition to face the future threat from Germany. Indeed, the impression this gave of Soviet bungling and incompetence led Hitler to believe that Operation Barbarossa, the invasion of the Soviet Union, could not fail. Stalin's paranoia and self-delusion nearly proved him right! In fact, the benefit derived from the war with Finland lay mainly in securing the approaches to the Arctic port of Murmansk, which was to become a lifeline for the Soviet Union once Germany invaded.

Alarmed by the Red Army's inability to crush even a smaller neighbour against whom it had overwhelming numerical superiority, Stalin turned to Marshal Semyon Timoshenko, who was given the task of reforming and rebuilding the Soviet Army.

The consequences for Finland were also very serious. The country was effectively cut off from what would have been its natural allies in the West. Sweden insisted on neutrality and would not help. The result was that the country came to depend on Germany for arms and equipment with which to counter any possible future Soviet onslaught. At first, the launch of Operation Barbarossa, the German invasion of the Soviet Union, helped Finland, with the recovery of those areas ceded in the peace of March 1940. Nevertheless, Finnish independence and the desire for neutrality also asserted itself when, in August 1941, the Germans asked the Finnish General Mannerheim to advance beyond the recovered territory and cut off Leningrad – he refused.

Chapter 3

Burying His Head
in the Sand

'Altogether, 36,671 officers were executed, imprisoned or dismissed, and out of the 706 officers of brigade commander and above, only 303 remained untouched,' wrote the historian Anthony Beevor in his prize-winning book, *STALINGRAD*. 'The most prominent victim was Marshal Mikhail Tukhachevsky, the leading advocate of mobile warfare. His arrest and execution also represented the deliberate destruction of the Red Army's operational thinking, which had encroached dangerously upon Stalin's preserve of strategy.'

Since the end of the Second World War, the British have often been critical of the way in which successive governments between the two world wars allowed the nation's defences to be neglected. The wildly optimistic 'Ten Year Rule' had been adopted as official policy and maintained that the nation would have ten years in which to prepare for war, yet in 1939 only six years had elapsed since Adolf Hitler had assumed absolute power in Germany. In the Soviet Union, the situation had been different. Belief in world revolution, the threat of rebellion in many of the nations subjugated unwillingly into the Soviet Union after the Russian Civil War, and the desire to reclaim those countries that had used the war to declare their own independence, such as Poland, Finland and the Baltic states, all combined to ensure that the Soviet Union was only a decree away from a war footing. The unrest in post-First World War Germany and the friction between opposing ideologies had only confirmed Soviet anxieties, and once Hitler assumed absolute power, the Soviet Union knew that it must prepare for war.

The period from the end of the First World War up until 1933 had nevertheless been a time of considerable German–Soviet cooperation. The Treaty of Versailles had severely limited German plans for defence and for defence-related industry. The size of both the army and the navy was limited, and Germany was banned from operating military aircraft, indeed from having an aircraft industry at all. Determined not to lose their world-class expertise, German designers and industrialists simply moved abroad, continuing their work in other European countries, including the Soviet Union. What might be described as Soviet *realpolitik* saw liaison between German and Soviet officers, with the former able to conduct experiments and studies in the Soviet Union. Not that the Soviet Union was completely without innovation and ideas itself, with the early experiments in the use of paratroops conducted there. For the Soviet Union, these contacts could have offered the incalculable benefit of dragging Soviet industry into the twentieth century. Many of the leading Russian engineers and designers had left following the Revolution, with perhaps the best known among them being Igor Sikorsky, who had built and flown the first large aircraft in 1913 and 1914, and who was to be a leading pioneer in flying boat and amphibian development while in the United States, before becoming effectively the father of the helicopter.

What weakened the Soviet position and made so many of the preparations pointless, was the series of damaging purges that Stalin inflicted upon the armed forces.

Industrial Weakness

The effects of the First World War, revolution and civil war, and the brutal nationalization programme that followed, had so undermined the economy that it was not until 1929 that coal production reached the levels recorded in 1913, while the same applied to iron and steel output. Rapid industrialization of the economy was boosted by a series of five-year plans, although a lack of entrepreneurial flair and poor infrastructure all combined to ensure that the targets in these plans were seldom, if ever, met, despite propaganda claims that the 1929–33 five-year plan had laid the foundations of an armaments industry. The Germans created what was in effect a shadow aircraft industry within the Soviet Union, while the Americans helped the Russians create a motor industry. The Germans acted through self-interest, planning to repatriate their developments once the international situation allowed, but, despite antipathy to Bolshevism as a political creed, many Americans did not share the hostility towards the Soviet Union that many Europeans possessed. Many

21

Americans simply saw yet another European monarchy crumbling and a republic taking its place. They also saw the potential of the vast Soviet market and the rich natural resources of the country.

Hitler's rise to power was a call to arms and a warning for the Soviet Union. It meant that military-might became a fundamental objective, even if it meant starving the Russian people themselves. Airfields were more important than homes, tanks more important than improved public transport, let alone cars. It was also a reflection that a counter-revolution could be a possibility. Just as many of the Soviet Politburo believed that the Soviet Union should export Communism, others believed that a newly aggressive and dominant Germany might want to export Fascism. The dominance of Fascist beliefs in Italy, which had been a model for Hitler, and then, later, in Spain, only showed that the creed of National Socialism could not only be planted elsewhere, but had in fact done so and taken root. The threat boosted Stalin's paranoia. Germany's annexation of Austria and much of Czechoslovakia, before Austria was swallowed whole in 1940, also caused warning bells to ring in the Kremlin. Even worse was the emergence of what effectively amounted to puppet states in Hungary and Romania, with the latter bringing with it the Ploesti oilfields.

The paradox was that Hitler and Stalin had much in common, apart from being dictators. Fascism, or to give it its true name of National Socialism, was not 'right', while Communism certainly was 'left' as both were left wing doctrines and both subjugated the rights and freedoms of the individual to the needs of the state. Both involved strict state control and direction, but National Socialism allowed the accumulation of wealth and allowed industry to remain largely in private hands provided that it fitted into the overall plan. While both dictators were ruthless, much of the evidence suggests that Stalin was the more cunning and devious. Certainly, being close to Stalin was never as safe for the individuals concerned as being close to Hitler.

The position of the two nations was far from similar. Germany had technology, but relatively limited natural resources apart from coal. The Soviet Union had considerable natural resources, although its oilfields were largely undeveloped, and the major breadbasket of the Ukraine. It also had massive quantities of manpower, but it was still under-industrialized and despite injections of support from the West, was still behind in technology.

Political differences may have been ones of degree to those accustomed to Western democracy and free speech, but between the two nations these were of fundamental importance. The Spanish Civil War gave both parties the chance to exercise their muscles on the battlefield and in the air above it. This was the last straw for any cooperation between the two countries. It was all the more surprising that the two nations came together again in the Molotov–Ribbentrop Pact, signed in secret, but both parties had much to gain. For both Germany and the Soviet Union, the Nazi–Soviet pact bought time. It meant that Germany would not have to face the danger of fighting the Soviet Union once the campaign in France began, and meanwhile it would not have to over-extend its lines of supply and stretch the armed forces too much by having to take and garrison the whole of Poland. For the Soviet Union, it brought back some of the territory lost during the civil war, and brought vital additional territory to increase the defence in depth of the region. This latter argument was many years later to lie behind Soviet intervention to curb nationalist movements in first Hungary and then Czechoslovakia. Nevertheless, what happened next was inexplicable. Stalin received many warnings about German intentions.

Ignoring the Warnings

Despite warnings from the West, which he instinctively distrusted, Stalin refused to prepare to fend off an invasion. The non-aggression pact with Germany meant that local commanders had no initiative or flexibility granted to them. Incredibly, Stalin had seized Poland to provide depth in which an invasion could be warded off, and had even driven a salient beyond Lvov to protect the vital Ukraine. He had warned that a spring offensive was likely, but still insisted that nothing should be done that might provoke a German response. This applied in the air as well as on the ground, with reconnaissance flights limited. The Soviet Union even continued to supply its future enemy with grain and oil up to the very day of the invasion. German ships were able to use Murmansk for refuelling, and earlier the German commerce-raider *Komet* had been rescued by Soviet ice-breakers after being trapped in the ice.

Stalin was desperately trying to buy time. The cost of the Winter War meant that the Red Army was stretched, with the 170 divisions deployed in the west not adequately supported and spread too thinly across Poland. The Red Army had lost almost 37,000 officers in the purges, further inhibiting initiative among those who remained. Despite the growing German menace, one can only assume that with the spring past and summer moving on, Stalin had assumed that Germany would wait until the following year, despite warnings by his own agents. Possibly, Stalin had expected some new reconciliation of his political interests and those of Hitler.

Yet the omens were there. Germans resident in the Soviet Union had already sent their families home. A prominent anti-Nazi had warned an American diplomat in Berlin as early as January 1941, and this information was eventually passed to Moscow. British 'Ultra' intelligence was already being decoded at Bletchley Park, and this information was also passed on to Stalin. As late as 18 June, the Lucerne-based 'Lucy' spy-ring, which comprised a German, a Russian, a Swiss and a Briton, had passed on a warning, indeed, given full details of the impending campaign including troop movements. Finally, a German deserter gave the date as Sunday 22 June. All of this was ignored, possibly because of Stalin's suspicions of the Western powers, or because he believed that it was an elaborate hoax, or because of his arrogant conceit that he could respond effectively to any attack – it is impossible to know. Another explanation could have been that he was in a state of denial.

Stalin trusted no one. Sir Stafford Cripps, the British ambassador in Moscow, believed that the Nazi–Soviet pact would collapse. When he pointed out to Stalin that, in default of an Anglo-Russian alliance, there could be a temptation for the UK to make its own peace with Germany, it was taken by Stalin as evidence that there was a British plot designed to draw the Soviet Union into war with Germany.

Invasion

Germany invaded the Soviet Union on 22 June 1941, starting at 03.15, attacking along a line drawn from the Baltic in the north to the Carpathian Mountains in the south. Belatedly, Stalin had ordered that all units were to be decentralized and camouflaged, but this message was received too late for the various headquarters to pass the message on to all units in time. The Soviet Union had some 18,000 aircraft, although only a fifth of those could have been regarded as modern, and many of the pilots were still undergoing training. Half of the aircraft were deployed in the West. Against this figure of around 9,000 Soviet aircraft, the *Luftwaffe* had 1,945 aircraft, with 1,400 immediately ready for combat, including 510 bombers, 290 dive-bombers, 440 fighters, 40 fighter-destroyers (fighter-bombers) and 120 long-range reconnaissance aircraft. This force was in three air fleets: *Luftflotte 1* under General Keller was assigned to Army Group North; *Luftflotte 2* under Field Marshal Kesselring was assigned to Army Group Central; and *Luftflotte 4* under General Lohr was assigned to Army Group South. The total *Luftwaffe* strength was augmented by that of Germany's allies, giving another 1,000 aircraft. Romania sent 423 aircraft, while Finland, still recovering from its war with the Soviet Union, sent 317, although only 41 of these were bombers. The Italian *Regia Aeronautica* sent a hundred aircraft to operate in the southern zone, operating as the *Comando Aviazione*, the air command of the Italian Expeditionary Force, but these did not arrive until late July! *Luftflotte 4* also had the Hungarian 'Express Corps' with a fighter and a bomber squadron, as well as some reconnaissance units, and the Croatian Air Legion, with a fighter group and a bomber group, another fifty or sixty aircraft.

From the start, the *Luftwaffe* caught most of the Soviet airfields by surprise, and a second wave was launched as the main attack, with 637 bombers and 231 fighters attacking 31 Soviet airfields. Later in the morning, 400 bombers attacked 35 Soviet airfields. Altogether, these 66 airfields accounted for seventy per cent of the Red Air Force's strength in the west. One Red Air Force officer, Lieutenant General Kopets, lost 600 aircraft without making any impact on the Germans, and committed suicide on 23 June. Almost half the Red Air Force aircraft were believed to have been non-operational on the first day of the invasion.

The Russian tactics as the German advance got under way showed considerable desperation. When Second Lieutenant S. Y. Sdorovzev found that, despite scoring hits on an He111 bomber, the aircraft continued to fly, he approached the bomber from the rear, and inserted his propeller into the He111's elevator. He tried again, and this time managed to get the aircraft to crash, before flying back to his base, a distance of almost 50 miles, with a damaged propeller.

Nevertheless, the *Luftwaffe* and the *Wehrmacht* failed to make the most of their technical superiority and their strategic advantage. In the first few months of the air campaign in support of Barbarossa, the *Luftwaffe* came across large marching columns of Russian troops and substantial troop concentrations. With the ground on either side of the roads baked hard in the summer heat, this was also being used as a roadway, so that often the roads were as much as 100 yards wide. Yet, because of a shortage of anti-personnel bombs, the *Luftwaffe* was unable to press home all the advantages which aerial supremacy had granted it. There is little doubt that the inability to disrupt these troop concentrations was a contributory factor at Moscow and Stalingrad.

The battles of envelopment which arose where strong Russian forces were trapped in large pockets by rapidly advancing German Panzer units, usually supported by small contingents of motorized infantry, might have been overcome had the *Luftwaffe* had the aircraft and the paratroops to act quickly, but these had been lost in the invasion of Crete. This meant that the more energetic and confident Russian commanders could often break out. There were at least seven major pockets of Russian ground forces. The Germans captured 2,256,000 Russian soldiers, 9,336 tanks and 16,179 artillery pieces, but again, these figures could have been much higher, especially for manpower.

When the weather began to change, the *Luftwaffe* faced serious operational difficulties. Some idea of the problems suffered because of the severity of Russian winter comes in extracts from a report written by Lieutenant General H. J. Rieckoff. This refers to the *Luftwaffe*'s experience during the winter of 1941–42, when the temperatures in the theatre stayed between minus 30 and minus 50 degrees centigrade for periods of several weeks, relieved only by those occasions when temperatures plunged to minus 70 degrees! The General commented that, for the most part, the problems were at their most serious when aircraft were on the ground, being prepared for operations:

> ... extensive icing of wings and tail assemblies ... cannot be removed manually ... Canvas covers are used to protect smaller aircraft ... a completely inadequate measure because the covers themselves freeze stiff and are then almost impossible to handle, especially when ... there is a violent wind. Closed ... hangars are rarely available. The attempt to prevent ice forming ... with water repellent oils has failed due to the shortage of lubricant supplies ... Snow-skid landing gear has proved ineffective except for the Fieseler Storch ... which can be kept ready under any snow conditions by this method.

The report also noted that the cold affected engines when they were started up, requiring precise observation of the instructions for a successful cold start, which was done by feeding a lubricant diluted with gasoline to the engine while starting. It took some twenty minutes of flying time for the gasoline additive to evaporate and for the engine to run at normal oil temperature. Often the problems were encountered with equipment used to start the engines, as oil froze in the pipes of the equipment rather than the problems being with the engines themselves. To improve matters, sometimes fires were started under aircraft and start-up equipment. Great care was needed as the starters' shafts sometimes broke if engaged abruptly. Propellers sometimes iced-up during flight, and on occasion damage occurred to aircraft and injuries were incurred among their crews from flying chunks of dislodged ice.

The report was comprehensive. The instruments of the aircraft seemed to cope very well with the cold, as did the communications equipment, although this did suffer badly from the effects of moisture. Aircraft guns, on the other hand, did not like the cold, usually because the oil lacked resistance to the low temperatures, while electrically-guided weapons suffered from the effects of condensation. Given a depth of snow of 3 feet or more, short-fused bombs, whether high explosive or fragmentation, were much less effective as the snow muffled the effects of the explosion. It was also noted that up to 75 per cent of the detonators on fragmentation bombs failed to work in deep snow, although they remained active and acted as land mines! Frozen hard ground shattered high explosive bombs without them exploding.

The Germans used one or two-piece sheepskin flying suits, which proved to be cumbersome if the wearer had to walk any distance, such as after an emergency landing. Thermal suits, apparently, were worse. They required attention in regulating temperatures, while being so fragile that they could be damaged in an emergency landing, after which, of course, they provided the wearer with little protection against the cold. The suggestion was made that lightweight fur or camel hair clothing, with waterproof linings, should be provided instead of leather (a material which the Germans loved to wear normally). Russian boots made of felt were regarded as more practical than German fur boots, which did not fit tightly enough. Good anti-slip soles were also required.

Between the start of Operation Barbarossa and mid-May 1942, the *Luftwaffe* lost almost 3,000 aircraft and another 2,000 were badly damaged. Of the losses, 1,026 were bombers and another 762 were fighters. Meanwhile, the Russians had gathered 3,164 aircraft on the Soviet Western Front, of which more than 2,100 were of modern design. A new commanding officer, General A. A. Novikov, took command of Red Air Force units on the front. A further indication of the way the tide was turning came from the battles around Kharkov in mid-May, when the Germans were outnumbered with their 1,500 aircraft facing twice as many Soviet aircraft.

A comparatively rare series of *Luftwaffe* strategic bombing raids on the Eastern Front was by the bomber wings of *Luftflotte 4*, under Field Marshal von Richtofen. On 3 June 1943 they raided the Molotov Collective Combine in Gorki, one of the few major armaments plants left west of the Urals after the massive evacuation of Soviet war industry to the east of the Urals. This was a major tank factory, reputedly producing 800 T-34 tanks per week, on a site about 2.5 miles square. At 20.00, 168 bombers, mainly He111s of the 3rd, 4th, 27th, 55th and 100th bomber wings, took-off from their base at Briansk, just within reach of the target. Most of the aircraft were carrying 1.7 to 2.4 ton mine bombs, but there were also large quantities of fragmentation, high explosive and incendiary bombs.

This was intended to be a precision bombing attack using the new *Lofte 7D* homing device, which was newly operational, although they also navigated using the Moscow transmitter, avoiding the city by flying in a wide arc to keep clear of its anti-aircraft defences. At midnight, 149 aircraft reached the target and began dropping 224 tons of bombs from altitudes between 13,000 and 20,000 feet. Five aircraft were shot down. This was the first in a series of raids, designed to help prepare the way for the summer offensive. The second raid was on the night of 4/5 June, sending 128 aircraft to the target, where they dropped 179 tons of bombs for the loss of just two aircraft. A third raid followed on the night of 5/6 June, with 154 bombers dropping 242 tons of bombs for the loss of one aircraft. Finally, on the night of 7/8 June, twenty bombers dropped 39 tons of bombs.

The result, according to German intelligence, was that production was suspended for six weeks, but others claimed that little disruption occurred. Two nights later, 9/10 June, 109 bombers were sent on another long-range operation to bomb the synthetic rubber plant at Yaroslavl. They dropped 109 tons of bombs.

It was to no avail. On 12 July 1943, Soviet forces mounted a massive counter offensive. From this time onwards the Germans were on the defensive. Hitler had other priorities by this time. Following the Allied invasion of Sicily two days earlier, he transferred important elements of the *Luftwaffe* from the Eastern Front to Italy, doubtless to the immense pleasure and relief of those involved.

Operation Barbarossa had been delayed because of the German armed forces' heavy commitments in Yugoslavia and Greece, where they had to take over after the Italians failed to occupy these two countries. Some commentators also believe that the operation could not have started much earlier because of the time needed for the ground to harden, having been too soft for tanks and other heavy vehicles after the winter snow had thawed. Nevertheless, the late start meant that the Germans were overtaken by the harsh winter before they had met their objectives. That such a supposedly efficient nation should have allowed their armed forces to advance so far into Russia without adequate precautions for the winter months almost beggars belief.

The failure to allow the Panzer units to advance even further ahead of the infantry has been mentioned by some as one reason for the slow progress across Russia, but even if this had been allowed, infantry would have been required to deal with prisoners, and this could only have been overcome by using paratroops. Both the *Luftwaffe* and the Red Air Force practised a strategy of operating in close support of ground forces, which would have been ideal had greater progress been made.

Most of Russia's heavy industry had been moved east of the Urals before the outbreak of war, and so once again the Germans reaped the bitter harvest of not being able to mount a truly strategic heavy bombing offensive.

The many omissions in the planning and execution of Barbarossa are all the more difficult to understand because one of the compelling reasons for mounting the campaign was to secure vital strategic supplies rather remain dependent on Soviet willingness to trade.

Chapter 4

Convoys

There was nothing new about the concept of a convoy, which dates from Roman times and was also used by the Spanish to protect ships trading with their colonies in the Americas from attacks by pirates. The concept continued through the Napoleonic wars, and the Royal Navy has been criticized for being reluctant to introduce convoys during the Great War.

Convoys were never compulsory, but it would have been a foolish master or shipowner who would not seize the opportunity if it presented itself, unless his ship was so fast that its security lay in its speed.

During the Second World War the nature of the convoys varied enormously. The heaviest attacks were almost certainly encountered by those crossing the Mediterranean to Malta, but the worst weather by far was on the Arctic convoys to the Soviet Union. The cruiser, HMS *Sheffield*, had the metal of one of her gun turrets folded back by a wave that crashed on to the ship.

Defensive measures for the convoys were developed. The British 2-pdr multiple pom-pom proved to be one of the most effective anti-aircraft (AA) weapons of the war, but even so, Oerlikons from Switzerland and Bofors from Sweden proved to be necessary, and both sides licensed these for production. Improved anti-submarine tactics included depth charge throwers, among them the 'hedgehog', which could throw the charges ahead of the ship.

New types of ship were developed, some even before war broke out. These included the sturdy corvettes based on the hull form of a commercial whaler, which were slower than a destroyer, but coped better with rough seas. The high speed of a destroyer was wasted on most convoys, plodding along at 6–8 knots. The need for more effective and larger ships saw the frigate reinvented for AA and anti-submarine duties. While the pride of the British Merchant Navy, the new ocean liners RMS *Queen Mary* and *Queen Elizabeth*, were needed as fast troopships, lesser vessels were converted to become armed merchant cruisers. But these suffered badly when they encountered German surface raiders, and many of those that did survive were converted to become AA ships.

The need for effective defence against submarines and aircraft saw the introduction of the merchant aircraft carriers, MAC-ships, with a basic flight deck laid over the decks of tankers or grain carriers. The tankers were able to carry three anti-submarine Swordfish biplanes, and the grain carriers four, while both continued to carry most of their normal cargo. Other merchant vessels became catapult-armed merchantmen, CAM-ships, with a single Hurricane fighter flown by pilots drawn from the RAF's Merchant Service Fighter Unit, initially augmented by a few Fleet Air Arm pilots. Best of all were the escort carriers, converted from merchantmen or, later, based on merchant hulls, able to carry both fighters and anti-submarine aircraft, and which were warships in the full sense.

Merchant vessels were armed, so that by March 1941, the Admiralty defensively equipped merchant ship (DEMS) organization had equipped 3,434 ships with anti-submarine guns and had also put one or more close range AA guns on 4,431 British and Allied ships. Initially, naval ratings and army gunners were seconded, but later merchant seamen were trained to take their place. The army gunners were members of the Maritime Regiment of Artillery. Initially, merchant ships received light AA armament, but many later received guns of up to 4-in calibre so that they could confront a U-boat on the surface.

Tankers were prime targets and so resorted to 'disguising' themselves. A dummy funnel was installed amidships and the tanker's own funnel aft was cut down and fitted with a spark arrester. They thus assumed the appearance of an ordinary freighter and became less attractive to the enemy. This action did not guarantee safety from attack, but it did mean that they were no longer at risk of being singled out.

Basically, on the North Atlantic, a MAC-ship was adequate once clear of German maritime reconnaissance aircraft shuttling between occupied France and Norway. On the Arctic convoys and across the Bay of Biscay, bombers were as big a hazard as U-boats, so escort carriers were needed. For the Mediterranean, where most convoys became fleet actions, fleet carriers were needed.

31

The Arctic Convoys

The early convoys to the Soviet Arctic were given the prefix 'PQ', while those on the return run were prefixed 'QP', which seems logical for convoys running in the return direction. The initials 'PQ' were chosen because these were the initials of Commander Peter Quellyn Russell, an Admiralty planner. While on many routes, convoys were loaded in one direction only, and return convoys were simply important because they returned 'the empties', this was not always the case. On the routes across the North Atlantic and to the Empire, convoys from the UK included many ships that were loaded with manufactured goods and other products, including whisky, for both the Empire and the United States. People working in such export industries were assured by official propaganda that they too were doing their bit for the war effort; the UK was short enough of foreign exchange as it was. The convoys to the Soviet Union, to Malta and to Alexandria in particular, also brought vital war supplies to these areas, and in the case of the Soviet Union, supplies that the UK was hard-pressed to provide, while the Soviet entry into the war also meant that American generosity had to be divided. On a small number of homeward convoys, ships were loaded with Russian timber, but overall there was little that the Soviet Union could provide.

Convoys for the Soviet Union from the UK normally left Liverpool or the Clyde and assembled at the Hvalfjord, the 'Whale's Fjord', in Iceland, although often the warships would use Seidisfjord as their base and the escort and escorted would rendezvous off Iceland. For the early convoys, a second cruiser would provide support out at sea west of Bear Island. Air support could only be judged limited by later standards, highlighting both a shortage of aircraft and a shortage of capability for the aircraft themselves, usually reflected in poor range and an absence of the anti-shipping radar that would be so useful later. Two RAF Coastal Command squadrons, Nos 269 and 330, were based in Iceland, while further cover was provided by flying boats from Sullom Voe in Shetland flying north along the coast of Norway looking for U-boats. Sometimes additional intelligence would come from Norwegian partisans.

The Arctic convoys not only had to run the gauntlet of constant enemy attack from above and below the sea, and at times on the surface as well, but they also had to face the weather. Even in summer, the polar ice cap tended to 'funnel' the convoys into a relatively confined stretch of water. This meant that an order for a convoy to scatter, which might have made sense in the Atlantic, was a nonsense in the Arctic as the ships had nowhere to scatter to, and simply lost the cohesion and mutual protection of being part of a convoy.

A major problem with the Arctic convoys was that while British warships were equipped with asdic, a highly effective submarine detection device now known by its American name of sonar, this did not work well in Arctic waters. Named after the Allied Submarine Detection Investigation Committee of 1917, some 200 warships were fitted with the device by 1939, and it remained a secret until 1940 when the Germans discovered equipment supplied to the French Navy. The problem in Arctic waters was that the thermal layering of the sea (creating streams of very cold water below the surface) distorted the signal. This was especially difficult closer to the shore as glacial water, colder than the surrounding sea and with much less salinity, was a prime culprit.

Radar and radar-controlled gunnery gave the Royal Navy a distinct advantage, especially at night or in poor visibility, but at the time, radar could not distinguish between friend and foe. As we will see later, it could also not distinguish between a land mass and an iceberg, so its use in navigation could be problematic. On the convoys it could have helped station keeping, except that few merchant ships were equipped with it at the time.

After experience with convoy PQ16, it was decided that rescue ships should be provided. These were usually small passenger ships with plenty of boats, being equipped with booms and nets, as well as weighted baskets for rescuing survivors from the water. Cabin partitions were taken down to provide mess decks so that survivors could enjoy the sense of community, being with others who had suffered the same traumatic experience. It was left to charities to provide the necessary clothing for survivors, whose own clothing could have been soaked in blood or engine oil, burnt, or simply become wet or frozen. The British Sailors' Society and the American-based British War Relief Society provided most of the clothing so that every survivor could be guaranteed underclothes, a woollen jumper, trousers, socks, shoes and gloves, a belt, a handkerchief, a raincoat or oilskin, and a cap.

Unfortunately, the rescue ships were indistinguishable at first glance or at a distance from other ships flying the blue ensign worn

33

by British auxiliaries, and so were regarded by the Germans as legitimate targets. These ships were also armed. It is open to question whether they would have been treated better if painted white as hospital ships and carrying the Red Cross, since the Axis powers were not reluctant to attack such ships, no doubt in part because they had employed them as troopships and supply ships themselves and assumed that the Allies did the same.

The use of the exposed Arctic convoy route was chosen because most of the material supplied to the Soviet Union by these convoys was British in origin, including Churchill tanks and Hawker Hurricane fighters, with the remainder being largely from the east coast of the United States or Canada. Most American aid went via the Arabian Gulf and Iran, although an increasing amount was shipped to Vladivostok as the war progressed, partly in the hope that the Soviet Union might declare war on Japan as the Trans-Siberian Railway itself was something of a bottleneck. Indeed, the use of the Iranian and Arctic routes was a reflection of the need to get equipment and ammunition as close to the battle front as possible. The choice of Archangel and Murmansk was forced upon the Allies. Archangel was the better port, but was inaccessible in winter because of ice when the White Sea froze completely, while Murmansk, built by the British during the intervention at the end of the Great War, lacked good port facilities and had a poor railway route, as well as being within range of German bombers. The proportion of supplies sent by these various routes varied, but by the end of the war it has been estimated as 25 per cent by the Arctic route, 25 per cent by the Iranian route and half via Vladivostok.

Once at sea, convoys were controlled by a commodore, who was responsible for the way in which the convoy sailed, including the positioning of ships within the convoy, the course they steered and the convoy's speed, as well as giving instruction to 'zigzag' in case of attack. Commodores were usually retired senior officers, many of whom dropped from flag rank to take charge of a convoy. The commodore sailed in one of the larger merchant ships and had a small staff, also provided by the Royal Navy. The convoy commodore's ship wore a variant of the standard Royal Navy commodore's pennant, with a blue cross instead of red. On the early Arctic convoys, the initial convoy commodores were often experienced and senior Merchant Navy masters, but later when naval officers took over, many Arctic convoy commodores were in fact captains in the Royal Naval Reserve. Even after the Royal Navy took control, experienced Merchant Navy masters remained involved, acting as vice and rear-commodores, not a naval rank, so that should the commodore's ship be lost, they could take over. In addition, there would be the senior naval officer aboard one of the escorts whose ship was not necessarily the largest or the fastest, indeed it was often an ocean minesweeper. Escorts were divided into 'close', which was the escort that mattered, and 'distant', with the latter usually including heavy units of the fleet, such as battleships and aircraft carriers, but usually too distant to be of any effective use. The problem was that placing such units too close would jeopardize the ships concerned, and already the Royal Navy had, by autumn 1941, lost three aircraft carriers and two battleships.

The distant escorts for the Arctic convoys were part of the Home Fleet, the force commanded by Admiral Sir John Tovey at the time of Operation Barbarossa. The convoys themselves were ordered into being by Churchill in the face of opposition from both the First Sea Lord, Admiral Sir Dudley Pound and Tovey, whom Churchill came to regard as 'negative'.

The Weather

The weather should not be underestimated. Aboard ships, especially the merchantmen, the cold was so intense that pipes froze and there was no running water, giving problems with sanitation. Spray froze as it was whipped through the air by the wind and pieces of ice hammered against superstructures like shrapnel. Sometimes the sea froze on decks, deck fittings, armament and rigging, and sailors had to spend time exposed on icy decks chipping away the weight of ice which could otherwise result in a vessel capsizing. This eventuality was more likely on the smaller ships. Anti-submarine trawlers were as much at risk as the merchantmen, and life aboard a destroyer was not always the fun it could be in warmer climes.

Henry Granlund, a British naval officer who sailed aboard a destroyer recalls:

> We did have some very serious problems with the heaviest seas in the world ... At sea, moving at just six or seven knots, very slow for a destroyer, the ship's motorboat was swept away. Part of the ship could be stove in or equipment swept away in the

35

middle of the night and in the storm it might not be noticed until the morning.

Lifelines were always rigged, but sometimes someone could be swept off the deck amidships and swept on again aft ... Some ex-United States Coast Guard vessels were being delivered to Russia, very small and they suffered terribly in the heavy seas.[1]

This view was echoed by those on the lower deck. David Walker, a signals rating aboard the destroyer HMS *Bulldog* remarks:

Escorting the cruisers, it was really horrendous. Cruisers were going at 30 knots and we were keeping up with them. Went on duty one night at 8 o'clock, was soaked by ten past despite wearing all my protective gear, leather sea boots and warm clothes.[2]

Not that life on a cruiser was that easy, according to Richard Steffans, a torpedo man who had also trained as a naval diver. He was pleased to have been posted from the cruiser HMS *Cairo* to another ship, *Dido*: 'Same cold conditions but I was in a better ship ... aboard *Cairo* water was sloshing around the decks. She dated from World War I. We had more space on *Dido*.'[3]

The issue of clothing for the Merchant Navy personnel is dealt with in *Appendix II*, but the Royal Navy also had special issues. 'Ships were Arctic-ised with considerable amounts of insulation fitted and crews fitted out with Arctic clothing', recalls Henry Granlund again. 'Duffle coats on top of sheepskin, special gloves, special waterproofs.'[4]

The clothing was also remembered by David Walker. It included:

Thermal long johns, vest, naval jersey, dungarees, sea boot stockings, sea boots, watchcoat, fleece-lined down to mid-calf, zipped up, life jacket ready to be blown up, balaclava to keep ears warm, gloves and mittens, and a McIntosh on top of coat if wet.[5]

Working in the open was difficult. 'It was not possible for a member of a gun's crew to touch the steel of the gun with bare hands or the cold would burn off the skin on his hand,' Henry Granlund recalled.[6]

Notes:

1. Imperial War Museum Sound Archive, Accession No. 8836.
2. Imperial War Museum Sound Archive, Accession No. 23186.
3. Imperial War Museum Sound Archive, Accession No. 10965.
4. Imperial War Museum Sound Archive, Accession No. 8836.
5. Imperial War Museum Sound Archive, Accession No. 23186.
6. Imperial War Museum Sound Archive, Accession No. 8836.

Chapter 5

The

Protagonists

Sea power remains our only safeguard against disruption in spite of the tremendous weapon of the air, but aircraft must be regarded as a part of sea power and not as an alternative. The essentials are that the Royal Navy, Merchant Navy and the Fleet Air Arm must be coordinated as one force. (Lieutenant Commander E. C. Talbot-Booth, RNR, editor of the journal *Merchant Ships* in 1939.)

On the outbreak of war in 1939, the Royal Navy was a smaller force than it had been in 1914, even taking into account the ships under construction as a result of the hurried and belated rearmament programme adopted in the late 1930s as war became inevitable. Initially, some of the new ships were seen as replacements for existing units of the fleet, with four new fast armoured aircraft carriers seen as replacements for older ships. It was soon clear, however, that the new ships would have to be additional vessels, and the order was increased to six while the older ships remained in service. Rather than being scrapped, older cruisers were converted for the AA role. It was scant consolation that the German Navy, the *Kriegsmarine*, was smaller. Germany had few overseas trade routes to protect, while the Royal Navy was stretched globally.

The most important point about the *Kriegsmarine* was that it was even less prepared for war in 1939 than the Royal Navy. Hitler had assured its chief, Admiral Raeder, that there would not be a war with the UK until 1944 or 1945, and that a decisive sea battle could not be expected before 1948. British and French weakness in the face of the Italian invasion of Abyssinia and of German demands for portions of Czechoslovakia followed by the occupation of Austria, had convinced the Führer that almost no matter what moves he made, the UK and France would be impotent.

The French Navy was even weaker than the Royal Navy, despite France's substantial empire. Where the Royal Navy had fleets, the French Navy had squadrons. Its Atlantic Squadron equated to the British Home Fleet; its Mediterranean Squadron to the British Mediterranean Fleet. In 1939, the French Navy had one elderly aircraft carrier, the Royal Navy seven, although four were elderly and only one was a modern ship, but it had six large, fast, armoured carriers under construction while the French had just two.

Nevertheless, by the time Operation Barbarossa was launched, France was effectively out of the fighting, although Vichy French forces in Madagascar, North Africa and Syria were a thorn in the side of the Allies.

The British

The start of the Second World War certainly did not catch the British armed forces completely unawares. War had been expected, and reservists were called up before war was declared while a massive shipbuilding programme was under way. Convoys were quickly instigated. As previously mentioned, convoys were never compulsory, and it was a foolish master or foolish shipowner that did not take advantage of the system, unless, of course, they had very fast ships, such as the famous Cunard ocean liners, *Queen Mary* and *Queen Elizabeth*, both of which were pressed into service as troopships. So concerned was the Royal Navy about convoy protection, and so alarmed by the shortage of flight decks, that at one stage these two ships were considered for conversion to aircraft carriers. Later in the war, the same consideration was given to completing the last British battleship, HMS *Vanguard*, as an aircraft carrier.

Before the outbreak of war, a number of elderly cruisers were converted to the AA role while additional warships suitable for convoy protection were ordered. Nevertheless, the fleet that went to war in September 1939 consisted of 12 battleships and battle-cruisers – including HMS *Hood*, 'The Mighty Hood', that despite its battle-cruiser designation had been the world's largest warship for many years – 7 aircraft carriers, of which 4 were either in reserve or earmarked for early retirement, a seaplane carrier, of little use in the carrier-age, 58 cruisers, 100 destroyers, 101 other escort vessels,

38 submarines and 232 aircraft. This compared badly with the 61 battleships, 120 cruisers and 443 destroyers, plus many sloops for convoy protection and two aircraft carriers of the previous global conflict with which the Royal Navy had struggled to maintain control of the seas. By 1945 this fleet was to grow to 61 battleships and cruisers; 59 aircraft carriers; 846 destroyers, frigates and corvettes; 729 minesweepers; 131 submarines; 1,000 minor vessels and landing craft; and 3,700 aircraft.

The two main fleets at the outbreak of the war, and until the Royal Navy was able to return in strength to the Far East late in the war, were the Mediterranean Fleet and the Home Fleet. It was the latter that had the responsibility for protecting the convoys to northern Russia. Under the pressures of wartime expansion, the Home Fleet was augmented by a new command, that of Commander-in-Chief Western Approaches, who had responsibility for the Atlantic convoys and those across the Bay of Biscay to Gibraltar, where convoys would divide for the Cape and for the run across the Mediterranean.

The commander-in-chief of the Home Fleet in 1939 was Admiral Sir Charles Forbes, but by the time the Arctic convoys started, the responsibility had passed to Admiral Sir John Tovey. On the outbreak of war, the Home Fleet consisted of 5 battleships, 2 battle-cruisers, 2 aircraft carriers, 3 squadrons with a total of 15 cruisers, 2 flotillas each with 8 or 9 destroyers, and some 20 or so submarines, but for much of the period covered by this book, the strength was less. American entry into the Second World War brought reinforcements, but these also varied from time to time, although a battleship, a couple of cruisers and a small number of destroyers were present on a number of occasions. The main forward base for the Home Fleet was Scapa Flow in Orkney. Scapa had been neglected since the previous conflict, and it was only as late as April 1938 that the Admiralty had decided that Rosyth would not be adequate for the coming conflict. All too soon, Scapa itself was to prove insecure, but in any case this was more of an anchorage than a base, lacking the heavy repair facilities available at Rosyth. On the other hand, Rosyth, on the north or Fife side of the Firth of Forth, was too far south, about twelve hours' steaming from Scapa.

Royal Air Force Coastal Command integrated its operations closely with those of both the Home Fleet and Western Approaches, with No. 18 Group being responsible for protection given to the convoys from its bases in Scotland. Later, RAF units were moved to northern Russia to help provide protection for the Arctic convoys and for ships turning round at Murmansk. The Royal Air Force also sent its bombers against the German battleship *Tirpitz* whenever she was within range. This reflected a problem that affected the Royal Air Force, and at times the Americans as well, which was simply that the supply of aircraft capable of adequate range was limited. The Consolidated B-24 Liberator bomber had the best range of any aircraft of its size during the war, but it was in demand for bombing operations for both the Royal Air Force and the United States Army Air Force, and for maritime-reconnaissance for the United States Navy. The Short Sunderland flying boat proved capable, and was feared by German U-boat crews because its formidable defensive armament made staying on the surface in an attempt to shoot down the aircraft a hazardous occupation. However, the Vickers Wellingtons that had previously done such sterling service were often hand-me-downs, having been replaced in Bomber Command by the new four-engined 'heavies'. The availability of the Consolidated Catalina flying boat under Lend-Lease was a boon.

Given the heavy units committed to the Malta convoys and the risks taken, it does seem that the Home Fleet was unduly cautious in its protection of the Arctic convoys, but in 1941 and 1942 the Fleet Air Arm still lacked adequate aircraft for both offence and defence, especially the latter. While the venerable Fairey Swordfish had done so well against the Italian fleet at Taranto and in the hunt for the German battleship *Bismarck*, sunk during her first sortie, it would have been suicidal to use them on attacks against heavily defended German airfields. Even the fast armoured carriers had shown themselves vulnerable to intense aerial attack, as had occurred to *Illustrious* off Malta and later to *Formidable* during the battle for Crete.

The Royal Air Force was somewhat limited in what it could do for the convoys because of the number of aircraft available and their performance, but after the disaster that was Convoy PQ17, aircraft began to be stationed in larger numbers in the Soviet Union, often with great difficulty in providing adequate accommodation, fuel, munitions and spares. It was also the Royal Air Force that maintained the Merchant Service Air Fighter Unit, whose aircraft operated from the CAM-ships.

The Merchant Navy had to bear the burden of the convoy system. It provided the ships and the manpower. At the outset of the war, the ships were not immediately in short supply, with many having been laid up during the recession of the interwar years. The problem was the lack of personnel to man them. Unemployed seamen had drifted away, and this was made worse by the call up of those who were also members of the Royal Naval Reserve.

The Germans

Having managed to occupy Norway in the face of British naval superiority, the Germans did not initially put the occupation to the best use after the invasion of the Soviet Union. It took some time before the Germans appreciated the true nature of the convoys and of their importance to the Soviet Union. Nevertheless, the Germans were already well placed to interfere, with airfields at Bardufoss, Banak and Petsamo, the latter well-placed for attacks on Murmansk, while they already had an Admiral Arctic.

Two main problems faced the German armed forces. The *Luftwaffe* had decided during the late 1930s not to pursue the development and production of long-range heavy bombers in favour of producing light-medium and dive-bombers. In part this was because the switch to smaller and lighter aircraft meant that higher rates of production could be maintained, in some respects a question of quantity before quality even though many of the individual aircraft types were a match for the opposition. It was also because the *Luftwaffe* was fully committed to the concept of blitzkrieg, with the air force operating in close coordination with ground forces and in particular with fast-moving Panzer, armoured, units. This was fine for continental warfare in which territory was seized; it was a failure when it came to the application of strategic bombing to first British cities and then to Soviet industry, most of which was beyond the range of the *Luftwaffe*'s aircraft. It also meant that the *Luftwaffe* was not as well prepared as it could have been to exploit its Norwegian bases.

The second problem was that the German Navy was far weaker than it should have been. A succession of ambitious plans had been laid by the German Navy before the war, with first Plan X, then Plan Y and finally Plan Z. In September 1939, the *Kriegsmarine* had 2 elderly battleships plus 2 new ships, *Bismarck* and *Tirpitz*, under construction; 2 battle-cruisers; 3 armoured cruisers or *panzerschiffs*, known to the British media as 'pocket battleships'; 3 heavy cruisers;

6 light cruisers; 22 destroyers; 20 torpedo-boats and small destroyers; and 59 submarines.

At its best, this was a modern navy, but it lacked what was to prove to be essential for any blue water navy in the war that lay ahead, aircraft carriers and naval aviation. Priority had been given in the period immediately before the outbreak of war to the development of the air force, the *Luftwaffe*, and while the army had massively expanded, it was not without its weaknesses, with artillery and most supplies still depending upon horses. The *Kriegsmarine* seems to have been at the back of the queue for modernization and expansion.

Looking ahead, the Germans had plans to create a navy that would be able to match that of the UK. The final form of long-term naval planning, Plan Z, called for 6 battleships; 8 heavy cruisers; 4 aircraft carriers; 17 light cruisers; 58 destroyers; 78 torpedo-boats and 223 U-boats. Over the longer term, Plan Z was intended to blossom into an even larger force than these figures suggest, with as many as eight aircraft carriers. As it happened, even the first two carriers were not completed and the first, the *Graf Zeppelin*, had its catapults stripped out and sent to Italy so that the Italians could complete a ship of their own. At the end of the war, *Graf Zeppelin* fell into Soviet hands, but capsized and sank while under tow, loaded with looted German equipment.

While there seems to have been some tension between Dönitz and Raeder, the extension of the submarine arm to 300 boats favoured by the former seems unlikely to have worried his then superior too much. In any case, as the war advanced, Hitler became increasingly disillusioned by the surface fleet and effectively committed this to the dustbin in 1943, concentrating most of the country's shipbuilding resources on the U-boat programme. The U-boat fleet peaked at 445 boats in early 1944, with more, almost 1,200, commissioned during the war years. But one authority on the *Kriegsmarine*, Jak Mallman Showell, maintains that around 800 never got within range of the enemy, and of the third that did, about half attacked fewer than five Allied vessels. Most of the damage suffered by Allied shipping was inflicted by 131 U-boats.

Inter-service rivalry between the *Luftwaffe* and the *Kriegsmarine* meant that the combined potential of both services was never fully realized. The disagreements extended to naval aviation since the *Luftwaffe* controlled all German service aviation other than a

43

small number of aircraft operated from battleships and cruisers for reconnaissance, and lay behind the lack of priority given to getting aircraft carriers into service.

Given the small number of major surface units, it was not too surprising that as the war progressed there was an increasing tendency for the Germans to harbour their battleships and battle-cruisers both literally and figuratively. To some extent, this policy was dictated by the shortage of heavy oil fuel for steam turbines, but it did not encourage an adventurous spirit among senior officers and while the presence of the *Tirpitz* was an ever present threat to the convoys, it never reached a convoy for fear of meeting the British Home Fleet. The big threat was seen by the Germans as British carrier-borne aircraft, which was why Hitler insisted that any aircraft carrier had first to be neutralized. The Germans were capable of doing this, as they had so successfully with first *Illustrious* and then *Formidable* in the Mediterranean, but only if a carrier came within range of their dive-bombers.

The Russians

If one leaves aside the inept and inexplicable conduct of the Soviet dictator Stalin immediately before the German invasion, the Soviet Navy was at a severe disadvantage when the country was attacked. Its fleets in the Baltic and the Black Sea were easily bottled up and incapable of venturing far given German superiority in the air. The fleet in the Far East, the so-called China Squadron, at Vladivostok was too far away and even bringing it back to European Russia would have been fraught with risk, and would not have been worthwhile as most of the ships were small patrol types. There were relatively few naval vessels stationed in the far north, in Arctic waters, nothing bigger than a destroyer, but there were also some minesweepers and a number of submarines.

Soviet Russia's economy was poor, but shipbuilding had been especially weak even during Tsarist days, with it taking as long as ten years to complete a ship, more than three times that needed for the British industry. In 1941, many of the ships in service dated from the early part of the century, in one case 1900.

Stalin's ignorance of maritime matters doubtless played a major role in the decisions taken by the Allies. This was a leader who viewed an obsolete Soviet battleship, the *Oktyabrskaya Revolutsia*

(*October Revolution*, so named because at the time of the Russian Revolution the country still used the Julian calendar), originally one of a class of four built between 1909 and 1915, as an asset, with some historians believing that he viewed battleships as having a prestige value. Inadequate and unable to produce her design speed in 1939, *Oktyabrskaya Revolutsia* and her two surviving sisters displaced just 26,000 tons deep load and had four triple 12-in turrets on the same level so that 'B' and 'X' turrets could not fire over 'A' and 'Y' turrets – a process known as 'super-firing'. Accommodation was inadequate by the still undemanding standards of 1939, but even so, *Oktyabrskaya Revolutsia* survived the war and was not withdrawn from the Red Navy until 1960! One commentator, James Talbot-Smith, writing in the 1939 edition of *All the World's Fighting Fleets* declared that they were:

> Dreadful ships to live in with practically no ventilation; a sister ship, *Pariskaia-Kommuna*, went for a voyage to the Black Sea in 1930 and has remained there ever since, as she is unable to risk the voyage back to the Baltic.

In pencil someone else added to the words 'no ventilation' the comment 'or sanitation'. By the outbreak of war in 1939, *Oktyabrskaya Revolutsia* was comfortably with the Baltic Fleet. On 18 December she bombarded the Finnish port of Koivisto with her sister ship, *Marat*, and a destroyer flotilla, but *Marat* was damaged by returning fire from the Finns. The ships then retired to the Kronstadt naval base, where *Marat* was sunk in an air raid, but *Oktyabrskaya Revolutsia* bombarded German forces during the siege of Leningrad.

Plans to build a fleet of destroyers were included in the Soviet Second Five-Year Plan, which began in 1934, based on French designs and with a 5.1-in armament. Twelve ships of the Leningrad-class were laid down, but work on three was suspended for the duration of hostilities.

Paradoxically, the real strength of the Soviet Navy at the outbreak of war was in submarines, with the largest fleet in the world at more than 150 boats in 1939, and almost 200 by the time the Germans launched Operation Barbarossa. Used effectively, this fleet could have crippled the German surface fleet and kept it in port, but it failed to realize its full potential. No more than a hundred German merchant vessels fell prey to Soviet submarines during the war years, and around thirty minor surface vessels. Most of the effective work was done as the Germans were attempting to withdraw in the face of the advancing Soviet armies, including the sinking of ships carrying civilian refugees, some of which ranked among the worst maritime disasters ever recorded.

The reasons for the poor performance of the submarine fleet were in part due to its rapid expansion, which meant that far too many of the personnel were poorly trained and inexperienced. Rigid bureaucratic control enforced by the Soviet system allowed little scope for individual initiative and individual boats were given tightly defined operational areas. There may also have been many technical failings, as when *K-21*'s torpedoes did not explode when fired at the German battleship *Tirpitz*. The K-class were the largest of the Soviet submarines during the war years, carrying twelve torpedoes and thirty-two mines, and they did in fact make a number of mining sorties in Norwegian waters.

The Soviet air forces were operated on a different basis from those in the West, with a separate Red Army Air Force, Naval Air Force and Long-Range Bomber Aviation. In practice, the Red Air Force was largely subjugated to the army, although at times this was concealed as being part of a larger, but still army-dominated, front command. For these reasons, the main thrust of Soviet military aviation was similar in concept to that of the German *Luftwaffe*, operating in conjunction with the army rather than developing as a strategic air arm, as in the case of the Royal Air Force or the United States Army Air Force. In contrast to the *Luftwaffe*, however, Soviet aviation was constructed on the basis of 'air armies' that were often over-sized and unwieldy, adding to the problems already created by the Soviet structure. Out of an estimated 18,000 aircraft in Soviet military service by 1941, only about a fifth could reasonably be construed as modern, and even these were technically inferior to those being produced by the American, British and German aircraft industries.

One reason for the poor air protection afforded to the convoys by the Soviet Union was the emphasis on the fronts, with convoys and their problems being little understood. Yet another was the loss of so many aircraft and aircrew within the first few days of Barbarossa. A third reason was the poor state of Soviet aircraft development by the late 1930s. As previously stated, the country had lost some of its most brilliant designers as they fled following the Revolution, including Igor Sikorsky. Another was Alexander de Seversky, who specialized in fighter design. One can hardly blame the designers, as some of them were expected to continue their work while imprisoned for trumped up charges.

The situation for the convoys was eventually eased by the stationing of RAF units in northern Russia.

As the war progressed, the British and the Americans made efforts to strengthen the Soviet forces. Apart from aircraft provided under Lend-Lease by both countries, a number of warships were also transferred, ranging from the battleship *Royal Sovereign*, which was transferred to the Soviet Union on loan in 1942, through American-built 'Town-class' destroyers that had been transferred to the Royal Navy first, to British submarines and minesweepers, the last-mentioned often being transfers direct from the United States Navy. At no time did the wartime Soviet Navy consider the construction or operation of aircraft carriers.

Despite the efforts made on their behalf, the Russians were consistently reluctant to open up their naval base facilities to Allied warships, although eventually the Royal Navy was able to establish a presence in the Soviet Union at Polyarnoe.

Chapter 6

Stalin Becomes
an Ally

The outbreak of war between Germany and the Soviet Union immediately highlighted Russia's lack of preparation and the weaknesses of Soviet industry. The Russians suddenly needed the means with which to fight a war. The immediate need was for almost anything and everything, including aircraft, tanks, guns and ammunition, but in fact the Soviet Union was to far outstrip Western aid through its own manufacture of these items, albeit many of the designs were poorer than the German, British or American counterparts. The real weakness was in the provision of vehicles. Soviet mobility was to be *the* big gift of the Western Allies. Soviet industry had not developed sufficiently after the Revolution, and at the onset of war, both industry and the products provided were generally far behind those of the West. Added to this there had been tremendous upheaval and disruption in the evacuation of heavy manufacturing industry east of the Ural Mountains. As previously stated, the movement of industry east was a necessary step, although this in turn made it difficult to copy the British system of shadow factories, which did so much to increase British war production.

In her time of need, Russia turned shamelessly to the much despised West for aid, expecting the shortfall in her needs to be met by British and, later, American output. Terrific moral pressure was brought to bear on the other Allies by the single-minded insistence by the Russians that they be given what they saw as the necessary support. At its most extreme, there were the almost hysterical demands for a second front, although as many of the surviving ex-Nazi leaders will maintain, the Allied bombing campaign was indeed the second front. Stalin worked hard to convey the impression that while Russia suffered, her new Allies were doing nothing. Insult was added to injury as later Russian records failed to note the achievements made possible by Western aid. One can scan official Russian accounts in vain for the mention of British and American equipment.

Politics were never far below the surface in the Western Allies' dealings with the Soviet Union. The two destroyers *Anthony* and *Norman* were put at the disposal of a TUC delegation, taking them to the Soviet Union, arriving there on 12 October and waiting for them to return, departing on 27 October to reach Scapa Flow on 2 November. The purpose of this visit was twofold, to impress the Russians and to get the TUC to encourage greater output by British workers. A little later, the cruiser and destroyer escort for the convoy PQ4 at Seidisfjord had a Soviet military mission aboard, waiting to return to the Soviet Union. The three ships flew the Soviet flag to mark the anniversary of the October Revolution (pre-revolutionary Russian calendar – November in the West), in an attempt to impress the leader of the mission, General Gromov.

In addition to making considerable sacrifices by diverting the output of British factories to the Soviet Union – the Hawker Hurricane fighters would have been very welcome in the Far East the following year – the British also had to make good the deficiencies in what the Soviet Navy could do to protect the convoys. In addition to basing submarines in the Kola area, ocean-going minesweepers were sent, so that a flotilla of five or six of these ships was permanently stationed in the Kola Inlet, being rotated back to the UK as convoy escorts. Most of these were of the Halcyon-class, sometimes classed as sloops, having a considerable anti-submarine capability. An oiler was also stationed, initially this was the *Aldersdale*, but as the war progressed, sometimes chartered tonnage was deployed. Some Polyarnoe-based Russian destroyers did help escort the convoys for the last few miles into the Kola Inlet, but while their AA support was welcome, as already mentioned these suffered from poor sea keeping.

Allied Aid

Taken at face value, it is easy to ask why Allied military aid was so necessary to the Soviet Union? The statistics suggest that in certain areas, such as tanks and combat aircraft, Allied aid at such huge sacrifice and for such scant recognition, let alone gratitude, was unnecessary.

Total Allied aid for the Soviet Union between 1941 and 1945 delivered by all convoy routes amounted to 21,621 combat aircraft and 12,439 tanks and self-propelled artillery. Yet, even in 1941, Soviet arms production had overtaken that of Germany. Soviet aircraft production over the same period amounted to 136,364 aircraft, but this included non-combat types such as trainers and some transport aircraft. The latter were also augmented by American production, while the ubiquitous Douglas C-47, known in the UK as the Dakota and in the United States as the Skytrain, was later produced under licence in the Soviet Union as the Lisunov Li-2. Production of tanks and self-propelled guns in the Soviet Union between 1941 and 1942 totalled 99,507. Inevitably, most of the aid for the country had to come from the United States, which provided 12,869 combat aircraft, compared with 8,752 from the UK, while the United States provided 7,747 tanks and self-propelled artillery, with 4,692 from the UK. Nevertheless, the figures conceal the fact that in late 1941 and throughout 1942, Allied supplies did provide an edge which ensured that the Red Army and Red Air Force were able to continue fighting and even start to take the battle back to the Germans.

Most important, the Allied contribution to the Soviet war effort was in the supply of lorries and jeeps, which gave the Soviet armed forces the mobility that was needed and also helped to ensure that the troops at the front were kept reasonably well supplied, at least by Russian standards. As it was, on the commencement of Operation Barbarossa the Red Army had raided agricultural communities, taking tractors and lorries, and even combine harvesters. By 1945, the collective farm system had just a quarter of the lorries that it had in 1940.

Allied help for the Soviet Union went far beyond military items, and in the case of American aid only 47 per cent of assistance consisted of military equipment. The Americans provided the Soviet Union with 4.4 million tons of food, with another 200,000 tons from Canada and the hungry UK. Despite the German admiration for the qualities of Russian army boots, mentioned earlier, the Allies provided 15.4 million pairs. There were also some 2,000 railway locomotives, all presumably to fit the non-standard Russian track gauge, more than 11,000 lorries for haulage rather than military use, 90 cargo vessels, 107 million yards of cotton cloth and 62.5 million yards of woollen cloth. Soviet production was also helped by supplies of otherwise scarce materials such as aluminium alloy, special steels and telephone wire, and aviation fuel. Allied aid at its peak provided more than 10 per cent of the Soviet Union's gross national product, GNP.

The Soviet Union had a far larger population and land area than Germany, and was able to move factories east of the Urals and beyond the range of most German bombers. Nevertheless, there were serious weaknesses in the economy. Throughout the war years, Soviet production of coal peaked at 151.4 million tons in 1941, while that for Germany, despite Allied bombing, peaked at 281 million tons in 1944, by which time Soviet production was 121.5 million tons, having plummeted to 75.5 million tons in 1942, doubtless due to the disruption caused by the invasion. Steel production for the Soviet Union fell from 17.9 million tons in 1941 to 8.1 million tons the following year, and by 1945 had only reached 12.4 million tons, while that for Germany was 31.8 million tons in 1941 and 35.2 million tons in 1944.

The victims of the war were the Soviet civilians, with estimates as high as 60 million deaths, the overwhelming majority coming from the Baltic States, Belorussia and the Ukraine, although at least 635,000 people died during the 900-day siege of Leningrad. Starvation was a factor in the total number of fatalities, as was warfare itself. Despite the pressure placed on the nation, Soviet citizens and those of the states absorbed by the Soviet Union were still being sent to the Gulag prison camp system, while 2.4 million were deported to Germany to work as forced labour. Members of the Soviet armed forces taken prisoner by the Germans could expect to be punished once they were liberated, even if they had escaped. On the farms, as vehicles and draught animals were taken by the armed forces, they were replaced by manpower, or more often womanpower, as men were called up for the armed forces or industry. Women were also called up, 800,000 being conscripted into the Red Army. Less than 60 per cent of draught animals were left on the farms by the end of the war, although some of these may have died from natural causes or been eaten. To make up for the loss of a third of agricultural manpower, the farming day was extended by 50 per cent. There was little reward for this effort, as the farms had to meet the quotas demanded of them and food consumption in rural areas fell dramatically. So too did production, with grain production falling from 95.6 million tons in 1940 to 26.7 million in 1942, while potatoes fell from 76.1 million tons to 23.8 million tons. This sharp decline in agricultural output was not simply the result of the loss of people and equipment to the armed forces: the Germans had swept across much of the western parts of the Soviet Union and down into the Ukraine.

For consumers as a whole, never a high priority in Soviet society, the index of clothing available to them fell from 100 in 1940 to 61 in 1941, and then 10 in 1942 and 1943, and by 1945 it was still only at 18. Cloth fell from 100 in 1940 to 73 in 1941 and 14 for 1942 and 1943, and rose to just 29 in 1945. For shoes, the fall was even more dramatic, down from 100 in 1940 to 65 in 1941, 8 in 1942 and 7 in 1943, and still only at 15 in 1945. No wonder army boots figured so prominently in the aid supplied by the Allies!

The Soviet Contribution

Operation Barbarossa was the largest military operation in European history, demanding nearly 3.6 million soldiers from Germany and its allies, including Italy, Hungary and Romania, 3,600 tanks and almost 3,000 aircraft. It immediately eased the pressure on British cities, bringing an end to the 'blitz', the German bombing campaign that had followed the Battle of Britain. Less well known, it also marked an easing of the aerial assault on the island of Malta. Nevertheless, the aid given by the Soviet Union to the Germans from the outset of the war had soured relationships even with those who did not have an instinctive suspicion of communism. The lack of any attempt to intervene while Germany rampaged through Denmark and Norway, and then France, had been bad enough, but earlier Soviet intervention could have made British and Greek efforts in the Balkans worthwhile.

Churchill broadcast to the nation on the evening of the German invasion, promising all possible effort against a common co-enemy, but initial approaches to the Soviet Union were, if not rebuffed, treated with remarkable coolness. This was despite the fact that Stalin was soon demanding all possible military aid from both the UK and the United States, and this included a Second Front. His demands clearly ignored the massive war being fought at sea by the Royal Navy and treated events in North Africa as irrelevant. Stalin was later to ignore the Anglo-German bomber campaign in the same way. Communists in the UK started a graffiti campaign demanding a 'Second Front Now', ignoring the realities of mounting an invasion of mainland Europe. Faced with Stalin's constant and growing demands, and conscious of the impact that German submarines, surface vessels and aircraft would have on the long convoy supply route to Murmansk and Archangel, Churchill wisely cautioned the Soviet dictator that the quantities promised would only be guaranteed at the port of departure, not at the port of arrival. This was also intended to encourage Stalin to provide Soviet ships to augment the Allied merchant vessels, but relatively few were forthcoming. Pre-war Soviet commerce had not called for a substantial merchant marine, and in any event, ships serving foreign ports could have been a means for many disenchanted citizens to leave the country!

Facing this large force were the 2.9 million men in the Red Army's western military districts, with more than 8,000 aircraft and between 10,000 and 15,000 tanks.

After the invasion, both German and Soviet forces embarked on a scorched earth policy, albeit for different reasons. Stalin wished to deny the invaders the use of the infrastructure, accommodation, food supplies and anything else that might make life easier for an invading army, and also ensure that his own people pulled back so that their labour could be used. Hitler planned to eliminate anything that could be construed as Slavonic, intending a ruthless 'Germanization' of the area, which was to be resettled by German immigrants after the war. The effect was unlike anything seen during the push north into Denmark and Norway, or west into the Low Countries and then France. The local populations were to be expelled, moved further east, with massive resettlement schemes involving as many as 30 million people.

It took Stalin two weeks to create a new military high command or *Stavka*, with three marshals, Voroshilov on the right of the line, Timoshenko on the centre, and Budenny on the left. Front line commanders who had survived the initial German onslaught were shot as scapegoats, partly for public consumption, partly to instil fear into their subordinates, now promoted into exposed positions. Political orthodoxy had become more important than military ability, with political commissars sitting alongside military commanders and having the power to countermand military decisions.

Chapter 7

The Convoys Begin

Clearly, space limits the depth in which the individual convoys can be covered, but it is worth looking in detail at some of the key convoys. Contrary to popular opinion, not all convoys suffered heavy attack, and indeed a number, especially in the early days and towards the end of the war, actually went unmolested. It is interesting to look at just how the delivery of aid to the Soviet Union started. There were difficulties from the outset in establishing a good relationship with the Soviet Union, and Stalin's ungracious approach at the top was, not surprisingly, reflected in the attitudes of those below him with whom naval officers and others had to work.

The first of what was to become a flood of supplies for the Soviet Union arrived at Archangel on 1 August 1941 aboard the elderly mine-laying cruiser HMS *Adventure*. The war materials aboard this ship included mines, which the commander of the Soviet Northern Fleet, Admiral A. Golovko, described as 'valueless'. This was to become the attitude of the Soviet Union to everything supplied to them, even though in the first half of September, four Russian destroyers laid these mines in northern waters to protect the approaches to Archangel. Stalin himself was always to press for a greater share of the available supplies, most of which came from the United States, despite this undermining the potential for the Western Allies to open the Second Front he claimed to need.

Rather more useful than the air attacks on Petsamo and Kirkenes mentioned in the next chapter, was the deployment of the submarines *Tigris* and *Trident* to the Arctic, soon to be joined by other British submarines, for offensive operations against German shipping.

On 9 August, Churchill and Roosevelt met for the first time when the battleship HMS *Prince of Wales* and the cruiser USS *Augusta* rendezvoused in Placentia Bay, off the coast of Newfoundland.

On 12 August, the two statesmen were able to cable Stalin assuring him of all the supplies that he would need. This it was recognized would mean that supplies from the United States for the UK's own war effort would be diverted to the Soviet Union.

Creating a convoy link with the Soviet Union was difficult. The demands of the existing war theatres and of the UK herself meant that few ships, naval or merchant, could be spared. The situation was made much worse as the Axis domination of the Mediterranean worsened, so that instead of the Mediterranean and the Suez Canal providing a short cut between the UK and the Middle East, Indian subcontinent and Australia, the Mediterranean was simply a battle-ground and convoys to Egypt went by the tortuous route of the South Atlantic, Cape of Good Hope and the Indian Ocean, with the Suez Canal being the final stage. The closure of the Mediterranean to shipping had effectively deprived the Allies of the equivalent of a million tons of shipping. Convoys to Malta were few and far between, heavily fought over and suffered losses as high as 100 per cent.

The shortage of British shipping had been eased considerably by ships that had escaped from occupied Europe, including the two other leading maritime nations, the Netherlands and Norway. The latter's contribution was considerably enhanced when the Norwegian government-in-exile radioed to all Norwegian ships at sea and contacted agents for those in neutral ports, with the order that they should head for a British port where management was transferred to British companies. The value of this instruction can be judged by the fact that it gave the British Merchant Navy more than 600 general cargo ships and no less than 233 tankers. 'Worth a million soldiers,' a delighted Churchill later wrote.

Two ports existed that were suitable for convoys to the Soviet Union, but Archangel could only be a summer port, with Murmansk, the port on the Kola Inlet built by the British in 1915 to supply the Tsar, the alternative all-year-round port. Admiral Sir John Tovey, Commander-in-Chief Home Fleet, was put in charge of the arrange-ments and sent two rear admirals, Vian and Miles – the latter already earmarked to head the British Military Mission in Moscow – to see Golovko to discuss the arrangements. Both officers pointed out that Murmansk was within easy reach of German forces at Petsamo, and that many of the population had already been evacuated. The port facilities at Murmansk had never been outstanding, but they had also been neglected between the two world wars. As it stood in 1941,

Murmansk had little in the way of AA defences and the largest crane could not lift a tank. While the Germans had not captured the town and port itself, they had succeeded in cutting the railway line to Leningrad, although the Russians had managed to lay new track between Belomorsk and Obozerskaya, where there was a junction with the Archangel–Moscow line. Vian, later to serve with distinction in the Mediterranean and the Far East, did not fit the mould expected of an officer in the Soviet Navy and Golovko did not like him, finding him opinionated.

Golovko was a peasant; scruffy and unpolished with poor table manners, according to another British rear admiral, Burrough. On the positive side, Burrough regarded the Russian as clever and far-sighted, 'likeable, friendly and frank', but probably ruthless.

The Russians were not prepared to help the British with the problems that using Murmansk would create, such as the lack of dry docks, always useful in any major port, but imperative in wartime, or the provision of refuelling facilities. There were additional wooden wharves available at Polyarnoe, a small port further down the Kola Inlet, and these were situated in a narrow fjord, or *guba*. Dry dock facilities were at the naval base of Rosta.

A suitable base for offensive naval and air operations against the Germans was a priority, but neither the Royal Navy nor the Royal Air Force had any real experience of the region. Casting around for a suitable base, the Norwegian territory of Spitzbergen was seized upon. Being some 450 miles to the north of Norway, this was hardly ideal, although its west coast was supposed to be ice free. On 27 July, Rear Admiral Philip Vian took the cruisers *Nigeria* and *Aurora* with two destroyers to investigate. Spitzbergen had been leased to Russian miners since Tsarist times, so the bleak Norwegian outpost was primarily occupied by Russian miners with a primitive camp above the coal mines. It was soon apparent that the difficulties of establishing and maintaining such a remote base, and one that was some distance from enemy targets, would not be worthwhile. As the war developed, the sole use for Spitzbergen was as a meteorological station and a refuelling rendezvous – for both sides! Vian instead decided to see if he could attack targets of opportunity on the Norwegian coast, but being discovered by enemy aerial reconnaissance, wisely decided against this. Shortly afterwards, as the first convoy for Russia was being assembled at Hvalfjord in Iceland, Vian was ordered to evacuate the Russian coal miners and any Norwegian personnel stationed in

Spitzbergen. Leaving on 19 August, again he took his two cruisers, escorted by five destroyers, with the Canadian Pacific liner *Empress of Canada* carrying Canadian troops, and the oiler *Oligarch*. This force landed at Barentsburg, putting the coal mines out of use and embarking some 2,000 Russian miners, before taking the miners to Archangel. Vian's force regrouped off Barentsburg on 1 September with the intention of destroying enemy shipping, which he did with the cooperation of the Norwegian military governor, who lured the Germans into believing that all was well. The result was that colliers, a whaler, a tug and an ice-breaker as well as two fishing vessels were captured as prizes. On 2 September the Canadian troops left, accompanied by 800 Norwegian service personnel and hardy colonists.

An aggressive officer anxious for action, Vian took his two cruisers towards the Norwegian coast, and in the early hours of 7 August, he found a German convoy to the east of the North Cape. The British cruisers sank the obsolete training cruiser *Bremse*, but not before her resistance had enabled the two troopships she was escorting to escape with 1,500 soldiers. In the action *Nigeria*'s bows were damaged by a mine.

Ungrateful and ungracious as ever, Stalin belittled the performance of the latest mark Hawker Hurricane fighters dispatched to him, demanded 30,000 tons of aluminium and also asked for 400 aircraft and 500 tanks each month! Arrangements were made to supply via Vladivostok 5,000 tons of aluminium from Canada, with another 2,000 tons each month, while half of the previously agreed American Lend-Lease supplies bound for the UK in October were to be diverted to the Soviet Union. Stalin's demands were completely unrealistic. At one stage he requested twenty or thirty British divisions to be dispatched to northern Russia.

The First Convoy

Code-named Operation Dervish, the first convoy left Liverpool on 12 August and Hvalfjord on 21 August 1941, and compared with many that followed later was very small, with just six elderly merchantmen, having Captain J. C. K. Dowding as Commodore. The convoy carried wool, rubber and tin – materials desperately needed by the Soviet Union – as well as fifteen Hawker Hurricane fighters dismantled and crated. As was usual, the make-up of the escort varied during the voyage, but included six armed trawlers and an AA ship, as well as three destroyers and three Halcyon-class minesweepers, accompanied by the cruiser *Aurora*. This was what was known variously as the 'ocean escort' or 'close escort'. The minesweepers had an anti-submarine capability and were due to be stationed in northern Russia. What also became known as 'distant cover', or 'heavy cover', was provided by the aircraft carrier *Victorious*, cruisers *Devonshire* and *Suffolk*, with a screen of three destroyers. This convoy had a relatively peaceful passage, arriving at Archangel on 31 August, after which the aircraft were offloaded and assembled, being available for service on 12 September.

Once Operation Dervish had arrived, Operation Strength got under way, with the elderly aircraft carrier *Argus*, which had been converted from a liner before the end of the First World War, carrying twenty-four Hawker Hurricane fighters and RAF personnel from No. 151 Wing. Other RAF personnel were also aboard the escort, which consisted of the cruiser *Shropshire* and three destroyers. As was usual with aircraft deliveries, the Hurricanes aboard *Argus* were flown off to the Russian airfield at Vaenga before the carrier reached port. While one might wonder at the choice of code-name, nevertheless, the aircraft supplied by Operation Strength were intended to provide fighter protection for the airfields at Archangel, Murmansk and Polyarnoe.

A major problem with the organization and protection of the convoys was that the British expected far more of their Soviet 'allies' than the latter were willing or able to provide. Having met Golovko, Vian proposed that the convoy routes could be protected by both powers, with the British providing air and naval cover for the long slog from Iceland and along the coast of Norway, but east of Bear Island he expected Soviet air and surface support, along with offensive operations against German shipping by Russian submarines. Collaboration with Soviet commanders proved difficult, particularly in the case of submarine operations, while Soviet air support simply did not appear. The Russian destroyers were poor performers in the open sea, while the heavier units of the Soviet Navy were obsolete, and seem to have been absent from northern Russia.

'Didn't recall anything larger than a destroyer,' stated Henry Granlund, who served aboard a convoy escort. 'In harbour at Polyarnoe, it was used as a British port with no other Russian escort vessels or destroyers in the same harbour.'[1]

Alongside the problems faced with the Russians, a member of the government and close friend of Churchill, Lord Beaverbrook, expressed doubts about even keeping the Soviet Union in the war, so Churchill assured Stalin in October 1941 that the British would provide a convoy every ten days to Archangel. This was an unrealistic promise intended to keep Stalin committed to fighting Germany. The British chiefs of staff had been counting on convoys every forty days, and estimated that simply providing the bare minimum of a cruiser and two destroyers per convoy, a convoy every ten days would require four cruisers and eight destroyers. Some have suggested that Churchill was playing politics, hoping that his promises would keep the Soviet leader committed, but the failure to live up to this unrealistic promise was soon held against the Allies by Stalin, who saw its failure as evidence of the superiority of Communism. Archangel could not be kept open during the winter months, but Churchill ignored this while his ally chose to believe that there was nothing the Soviet ice-breakers could not do. Stalin had no concept of the sheer difficulty of running convoys through in the winter storms, nor of the threat to plodding merchantmen of the German attacks.

Hitler had a far better idea of what was involved, and despite his preoccupation with the advance on the Ukraine, his 36th Directive on 22 September 1941 advised that the British would deploy strong air forces around Murmansk, while his 37th Directive the following month demanded close collaboration between the *Kriegsmarine* and the *Luftwaffe* to prevent the British sending large quantities of supplies to the Soviet Union. His big mistake was to see the build-up of substantial British naval forces off Norway as an indication that the British intended to invade Norway as a first step in driving German forces out of western and northern Europe. This was one reason why maintaining heavy units of the German fleet in northern waters was regarded by Hitler as so important. However, the paradox was that these ships, intended to protect Norway, were seen by the British as a major threat to the Arctic convoys! Hitler's strategy might have been more successful if the German Navy and the *Luftwaffe* had truly cooperated, but the command structures were different, and only at Kirkenes were the senior officers in close touch, while rivalry between the two services ran deep. Nevertheless, it was also a weakness from the German point of view that their German mountain troops had not been able to seize Murmansk at the outset of Operation Barbarossa, a move that would have made the re-supply of the Soviet

Union in the Arctic virtually impossible, and overloaded the only two other routes.

The first of the regular convoys to the Soviet Union, PQ1, was more substantial than Operation Dervish, with ten ships, mainly British, but also including Panamanian-flagged vessels and a Belgian ship. The cargoes included no less than 193 fighter aircraft and twenty tanks. PQ1 assembled at the Hvalfjord before sailing on 28 September. The commodore was a Merchant Navy officer, Captain D. Ridley, master of the SS *Atlantic*. Another merchant vessel was the fleet oiler *Black Ranger*, albeit there for the sake of the escort rather than a convoy vessel in the proper sense. A small escort was provided, consisting of the cruiser *Suffolk*, two destroyers and four fleet minesweepers. The latter had been suitably armed in order to be classified as sloops and were making a one-way trip for a tour of duty in the Kola Inlet. Despite an engine breakdown on one merchantman, which her crew managed to repair, the convoy was unchallenged as it proceeded to Archangel, reaching it a day early on 11 October.

Departing from Archangel on the same day was the first convoy from the Soviet Union, QP1, and with it were the ships of the Operation Dervish convoy with seven additional Soviet ships. When this convoy crossed with PQ1, the destroyer *Anthony* and the oiler *Black Ranger* transferred to it. The main escort was provided by the cruisers *London* and *Shropshire*, two destroyers and four armed trawlers, although one of these, *Ophelia*, broke down. This convoy also had an uneventful passage. Most of the ships made even better time than those of PQ1, reaching Scapa Flow in Orkney on 9 October. Even two Russian stragglers managed a safe arrival.

'Generally it was a pleasure to act as ocean escort to such a well-mannered convoy and credit is due to the Russian masters, probably none of whom had been in a convoy before,' reported the commanding officer of HMS *Shropshire*.

The returning Operation Dervish ships were not empty, carrying large numbers of Polish soldiers who had escaped the German invasion only to find that the Soviet Union was also invading their country.

Certainly, the early convoys seemed to have led a charmed life. The next convoy, PQ2, consisted entirely of six British ships, escorted by the cruiser HMS *Norfolk*, two destroyers and three ocean-going minesweepers. Sailing from Scapa Flow on 17 October, the convoy reached Archangel on 31 October completely unscathed. The three larger warships then accompanied convoy QP2 home, which again not only included the ships from PQ1, but had three Soviet merchantmen added. QP2 left Archangel on 2 November, reaching Kirkwall in Orkney on 17 November.

By this time, both sides were becoming increasingly nervous. The Germans expected British attacks on the coastal convoys, which were not only important in supplying German forces scattered along Norway's heavily indented and rugged coastline, but also carried the precious nickel from Petsamo and iron ore from Sweden for the German war industry. These materials were shipped via Norwegian ports as the Gulf of Bothnia froze in winter. The British knew that the Arctic convoys were vulnerable to German attack, from the air and from under the sea, and from major surface units of the *Kriegsmarine*. Although the German battleship *Tirpitz* had been commissioned, the Führer chose to harbour this asset, literally, for fear that she might share the same fate as her sister, *Bismarck*. There was also a shortage of heavy oil fuel for steam turbines. Hitler did at least allow Admiral Raeder to move the heavy cruiser *Admiral Scheer* into position, largely because she was diesel-powered and diesel was plentiful at this stage in the war. Raeder also made other improvements to the disposition of his forces, moving the T-class torpedo-boats, in effect small destroyers compared to the high speed E-boats and replacing them with five destroyers with 5-in guns and eight 21-inch torpedo-tubes, more powerful than their British counterparts. He also placed a patrol line of three U-boats across the Arctic convoy routes.

A good indication of how concerned the Admiralty was by this time was that the Commander-in-Chief Home Fleet, Admiral Tovey, tried to stop QP2 sailing. While too late to prevent this, he did manage to delay PQ3. Considerations other than the German threat also played a part in this decision, as the destroyers used on convoy escort duties at this stage of the war were ill-suited to the hammering of the heavy seas found on the Arctic convoys, and repairs were needed to the destroyers assembled at Seidisfjord.

In the end, PQ3 sailed on 9 November, with eight merchantmen, although one of these, the *Briarwood*, suffered ice damage and had to turn back, escorted by the armed trawler *Hamlet*. Convoy PQ4, which sailed on 17 November, then caught up with PQ3, making a total of fifteen merchantmen arriving at Archangel on 28 November, while a sixteenth ship fell behind but still arrived safely. PQ3 had as an escort the cruiser *Kenya* with two destroyers, and just one trawler after *Hamlet* had left to escort *Briarwood* to safety. PQ4 had been escorted by the cruiser *Berwick*, also with two destroyers and two armed trawlers.

After reaching Archangel, Rear Admiral Burrough in *Kenya* led two British destroyers and two Soviet destroyers to bombard enemy shore batteries at Vardo, an operation which at last produced a note of appreciation from the reticent Admiral Golovko.

The UK-bound convoy QP3 consisting of ten ships sailed on 27 November. Two of the ships turned back, but the remainder reached their destinations safely with two Soviet ships reaching Kirkwall in Orkney escorted by two destroyers, while the six British ships reached Seidisfjord on 7 December escorted by the cruiser *Kenya* and two destroyers.

Next to leave Hvalfjord was PQ5, on 27 November 1941. The seven ships of this convoy included the British *Briarwood*, repaired after her earlier problems with ice, escorted by the cruiser HMS *Kent*, later joined by the cruiser *Sheffield* and a number of minesweepers, while three destroyers eventually joined after searching in vain for the convoy for six days, having been given the wrong coordinates by the Home Fleet. This was the last convoy of the year to reach Archangel, with the help of Russian ice-breakers.

Convoy PQ6 had eight merchantmen, but was very lightly escorted with just three armed trawlers. Two of the ships had to turn back. The rescue ship *Zamalek* escorted the merchantman *Hermatris*, which had fallen behind the convoy and then encountered bad weather before discovering that a lorry had caught fire and broken loose, damaging much of her cargo. The fire was in danger of spreading to explosives in her cargo and it took heroic efforts by the mate and a chief steward before the fire could be brought under control.

Earlier mention was made of the RAF personnel who went to Russia in Operation Strength. These returned home early in December 1941 after handing over their Hawker Hurricanes to the Russians, taking passage in the cruisers *Berwick* and *Kenya* and two destroyers. As an indication of just how quickly the weather could change, two other destroyers had left a day earlier and so missed the severe weather that the ships carrying the RAF contingent encountered. The weather was so bad that not only were the lightly-built destroyers damaged, but even the cruisers suffered damage to their superstructures and deck rails. Nevertheless, a week later *Kent* was able to take the Foreign Secretary, Anthony Eden, to Murmansk along with the Soviet ambassador to London, Maisky. Despite

German troops being just 25 miles from Moscow, they travelled on to the city, where Stalin pressed for further supplies and also sought British recognition of the Soviet Union's annexation of the Baltic States.

Eden soon realized that Stalin was not at all concerned with the plight of the Americans, by this time drawn into the war by the Japanese attack on the United States Pacific Fleet at Pearl Harbor. This did have the advantage that the United States could now help openly and the volume of aid increased considerably during the first few months of 1942, as did the number of ships available for the convoys, with American merchantmen now available. Later, it was also to see the arrival of the escort carrier to increase the protection available to the convoys.

Meanwhile PQ6 was heading north towards the Soviet Union under the sole and very limited protection of the armed trawler *Hugh Walpole*. The cruiser HMS *Edinburgh*, having bunkered at Seidisfjord, raced north with two destroyers to catch the convoy. By this time, PQ6 was down to seven ships, led by the *Elona*, which carried the convoy commodore, with three other British ships, two Panamanian ships and one from the Soviet Union.

The extreme cold meant that *Edinburgh* encountered difficulties refuelling one of the destroyers, as the fuel solidified in the exposed refuelling line. The breath of those on deck and on watch in the bridge, froze on their duffle coats. On 18 December, *Edinburgh* heard that two ocean minesweepers outward bound from Kola to clear the approaches had encountered four German destroyers of the 8th Flotilla under *Kapitän zur See* Ponitz, busy laying mines. Fortunately, at first the Germans mistook the two ships for their own G-class destroyers, allowing them to make their escape in the dull winter light as they hastily laid a smokescreen. The Germans then realized that something was amiss and fired starshell before opening fire, hitting the minesweeper HMS *Speedy*, which retired to Kola.

HMS *Kent*, waiting at Kola, immediately set out to intercept the German destroyers accompanied by two Soviet destroyers, while another minesweeper set out to replace *Speedy*. The minesweepers took most of the convoy to Molotovsk, which it reached safely on 23 December, while the cruiser and her destroyer escort ran along the coast towards Murmansk.

The merchant ships soon found themselves frozen in at Molotovsk, along with the ice-breaker that had enabled them to enter the port.

Conditions aboard the ships which had not been built with such conditions in mind were barely habitable, with fresh water supplies frozen, toilets and washing facilities unusable, and an outbreak of scabies passed through the crews. Even more miserable were the German prisoners of war who were used as forced labour to unload the cargoes, and who were pathetically grateful for the scraps of food thrown overboard by the crews of the ships, not so much out of charity or compassion for the Germans, but because the food was deteriorating so badly that they refused to eat it. Conditions for the Russians themselves in an outpost of the Stalinist Soviet Union were bleak enough, but eventually they supplied yak carcasses for the crews of the merchantmen. It was not until the following June that the ships were able to leave on their return voyage. These hardships could have been avoided and the ships kept in use on subsequent convoys had not the centralized control exercised by Moscow continued to interfere with the efficient conduct of the war. Ships were still being sent to ports that would become ice bound, while the local naval commander waited in vain for instructions to divert all incoming shipping to Murmansk.

Before this, however, the convoy encountered problems at the last minute. As the weather worsened, the destroyer *Escapade* was detached in order to look for a straggler, while the other destroyer, *Echo*, was sent to escort the fast Soviet merchantman *Dekabrist* into Murmansk, both ships proceeding at 18 knots, a speed almost unheard of among the cargo ships of the day. The forces thus divided, *Edinburgh* was alerted by the sound of gunfire to the fact that the *Dekabrist* was under attack from two Ju88 fighter-bombers. The Russian freighter had been shaken by near misses while two unexploded bombs rolled about on her deck. *Echo*'s 4.7-in low angle guns were ineffective against the aircraft, and she lost two men washed overboard from the open 'A' turret into the freezing seas as she zigzagged and worked up to her maximum speed. The cruiser and a flight of six Russian Hurricanes drove the Ju88s away, although they had already dropped their bomb load. The other straggler, the freighter *El Mirlo* had not simply had a lucky escape, she had managed to reach Murmansk before her escort.

QP4 was due to leave Archangel on 20 December. The cruiser *Kent* left Murmansk on 25 December, after sitting there waiting to take the Foreign Secretary home.

American Support

The first British ship to load supplies for the Soviet Union in the United States was the SS *Waziristan*, owned by Common Brothers of Newcastle, which loaded in mid-December 1941. She left New York with two other cargo ships and joined eastbound convoy SC60. The three ships left the convoy in mid-Atlantic and headed for Reykjavik with an escort of two armed trawlers. Convoy PQ7A was one of the smallest to be graced with the title, having just two ships, the *Waziristan* and the *Cold Harbour*, a Panamanian ship. PQ7A departed from Hvalfjord on 26 December with an escort of just two armed trawlers, the *Hugh Walpole* and *Ophelia*.

The escort was due to be changed over while on passage, but the two trawlers had to leave before the rendezvous with two ocean minesweepers, which was missed in the poor weather and unremitting gloom. The two merchantmen found themselves proceeding unescorted, eventually finding thick ice and an easterly gale, and on New Year's Day 1942, the two ships lost contact in the bad weather and darkness at 16.00 – neither ship was equipped with radar.

At just before 07.00 on 2 January, the *Waziristan* was found by *U-134*, torpedoed and sunk, with the loss of forty-seven lives. Her erstwhile companion, *Cold Harbour*, was luckier, arriving in the Kola Inlet on 12 January. The previous day, Convoy PQ7B, made up of the other ships that together with those in PQ7A would have constituted Convoy PQ7, had arrived safely.

Meanwhile, QP4 had struggled out of the White Sea led by the new Soviet ice-breakers *Lenin* and *Stalin*, and was heading for home. Leaving Archangel on 29 December, QP4 consisted of thirteen merchantmen escorted by trawlers and minesweepers. It had suffered a false start as the ice-breakers had headed into thicker ice and were forced to change course, searching for thinner ice. It then had to refuel, or to be precise re-coal, at sea – a time-consuming and messy operation – but the use of coal-fired ships could have been dictated by experience of the difficulty in transferring fuel oil in extreme cold. *Edinburgh*, accompanied by two destroyers, followed, hoping to rendezvous with the convoy minesweepers, but instead found one of them, *Hazard*, heading in the opposite direction escorting a merchantman that was short of fuel to Murmansk. Shortly afterwards a second merchantman also had to return to Murmansk for the same reason. Soon after joining the convoy, found by moonlight rather than by the use of radar, *Edinburgh* was warned that U-boats were in the vicinity of Bear Island, and on 8 January the cruiser was ordered to disperse the convoy and patrol south of the convoy route, finding extreme weather conditions the following day. In this case, the cruiser found winds so severe that instead of creating a heavy sea, it whipped the surface of the sea and created spindrift, a thick fog of fine spray that froze on the superstructure, the guard-rails and the guns. On 10 January, the temperature rose suddenly, the ice melted and the sun shone. Even more welcome when the cruiser reached Scapa Flow the following day was the 180 bags of mail for her crew, as well as fresh meat, vegetables and potatoes. Despite the concerns raised by the reports of U-boats and the earlier mine-laying activities of the German destroyers, QP4 reached Seidisfjord on 16 January 1942 safely.

Meanwhile, taking advantage of the harsh winter weather, the Soviet Union mounted a counter-attack against the German armies, who were from this time onwards to be in an increasingly unfit state. This called for no less than fifty-three merchant ships to be sent to Archangel and Murmansk, fifty to Archangel with just three to Murmansk. These ships carried the staggering total of 800 fighters, 750 tanks and 1,400 assorted military vehicles, as well as ammunition and other supplies, including the aluminium, rubber and other raw materials needed by Soviet industry. The Soviet Union was ill-equipped to handle such largesse smoothly and efficiently, and in London, the War Cabinet was concerned at the reports of neglect and bad handling of these valuable cargoes, sent at a time when the British armed forces could have made good use of them.

Churchill wrote to Stalin: 'Please make sure that our technicians who are going with the tanks and aircraft have full opportunity to hand these weapons over to your men under the best conditions.' Stalin's response was as always ungrateful and ungracious, maintaining that tanks, planes and artillery were arriving 'inefficiently packed, that sometimes parts of the same vehicle are loaded in different ships, that planes, because of the imperfect packing, reach us broken'.

Stalin's attitude also reflected the fact that he wished Churchill to declare war on Finland, which the British premier was reluctant to do. Finland had been reinforced by the Germans after throwing its lot in with the Axis, but the British appreciated that the Finns had been placed in an impossible position by the Soviet invasion of 1940, and the Finns had much popular support in the UK because of this.

Facing the Wolf-Pack

The first northbound convoy of 1942 was PQ8, consisting of seven ships, which departed from Hvalfjord on 8 January, with Captain R. W. Brundle of the *Hermatris* as commodore. The master of the first American ship to appear on an Arctic convoy, the *Larranga*, acted as vice commodore. At the outset, the close escort was just two ocean minesweepers, but these were joined on the night of 10/11 January by the new light cruiser *Trinidad* and two destroyers, which had departed from Seidisfjord after refuelling on 9 January. The convoy enjoyed unusually calm and clear weather at first, but was forced south by ice. Fog kept the Russian-based minesweepers in port at Kola, but two others were on their way. As usual, the Soviet Navy was conspicuous by its absence.

The feared U-boat group now put in an appearance during the early evening of Saturday, 17 January. At 19.45, *U-454*, one of the Ulan group of three U-boats, fired a torpedo that struck *Hermatris* on her starboard bow by her No. 1 hold. Her first officer ordered engines to reverse in order to stop the ship and to avoid her being swamped by water flooding through the hole, although unknown to him, the blast of the explosion had also dropped the starboard anchor. *Hermatris* had been lucky as the hold contained a cargo of torpedo warheads that could have been blown up by the oncoming torpedo, but instead they had fallen safely through the bottom of the ship, while clothing intended for Polish refugees had been blown upwards on to the ship's rigging.

The initial reaction of the escort was that the merchantman had struck a mine, but one escort reported torpedo noise and another reported a torpedo passing under her. The convoy was escorted past the *Hermatris* under the command of the vice commodore aboard *Larranga*, while a minesweeper stood by the stricken vessel whose master and mate conducted a survey of the damage. They had just decided that the ship could be saved when a second torpedo from *U-454* struck the port side, but failed to explode. A minesweeper came alongside and rescued most of the crew from the damaged freighter, while her commanding officer called for volunteers so that she could be towed. It took some effort to pass a towing line between the two ships, and it was only when the *Hermatris* refused to budge that the dropped anchor was noticed! It was not until after 22.00 that the tow got under way.

Meanwhile, showing considerable skill and determination, *Kapitänleutnant* (lieutenant commander) Hacklander took *U-454* ahead of the convoy, and seeing the tanker *British Pride* highlighted against the beams of a lighthouse on Cape Teriberski, fired a salvo of torpedoes. None of the torpedoes struck the tanker, but one hit the destroyer *Matabele*, causing her magazine to explode. As the destroyer exploded in a sheet of flame, many of her crew were killed outright, but others made it into the water only to be killed as she sank and her depth charges exploded. Others succumbed to the cold, leaving just two ratings to be rescued.

By this time *Hermatris* had stopped. It proved difficult to handle the towing cable in the intense cold. Her master joined his crew on the minesweeper, which circled the crippled freighter throughout the night, keeping on the move to minimize the risk of being torpedoed. On returning to his ship at 06.00 on the morning of 18 January, Captain Brundle found the boilers almost dry as steam had escaped through a cracked valve, and the steam pipes forward serving the windlass had frozen. An anchor cable was slipped and towing resumed at 08.00. A welcome sight shortly afterwards was the arrival of two minesweepers, whose AA armament augmented that aboard *Hermatris*. At noon a Heinkel He111 attacked at low level, but was driven off by the intensive AA fire. Another aircraft made a pass, but it was indicative of the morale of the *Luftwaffe* on the Russian front that it contented itself with dropping its bombs a mile or so away. Despite the supply of fighters to the Red Air Force, once again Soviet support was conspicuous by its absence.

The towing operation seemed to be dogged by bad luck, for at 14.30, a high pressure steam pipe in the engine room of the minesweeper *Speedwell* burst, scalding three men badly. As the minesweeper lost way, her commanding officer signalled for a Soviet tug. A first tug arrived promptly, in less than an hour, and after emergency repairs, *Speedwell* set off to get medical assistance for her injured ratings. Two further Soviet tugs arrived by 17.00, and between them the three vessels nursed *Hermatris* into Murmansk, arriving during the morning of 20 January.

While QP8 had been making its way to the Soviet Union, QP5 with four ships had been escorted safely to Iceland by the cruiser HMS *Cumberland* and two destroyers. They arrived on 24 January 1942.

This was the first Arctic convoy in which a badly damaged ship was saved. It was also notable for being escorted by a new light cruiser with an all-welded hull. The Admiralty was suspicious about the suitability of welded construction for Arctic conditions, and had commissioned British escort carriers with riveted hulls for such operations! More seriously, the lack of Soviet support at sea and in the air showed that the convoys were on their own.

This was a messy episode of the war. On arrival at Vaenga, after refuelling, the cruiser *Trinidad* embarked 250 Poles who had been interned by the Soviets, many of whom wept with relief on boarding the cruiser; some even kissed the deck. They returned with the convoy QP6, which included six ships escorted by *Trinidad* and the surviving destroyer. After being spotted by a Junkers Ju88, the convoy experienced a foretaste of what was to come. On 31 January the *Empire Redshank* was bombed by *Luftwaffe* aircraft and took some damage. QP6 reached the Clyde on 2 February.

A far larger convoy with ten merchantmen resulted when PQ9 and PQ10 were merged after PQ9 had been delayed due to reports that the largest ship in the *Kriegsmarine*, the battleship *Tirpitz*, had been seen at sea moving northwards along the Norwegian coast. There was, however, no significant increase in escort strength as the additional ships consisted of a cruiser, HMS *Nigeria*, flagship of Rear Admiral Wake-Walker, with two destroyers, albeit augmented by two Norwegian armed whalers. By this time, the convoys were firmly international affairs with British, American, Soviet, Norwegian and Panamanian ships. Leaving Iceland on 2 February, the convoy passed through unchallenged and reached the Kola Inlet on 10 February, being escorted on the final stages by two ocean minesweepers. It was followed by a British trade delegation on 15 February, which arrived on the cruiser *Cairo*.

The next convoy, PQ11, left Loch Ewe on 6 February for Kirkwall on the mainland of Orkney, where it became weatherbound and was unable to sail until 14 February. The largest convoy thus far, PQ11 had thirteen ships, described by one naval officer aboard the escorts as 'an undistinguished collection of grey-hulled ships low in the water'. Once again, an increase in size did not mean an increase in the cover available. PQ11 had no cruiser, but two destroyers and two ocean-going minesweepers, two corvettes and three armed trawlers. On 17 February the destroyers and trawlers were detached, being returned to Londonderry having been on loan from Western

Approaches Command. Had the convoy left Kirkwall on schedule, they could have covered it for most of the way north, but the withdrawal of these ships demonstrated the ever increasing strain being placed on the Royal Navy's resources by this additional convoy route. It was fortunate that this convoy was not attacked, but it was the last to be unmolested for some considerable time, being protected by the appalling weather encountered, with rain and snow boosted by gale force winds interspersed with fog. The escorts were fitted with the new Type 271 radar, which although described as 'basic' or 'primitive', did at least make station-keeping much easier, especially in poor visibility. The small escort vessels had to contend with the spray that froze on their decks, requiring the crew to spend much time and effort chipping it off. Without this course of action, the stability of the vessels would have been compromised. Depth charges were similarly frozen to their racks.

Cruiser cover did not appear until PQ11 approached the Russian coastline, when *Nigeria* appeared, and eventually, on the last day at sea, two Soviet destroyers put in an appearance. PQ11 reached its destination on 23 February. The escorts were ordered back to sea on 1 March to join the Kola-based 6th Minesweeping Flotilla in escorting QP8.

While PQ11 had been stuck in Orkney prior to battling its way northwards, QP7 had sailed from Murmansk on 12 February to reach Seidisfjord ten days later, with seven ships from the combined PQ9/10 convoy plus the Soviet *Stalingrad* and two destroyers from the earlier combined convoy.

Note:

1. Imperial War Museum, Accession No. 8836.

Chapter 8

Encouraging
our Allies

The Soviet Union was an unreliable and uncertain ally for the UK as the two nations had nothing in common. It was also a demanding ally, expecting the hard-pressed British to demonstrate their commitment to Russia's survival. The British, not without some cause, were concerned that Russia might try to reach an accommodation with Germany – ceding parts of the Soviet Union's territory was considered by Stalin both before and immediately after the German invasion. While the British wished to help the Russians, opportunities for doing so were limited.

German possession of the ports of Petsamo and Kirkenes, north of the Arctic Circle made it more difficult for Russia's new allies to send supplies, since the direct route through the Baltic was completely out of the question!

Kirkenes, in Norway, had been taken by the Germans as they advanced in the spring and early summer of 1940. Petsamo, or Pechenga to the Russians, had changed hands on a number of occasions. Originally part of Russia, it became part of Finland when that country became independent in the wake of the Bolshevik Revolution, but it was one of the towns lost again as the price of peace in the Russo-Finnish War of 1940–41, and then regained as the Germans advanced towards Moscow.

In 1941, the only possible means of making an impact on the German forces attacking the Soviet Union lay with the Royal Navy, and especially with naval air power. The Commander-in-Chief, Home Fleet, was urged by the UK's wartime leader, Winston Churchill, to carry out an attack which would be 'a gesture in support of our Russian allies to create a diversion on the enemy's northern flank'. This led to Operation EF, with the cruisers HMS *Devonshire* and *Suffolk*, and the aircraft carriers *Victorious* and *Furious*, under the command of Rear Admiral W. F. Wake-Walker, leaving Scapa Flow on 23 July, refuelling at Iceland, and then heading for the operational zone. They found no German coastal convoys, and then, as they decided to attack the two ports, found little German shipping. On the other hand, while the *Luftwaffe* had moved its main strength to support the advance on the Russian front, the British force was discovered by German long-range reconnaissance on 30 July, and the *Luftwaffe* was waiting for them!

Operation EF saw the Royal Navy deploying one of its newest aircraft carriers, *Victorious*, and its oldest, *Furious*. Aircraft from *Victorious* included twenty Fairey Albacore torpedo-bombers from 827 and 828 naval air squadrons, escorted by Fairey Fulmar fighters from 809 Squadron. The elderly *Furious* sent nine Fairey Swordfish of 812 Squadron and nine Albacores of 817 Squadron, escorted by the Fulmars of 800 Squadron.

Although the Albacore was intended as a successor for the Swordfish, it was another biplane, with its main concession to the changing times being an enclosed cockpit. If providing yet another museum-piece for the Fleet Air Arm was not bad enough, the Albacore was notoriously unreliable, resulting in the Swordfish outlasting the Albacore in front line operational service.

The Operation

Operation EF was forced to take place in daylight because of the almost twenty-four hour summer sun of the far north. Neither port had the mass of significant warships that had been waiting at Taranto. The final approaches to the targets were also far more difficult.

Aircraft were flown off late in the afternoons of 22 and 25 July 1941. *Victorious* was to send twenty Albacore torpedo-bombers to Kirkenes, escorted by Fulmar fighters, while *Furious* was to send nine Albacores and nine Swordfish, again escorted by Fulmars, to Petsamo (Pechenga). The aircraft from *Victorious* had to fly over a German hospital ship on the way to the target, and were ordered not to attack, although, of course, those aboard could warn those ashore.

At Kirkenes the aircraft had to fly over a mountain at the end of the fjord before diving into the bay, where they found just four ships. After enduring heavy AA fire from positions on the cliffs, the attackers were themselves attacked by German fighters, and most of them had to jettison their torpedoes in a desperate bid to escape. They managed to sink just one cargo vessel of just 2,000 tons, and set another on fire. The slow and lumbering Fulmars did well to shoot down four *Luftwaffe* aircraft.

Petsamo was even worse, for the harbour was empty. Frustrated aircrew could do nothing more than aim their torpedoes at the wharves, hoping to do at least some damage.

Having received such a hot welcome for so little of any value in the target area, the attackers attempted to make their escape. This was easier said than done, for the aircraft were easy prey for the German fighters. The normal defensive drill in such circumstances was for the Swordfish or Albacore pilots to go right down on the water and wait, with the telegraphist/air-gunners watching for the cannon shells hitting the water, and at the last second calling out to the pilot, 'hard-a-starboard' or 'hard-a-port'. Flying just above the surface of the water also meant that the fighters had to pull out early or risk a high speed dive into the sea.

In the operation, *Victorious* lost thirteen of her aircraft, while *Furious* lost three. Altogether, forty-four aircrew were lost, seven of them killed, the remainder taken prisoner. Had the losses at Taranto been on a similar scale, seven aircraft would have been lost rather than just the two.

No. 809 Squadron had managed to shoot down three German fighters, although two of its aircraft were lost. Wake-Walker visited the wardroom of *Victorious* and attempted to boost morale by pointing out that the operation had shown the Russians that the Royal Navy was supporting them.

'However, the pilots and observers were so angry about the mishandling of the operation that they received what he had to say in stony silence,' remembered John Copper, one of the Fulmar pilots. 'The atmosphere was both eerie and embarrassing and he had no course but to withdraw.'[1]

Tovey's reaction was simple and straightforward:

The gallantry of the aircraft crews, who knew before leaving that their chance of surprise had gone, and that they were certain to face heavy odds, is beyond praise … I trust that the encouragement to the morale of our allies was proportionately great.

In short, great risks had been taken and heavy losses suffered for no material or strategic benefit at all!

Note:

1. *Daily Telegraph*, 24 February 1998.

Chapter 9

The *Tirpitz*
Ventures Out

With their ground forces bogged down in the Soviet Union and suffering from counter-attacks by the Red armies, Hitler decided to increase his naval power in Norway. This was partly because of the bombing of the *Scharnhorst*, *Gneisenau* and *Prinz Eugen* at Brest, which while never fatal to the ships, was nevertheless taking up resources that were needed to maintain the U-boat campaign in the Atlantic and the Bay of Biscay, and partly because Hitler was convinced that Norway was the weakest link in his defence structure. He believed that Norway was likely to be the point of entry for any Allied invasion of Europe, and of course, the Arctic convoys were enabling the Soviet Union to maintain its struggle against his invading forces. Hitler also had his own convoys down the Norwegian coast to think about, which were vulnerable to attack by the Allies. Operation Cerberus saw the battle-cruisers *Scharnhorst* and *Gneisenau*, and the heavy cruiser *Prinz Eugen*, moved from the Atlantic coast of France through the English Channel, shrugging off belated British efforts to attack the three ships, to the relative safety of northern waters. The result was that Germany established a strong naval battle group in the area. The battleship *Tirpitz* in the Aasfjord, 15 miles east of Trondheim, was joined by the *Admiral Scheer* and the *Prinz Eugen* on 20 February, and later still by the *Scharnhorst*, after the *Gneisenau* was damaged first by mines and then by heavy bombing. *Prinz Eugen* had a lucky escape on 23 February when she was torpedoed by the submarine *Trident* at 06.00, stopping her in the water, but not managing to inflict mortal damage.

This concentration of German naval force forced the Home Fleet to deploy the aircraft carrier *Victorious*, the battleship *King George V* (flagship for Admiral Tovey) and the cruiser *Berwick*, with four destroyers, to the area. Further north, the 10th Cruiser Squadron under Rear Admiral Burrough in HMS *Nigeria* was to provide support around Bear Island.

Churchill, when told of the risks to the convoys and indeed to the much overstretched Royal Navy, was unsympathetic, viewing the situation in stark political terms, anxious to keep the Soviet Union in the war at all costs. Meanwhile, the Russians ignored or simply made token gestures in response to British requests that they should mount anti-submarine patrols in Soviet waters and ensure that convoys received air cover when within range of Russian air bases. All of this was viewed by the British as being within Soviet capabilities, and indeed, something to be expected of them. By comparison, as early as September 1941, the United States Navy had started escorting convoys to and from the 'mid-Ocean meeting point' in the Atlantic, although the USA was still neutral.

The strengthening of German naval forces in Norway led to the homeward convoy QP8 being held back from 26 February to 1 March, by which time it included fifteen ships. At about the same time, the northbound convoy PQ12 with eighteen ships was leaving Iceland. PQ12 had as commodore, Captain H. T. Hudson, a Royal Naval Reserve officer flying his pennant in the *Llandaff*. Despite the presence of the main body of the Home Fleet and increased attention from RAF Coastal Command, this was to be the first convoy that would actually have to fight through to Murmansk. A fleet oiler was included, taking fuel to top up storage tanks at Polyarnoe for the ocean minesweepers stationed there by the Royal Navy, showing the high degree of self-sufficiency the Russians expected of this remote force. PQ12 was escorted by a cruiser, *Kenya*, and two destroyers, augmented by a small number of Norwegian whalers fitted for anti-submarine operations. The distant escort was much heavier, and included the battleship *Duke of York* with the battle-cruiser *Renown* and six destroyers. Meanwhile Tovey was on his way to join this force under Vice Admiral Curteis, with the battleship *King George V*, the carrier *Victorious*, the cruiser *Berwick* and six destroyers. *Berwick* was slow, but plans to relieve her with the more capable *Sheffield* had to be abandoned after the latter was mined.

Tirpitz is Spotted

On 5 March, a patrolling Focke-Wulf Fw200 Condor spotted the convoy, and at 17.00 on the following day, the submarine *Trident* spotted the *Tirpitz* at sea, but was out of radio range and could not report to the Admiralty. Another British submarine, the *Seawolf* spotted the German battleship at 18.01 but could not report until surfacing at 19.40. *Tirpitz* had *Vizeadmiral* Otto Ciliax aboard and was escorted by four destroyers. That same day, PQ12 ran into pack ice. Some of the ships were already straggling by this time, including some of the Norwegian whalers. The ice, while loosely packed, presented difficulties, for it slowed all the ships and also forced the commodore to attempt to segregate those ships not strengthened for operations in ice, from their sturdier companions, breaking up the convoy and making effective escort more difficult. The lightly built destroyers were also vulnerable, with *Oribi* suffering damage to her slender bows early on.

Kenya's commanding officer, Captain Denny, was later to say that he would never take a convoy anywhere near ice again following his experience with PQ12, taking any other risk in preference.

Meanwhile, the intelligence report from *Seawolf* did not reach Tovey until past midnight on 7 March. The report presented him with a dilemma. His initial reaction was to send Curteis to cover the convoy and attempt to confront *Tirpitz* himself, but the Admiralty felt that his force would be at danger from air attack if he went too close to the Norwegian coast. This was a wise assumption since at this time the Fleet Air Arm, while maintaining combat air patrols over the surface ships, was doing so with aircraft that were no real match for the *Luftwaffe*'s fighters. Tovey decided that he would disengage if *Tirpitz* really was their foe, wanting to avoid a repeat of the loss of the battle-cruiser *Hood*, or the severe damage inflicted on the aircraft carrier *Illustrious* off Malta in January 1941. *Illustrious* and *Victorious* were sister ships. Instead, if contact was made, the destroyers were to make a torpedo attack, and once within range, *Victorious* would have her Fairey Albacore torpedo-bombers ready.

As the weather worsened, the two opposing commanders were reduced to playing guessing games. Tovey's assumptions about the position of PQ12 were wrong, but Ciliax's intelligence was even worse, being more than two days out of date, and the severe weather prevented *Tirpitz* from launching one of her Arado reconnaissance aircraft. Like Tovey, caution was urged on Ciliax, and on no condition was he to engage superior forces, and even equal forces were only to be engaged on condition that it made the convoy's destruction likely. While Tovey's destroyers were likely to suffer if they strayed into the ice,

Ciliax's destroyers suffered from poor sea-keeping and mechanical unreliability. His one advantage was the line of four U-boats that he had deployed across the projected convoy path. In this game of cat and mouse, the fatal flaws were that Ciliax had underestimated the convoy's speed – PQ12 was moving clear of the German dispositions – while Tovey had overestimated the progress of QP8, and instead of sending his heavy units after the convoy, they were steaming away from it.

QP8 was indeed vulnerable. The escort consisted of just four small vessels, two minesweepers and two corvettes. The senior officer, Lieutenant Commander J. R. A. Seymour, had technical problems to contend with, since the asdic on two escorts was not working and another had her radar out of action. By this time the convoy was well clear of the local escort that had seen them out of Russian waters, which consisted of two minesweepers and two Soviet destroyers that had followed their own agenda, making searches independently, obscuring the escorts' asdic and then returning to base early. By 7 March the convoy had been scattered in bad weather, but twelve of the ships were back in position when QP8 and PQ12 passed at around noon. When one escort compared her longitude calculations with those of *Kenya*, they found a difference of 95 miles. This was a reflection of the difficulty of accurate navigation in polar latitudes where the longitude lines converge, especially after some time without making an accurate sight. Changing course to avoid the ice on the advice from *Kenya*, QP8 had the Germans across its course at a distance of some 50 miles for the heavy units, but the nearest German destroyer was just 10 miles away.

As PQ12 continued eastwards, *Kenya* chased after a tell-tale column of smoke that in the suddenly clear air turned out to be 30 miles away, and then proved to be a straggler from QP8. Later, on receiving reports from a straggler that she was being shelled by a warship, *Kenya*'s Walrus amphibian was put into the air on a reconnaissance mission, on strict orders not to lead any German ships towards the convoy, which was turned east-north-east at sunset. Confusion continued, but the ship was shelled and sunk by the destroyer *Friedrich Ihn*, which then headed for Tromso to refuel, followed by the rest of the destroyers. The British destroyers searching for the Germans then suffered the same problem and were ordered to Iceland to refuel.

The situation the following morning, 9 March, was that *Tirpitz* and PQ12 were on diverging courses until Ciliax decided to turn north. Believing, correctly, that he was to the east of the convoy, he started zigzagging in the hope of finding it. However, at 18.00, not realizing that he was little more than a hundred miles from PQ12, Ciliax gave up and set a course for the Vestfjord. PQ12 finally reached Murmansk and safety on 12 March, although some stragglers were still at sea the following day when one of the anti-submarine whalers, the *Stefa*, shot down an aircraft trying to bomb the merchantman *Sevaples*. One of the other stragglers joined the following convoy, PQ13.

The weather was not simply a hazard for the merchantmen. Two of the sturdy Norwegian armed whalers, designed to operate in the worst conditions, were sent from Iceland on 9 March 1942 to provide additional support for the convoy PQ12, but one of them capsized on 12 March due to the weight of ice on her upperworks, leaving just three survivors, who were picked up by the other whaler.

On 9 March Tovey again expected to encounter the *Tirpitz*. He realized that she would have to pass the Home Fleet, which was heading for the Lofoten Islands, on her way back to the Vestfjord. Aboard the aircraft carrier *Victorious*, the Fairey Albacores were again readied. Their opponents aboard the *Tirpitz* were alerted by the *B-Dienst* intelligence crew, which monitored British radio transmissions, that a battleship and a carrier were searching for them.

At 06.40, six Albacores were flown from *Victorious* to search for the Germans, while at 07.30 twelve Albacores armed with torpedoes took to the air. Tovey signalled Captain Bovell aboard the carrier: '... a wonderful chance which may achieve most valuable results. God be with you.'

At around 08.00, an Albacore spotted the *Tirpitz* with a destroyer 80 miles from the Home Fleet, but the aircraft itself was soon spotted, and while her AA gunners stood to and an Arado seaplane was flown off to watch out for the approaching British ships, *Tirpitz* turned east to try to outpace the Home Fleet. The evasive manoeuvre became all the more successful as the observer in the Albacore wrongly reported the change of course. Later, Albacores armed with torpedoes finally found the *Tirpitz*, framed by the rising sun, but then struggled to overtake her while flying into the wind, edging closer at an agonizingly slow 30 knots. In an attempt to get ahead of the *Tirpitz*, the squadron commander took his aircraft into cloud, but on overflying the *Tirpitz* and a destroyer, a gap in the clouds exposed the lumbering aircraft to heavy AA fire. The aircraft then manoeuvred into flights, aiming to attack the *Tirpitz* from all quarters. Had the attack been properly coordinated, the ship could have been trapped, but it was not to be. The first flight of three aircraft launched their torpedoes at the battleship's port bow, but her commanding officer, *Kapitän* Karl Topp, ordered his ship to turn to port and combed the tracks of the approaching torpedoes. The second flight attacked the starboard quarter, without success, and was followed by the third and fourth flights, which attacked on the starboard side but had difficulty getting into position given the wind and the high speed of the ship. As Topp ordered his ship to turn to starboard, he once again succeeded in combing all of the torpedoes. Two of the final six Albacores were shot down, and the Germans were sure that many of the others had suffered damage. The *Tirpitz* then completed her hasty return to Vestfjord. Had the *Luftwaffe* made aircraft available, the losses among the Albacores could have been far more serious. As it was, three Junkers Ju88 bombers attempted to attack *Victorious* at 15.45 on 9 March, but their bombs missed their target. Plans for the Fleet Air Arm to attack coastal targets in Norway were abandoned for want of suitable air cover.

A large flotilla of seven British destroyers was sent to intercept the *Tirpitz* should she move south to Aasfjord, arriving in position at 01.30 on 13 March, while a patrol line of submarines was deployed, with five boats spread between three positions. By the time the *Tirpitz* and her five escorting destroyers steamed south, the British destroyers had been withdrawn in high winds and blizzard conditions. Only one submarine, HMS *Trident* picked up the German force on her hydrophones, but was unable to distinguish between the battleship and her escorts, who were launching depth charges to keep British submarines away. Five days later, aerial reconnaissance showed the *Tirpitz* back in the Aasfjord, unscathed. The withdrawal of the destroyers may have seemed premature, but the attack on the *Tirpitz* would have been unlikely to succeed, given the weather and the strength of the escort, with German destroyers being larger and more powerful than their British counterparts.

Nevertheless, British strategy was increasingly based on the view that the destruction of the *Tirpitz* was of 'incomparably greater importance to the conduct of the war than the safety of any convoy', according to the Commander-in-Chief of the Home Fleet, Admiral Sir John Tovey. This preoccupation with big ships and their safety, or lack of it, was to mark the progress of the convoy war by both sides.

For their part, the British carefully husbanded their cruiser strength, withdrawing them when they were considered vulnerable. This left those aboard the merchantmen and even the smaller escorts feeling vulnerable, of little consequence and quite simply abandoned. On the other hand, bombs could seriously damage a cruiser, which was also vulnerable to submarine attack.

A change in strategy also now emerged from the Germans, who were convinced that their remaining major surface units were at serious risk, especially from British aircraft carriers. The convoys to Russia were now recognized as being significant, and Hitler himself called for this supply line to be cut, believing that renewed Russian counter-attacks were made possible by the supplies being carried by the convoys. Work on the aircraft carrier *Graf Zeppelin*, abandoned because of *Luftwaffe/Kriegsmarine* rivalry, was ordered to restart, while the cruiser *Seydlitz* was considered for conversion to an aircraft carrier and the liner *Potsdam* for conversion to an auxiliary carrier. Meanwhile, the U-boats and the *Luftwaffe* were to take the burden of countering the convoys.

The Germans Intensify the Attack

The Germans wasted little time in moving to the offensive. It is difficult to understand why it took them so long, for even had the *Wehrmacht* and *Luftwaffe* not been engaged in a life and death struggle with the Soviet armed forces, the importance of sinking so many Allied ships should have been obvious. After all, in two world wars, the *Kriegsmarine* had sought to destroy as many British convoys as possible with U-boats and surface raiders.

The position was summed up aptly by the commanding officer of the cruiser, HMS *Trinidad*, Captain L. S. Saunders, who told his crew after the morning service on Sunday, 22 March 1942, that the ship had been moved from patrolling to convoy escort, and that meant sailing between Bear Island and the North Cape, an area effectively controlled by the enemy. Worse, by March the hours of daylight were increasing.

'We can almost certainly expect to meet their ships, U-boats and planes,' Saunders continued. 'And many of you will receive your baptism of fire.'

Despite this warning, *Trinidad* was accompanied by just two destroyers as the escort for the convoy. There were three of the sturdy Norwegian whalers, intended for the Soviet Navy in the hope that they would boost the number of escorts operating out of Kola. The destroyer *Lamerton*, which had accompanied the convoy out of Reykjavik, was to remain as an escort to the fleet oiler *Oligarch*, but these two ships comprised Force Q, not formally part of the convoy as they were heading to refuel the destroyers accompanying the distant escort.

PQ13 was another international convoy with British, Swedish, American, Panamanian, Honduran and, surprisingly and even insensitively bearing in mind all too recent history, Polish ships. The commodore was a Royal Naval Reservist, Captain D. A. Casey, flying his blue and white pennant in the merchantman *River Afton*.

The heavy cruiser *Admiral Hipper* left the River Elbe at around this time and made a safe passage to Norway to be close to the *Tirpitz*, which she reached on 21 March. This gave the *Kriegsmarine* a battle group close to the convoy routes. Nevertheless, a powerful distant escort was assembled by the Home Fleet under Vice Admiral Curteis, with the battleships *King George V* and *Duke of York*, and the battle-cruiser *Renown*, the aircraft carrier *Victorious* and the cruisers *Edinburgh* and *Kent*, as well as eleven escorting destroyers.

As PQ13 steamed north, the homeward convoy QP9 was scheduled to depart from northern Russia at the same time, but was delayed by a couple of days by reports of U-boats off Kola, and it was not until 21 March that nineteen 'empties' started back. QP9 was under the charge of PQ12's commodore, Captain Hudson, but once again had a small escort composed of a destroyer and two minesweepers. The cruiser *Kenya*, intended to provide heavier support for the convoy, and which left Kola on 22 March, failed to find the convoy in worsening weather and radio silence. One cannot but wonder, however, whether *Kenya*'s failure to find the convoy was a tactical decision as her commanding officer had concerns of his own – she was carrying 10 tons of gold bullion from the Soviet Union to the UK; an important cargo given the immense support the bankrupt country was providing for its newfound Soviet 'ally'. For the first two days, QP9 had the support of five British minesweepers, the damaged wartime emergency destroyer *Oribi* and two Russian destroyers, although one of these lost contact with the convoy within hours of leaving Kola and can be counted as having been of no value whatsoever.

On 23 March, QP9 steamed into a severe gale blowing from the south-west bringing heavy snow, but despite this the convoy kept together. The weather eased late the following day allowing the watch aboard the minesweeper *Sharpshooter* to spot a surfaced U-boat during a break between snow storms, and with quick thinking, Lieutenant Commander Lampen, her commanding officer, succeeded in turning towards her, increasing speed and ramming *U-655*, sinking her before she could dive. His prompt action may have saved many ships, but it also meant that *Sharpshooter* herself was badly damaged. He had to hand over his role as senior officer of the escort to Lieutenant Commander Ewing aboard the destroyer *Offa*, allowing his ship to make her way home independently. Despite this inauspicious beginning, all the ships of the convoy and of the escort continued unmolested.

PQ13 was to enjoy no such luck. At first, all went well, with a stiff south-westerly wind actually helping rather than hindering the convoy, but early in the afternoon on 23 March, the convoy was re-routed eastwards after Ultra intelligence alerted the Admiralty to a line of U-boats, taking the convoy closer to the Norwegian coast and German airfields. The north-easterly course was resumed twenty-four hours later, but despite the diversion, the convoy was still some 40 miles ahead of its planned schedule. During the night of 24/25 March, the convoy ran into a severe north-easterly storm, and despite the time of year, spray began to freeze on the decks, superstructure, rigging and guns aboard the ships. Speed was reduced, but in the poor visibility and extreme conditions, station keeping suffered. Such were the difficulties that late on 25 March, Captain Saunders decided to disobey his strict orders to maintain radio silence and contacted the Admiralty and Rear Admiral R. H. Bevan, who was Senior British Naval Officer, North Russia, to make them aware of the situation. He also radioed the convoy to organize a rendezvous south of Bear Island for 27 March, a necessary step in the circumstances as it would give the convoy an opportunity to regroup rather than leaving solitary merchantmen at the mercy of German forces. The severe gale lasted well into 26 March, so that too few ships were able to keep the Bear Island rendezvous, and the distant escort suffered damage not only to the destroyer *Tartar*, but also to the fast armoured aircraft carrier *Victorious*, forcing it to return to Scapa Flow. The threat from the Germans had already been brought home to those aboard the ships, as during the afternoon of 26 March a German aircraft found four merchantmen. Together they fought off the attacker, with DEMS gunners claiming a possible kill. During the storm, the cruiser *Nigeria* met *Trinidad*.

Worse was to follow. Shortly after midnight on 26/27 March, the Admiralty sent the first of three messages warning of German surface raiders. Lieutenant Commander C. H. Campbell, the escort's senior officer commanding the destroyer HMS *Fury*, was still attempting to gather the merchantmen together, but almost twelve hours later he received a distress message from the whaler *Sumba*, which was desperately short of fuel. Fortunately, a radio operator aboard the destroyer obtained a radio bearing of *Sumba*'s signal, and Campbell turned his ship onto a course west of south-west, eventually finding *Sumba* at 16.00. It took almost five hours to refuel the former Norwegian vessel, during which both it and the destroyer were at risk from any U-boat or aircraft that happened to stumble across them.

Almost equally at risk was the *River Afton*, carrying the convoy commodore, which was unable to head into the wind and was being forced shorewards. It was not until noon that the ship was able to resume her course, but far from leading the convoy, she made a solitary voyage to the Kola Inlet.

Despite the odds being against them, the convoy escorts did manage to gather some of the merchantmen together, with *Trinidad* finding two ships by 22.00 on 27 March. The destroyer *Eclipse* found another ship, while five more were together but to the south of the convoy escort. Rather than hang around with the merchantmen, *Trinidad* hastened back to the rump of the convoy, anxious to rejoin the two destroyers. There was mutual defence in this, as the cruiser's heavier armament would be needed if surface raiders appeared, although it would be hard put to cope with the heavy cruiser *Hipper*, let alone the battleship *Tirpitz*. On the other hand, the cruiser would be at the mercy of the U-boats, for which the destroyers with their asdic would be best suited. The cruiser also carried a substantial AA armament, but when, shortly after 10.00, her lookouts spotted a Blohm und Voss Bv138 reconnaissance flying boat, and her AA batteries opened up, the aircraft was too far away to be caught, and the confident German aircrew reputedly signalled that 'your shots are falling short'. The remaining ships of the convoy had by this time formed up into isolated groups of as many as half a dozen vessels.

The Bv138 had a distinctive appearance and was easily recognized at a time when aircraft recognition, especially friend or foe, left much to be desired. The aircraft had three engines, and a twin-boom fuselage – the tailplane was supported by booms running from the wings rather than sitting on the end of the fuselage.

Unknown to the British, the *Kriegsmarine* was suffering a serious shortage of fuel, especially boiler oil, and the intervention of heavy units of the fleet was unlikely. In any case, the convoy was by this time too far north from their base near Trondheim, but the local commander, *Konteradmiral* (Rear Admiral) Hubert Schmundt, 'Admiral Arctic', had three large destroyers from the Eighth Destroyer Flotilla, also known as the 'Narvik Flotilla', at his disposal in Kirkenes, and at 13.30, the *Z26* led the *Z24* and *Z25* to sea. Despite their classification as destroyers, their guns equated to 5.9-in. and were a match for the 6-in of the *Trinidad*. In theory, the destroyers were faster than the cruiser, but in the open sea the cruiser's greater length and tonnage would have given her an advantage.

Meanwhile, an anti-submarine trawler was attacked by aircraft from Banak at 11.27, while two ships were twice bombed by Junkers Ju88s of *Luftflotte 5*. Two more ships suffered near misses, which could often be as devastating as a direct hit, and indeed one merchantman, *Ballot* suffered burst pipes and lost way, the master deciding to allow a partial abandoning of his ship and sending sixteen men to the whaler *Silja* by lifeboat. Emergency repairs were put in hand, and the crippled ship eventually reached her destination safely.

With their location known to the Germans, there were frequent but brief radio transmissions from *Trinidad* as her commanding officer desperately sought the other ships of the convoy. At 13.15 her radar found a solitary aircraft that dropped three bombs, all of which were near misses. These were followed by a more sustained attack by Junkers Ju88 bombers, again near misses, but this time so close that the radio transmitters were damaged. Fog banks provided welcome relief as the cruiser raced and twisted and turned to avoid her attackers, while her crew, by now thoroughly blooded, put up heavy AA fire. Meanwhile two merchantmen were bombed, although both survived. Less fortunate was the *Empire Ranger*, bombed as darkness fell at 19.30 and sunk. Her survivors were picked up at 22.45 by one of the German destroyers before the trawler *Blackfly*, alerted by her distress signal, could reach the area. The three German destroyers spent the night steaming west in line abreast, three miles apart, steaming at a comfortable 15 knots. The destroyer leader, *Z26*, commanded by *Kapitän* Ponitz, found the merchantman *Bateau*, ordered her crew to abandon ship and then sank her by gunfire and torpedo. The crew from this ship were also rescued and interrogated, while the Germans

85

loitered before Ponitz decided that he was too far north and turned his small force south-eastwards, increasing his speed to 25 knots, before turning north again at 05.30.

Meanwhile, at 04.00 on 29 March, *Trinidad* and *Fury* were heading east by north-east to rendezvous with a group of convoy stragglers. In the early morning haze another vessel was spotted on the starboard side at a distance of some 4 miles. Believing this to be a surfaced U-boat, *Trinidad*'s 6-in armament opened fire, but firing ceased after three salvoes as the possibility that the target could be a lifeboat under sail occurred to those on the bridge, but the 'lifeboat' dived. At about this time the two ships were joined by the destroyer *Oribi* and two Soviet destroyers.

This time, two days later than planned, the rendezvous finally happened. Saunders immediately attached the two Soviet destroyers to the escort and sent *Oribi* on a sweep to find any other stragglers, after which she was to rejoin the Russians. *Oribi* headed off with *Fury* to search for a group of stragglers who had strayed some way to the east.

The eastern group had been led by a whaler, *Silja*, and consisted of five merchantmen having already lost one that had fallen behind with bomb damage. During the hours of darkness, these ships ran into heavy ice. The whaler, a class of ship notoriously short on range, was by this time short of fuel and was taken in tow by one of the merchantmen, *Induna*. The men ordered off the *Ballot* crossed an ice floe on foot to join the *Induna*, adding another sixteen men to her ship's company of fifty. Shortly afterwards, the two ships were stuck firm in the ice, but eventually managed to move astern. Still with the whaler in tow, they followed a course through the ice that the *Empire Starlight* was managing to force through heavy blizzards that contributed to the poor visibility. Shortly after daybreak, this force was joined by the armed trawler *Blackfly*.

The Ship that Torpedoed Herself

Having found nothing more during the night, Ponitz took his three destroyers back westwards at 17 knots, with *Trinidad* and *Fury* steaming at 20 knots on a reciprocal course towards them. As the morning passed, visibility deteriorated with a leaden sky and fog drifting off the ice floes. Fortunately, Saunders had already identified the three destroyers earlier, and when his radar operator picked up three ships at 6.5 miles, confirmed as probably hostile at 4.5 miles, the crews of the cruiser and destroyer closed up to action stations at 08.45. At 08.49 the three destroyers were seen, but before his duty signalman could complete the challenge, Saunders ordered fire to be opened at 08.51. The Germans must have done the same, for almost immediately two shells from Z26 struck *Trinidad*'s aft 'Y'-turret while her own fire hit Z26 amidships. The cruiser redirected her fire to a second destroyer, but the destroyers then changed course and vanished into the fog. Expecting a torpedo attack, Saunders changed the cruiser's course and was gratified to find shortly afterwards that he had successfully combed two torpedoes. The cruiser regained radar contact with Z26, as damage control parties struggled with a shell hole in her hull, and started to gain on the destroyer, while the other two German destroyers started evasive manoeuvres fearing a torpedo attack from *Fury*. At 1.5 miles, Saunders could see Z26, and altered course to starboard to bring all his guns to bear, while also preparing a torpedo attack. The German destroyer started to zigzag as 6-in shells fell around her, and as the cruiser prepared to launch her torpedoes. The first torpedo was launched from the port triple tube, but the torpedo officer then delayed firing the second and third as he adjusted the angle of attack, only to find that both had frozen in their tubes. Meanwhile, the first torpedo, either because of a gyro problem or because the gyro had been toppled by the British shells falling around it, promptly reversed course and headed back towards *Trinidad*. At 09.24, the cruiser was struck by her own torpedo on the port side, rupturing a fuel tank. The men from the gunnery direction transmitting station deep between the two main bunker tanks were left struggling to escape. Four managed it before an armoured hatch fell and broke the back of the fifth man, and at the same time the inner bulkhead of the port fuel tank gave way and the remaining seventeen men were drowned in heavy fuel oil. In the forward boiler room, other men were suffering the agony of being scalded by super-heated steam from fractured pipes as sea water poured in. The cruiser rapidly listed to port while steering and command were moved to the emergency position aft.

Seeing her opponent's distress, Z26 attempted to escape, but found herself being chased by *Fury* and heading towards two British and two Soviet destroyers. Confusion reigned as *Fury* emerged from the fog. Those aboard the British destroyers were expecting *Trinidad*, having heard her gunfire earlier, while one of the Soviet destroyers opened fire before realizing her mistake. *Fury* herself fired a couple of salvoes before returning to stand by the crippled cruiser. One of the British destroyers, *Eclipse*, then raced after an unidentified vessel, anxious to take part in the destruction of a German destroyer. It was not until 09.50 that *Eclipse* was able to identify the fleeing *Z26*, but the Germans believed that her pursuer was one of her own group and flashed a challenge at her. A destroyer to destroyer engagement now commenced, with the British ship housing just 4.7-in guns, heavily outgunned. The Germans had lost their after armament in the earlier engagement with *Trinidad*, but the forward gun, 'A', on *Eclipse* was frozen and unusable. Despite blizzards and frozen spray and the zigzagging of the Germans that made accurate gun laying impossible, over a period of around thirty minutes, six shells from *Eclipse* struck *Z26*, one causing an explosion in an ammunition store and another hitting the boiler room. It was now the German's turn to lose speed and list to port, her stern sinking fast. By 10.22 she was dead in the water. *Eclipse* had not come off lightly, having taken two hits and having several of her crew wounded when a ready use ammunition locker exploded. She had also lost most of her torpedoes when a torpedo man fired three by mistake.

As *Eclipse* prepared to use her remaining torpedo for the *coup de grâce*, *Z24* and *Z25* suddenly appeared on the scene, and opened fire on the British destroyer, which was caught in the open during a break in the weather. The commanding officer had no option but to turn and head at full speed for the cover offered by a blizzard, but although the Germans did not pursue, they continued to fire and *Eclipse* was hit at least four times, twice aft and twice forward as shells fell under her bow, while her aerials were swept away. By 10.35 she was safely hidden, and fifteen minutes later *Z26* sank beneath the waves. Her survivors were picked up by the other two ships which then withdrew at speed to Kirkenes.

Eclipse emerged from the blizzard badly damaged, only to find a surfaced U-boat ahead, but the destroyer's commanding officer managed to comb the track of the two torpedoes that were loosed in his direction before the German dived. The area was depth charged, but eventually the crippled destroyer was forced to give up the fruitless search for her opponent. *Eclipse*, short of fuel, nevertheless managed to reach the Kola Inlet the next day, 30 March, with her tanks almost empty.

Two days earlier, on 28 March, four British minesweepers from Kola had been sent to help bring the convoy to safety, with one ordered to look for survivors from the *Empire Ranger*, but they were unaware that the boats had been sighted, fully provisioned but empty. They also had to look out for the *River Afton*, but these orders were soon changed and the minesweepers were sent to help the crippled *Trinidad*. The cruiser was in a bad way, with no lighting other than a battery circuit for the crowded sick bay, and while hot drinks were served to her crew, only cold food could be provided. Two destroyers provided an anti-submarine screen as she limped south-east at just 6 knots. Efforts were made to correct her list by transferring fuel between tanks, and speed increased to 12 knots, until salt in the boiler water brought her to a halt. Now a sitting duck, her destroyer screen at least managed to drive off a U-boat after an earlier depth charge attack had failed, but the U-boat concerned was sunk by a minefield. While waiting for tugs from the Kola Inlet, just 70 miles away, to arrive, the engine room crew managed to rectify the problem and again the cruiser got under way at 7 knots. Badly crippled after being blown off course by the rising wind, the only way to correct her course was to go astern and bring the stern round, before resuming her laboured forward progress. Nevertheless, at 09.30 on 30 March, the cruiser entered the Kola Inlet under her own steam, and the tugs that eventually arrived were not needed as she managed to anchor off the dry dock at Rosta.

While the mainstay of the escort for PQ13 was by this time safe, most of the convoy was still at sea, and in danger. At 07.30 on 30 March, *Induna* was torpedoed and sunk by *U-435*. The torpedo ignited gasoline in No. 5 hold and the resulting explosion blew barbed wire rolls across the deck, preventing men from reaching the boats. Many of those aboard, including those from the *Ballot*, were horribly burnt while others dived overboard into the cold sea. There were difficulties in getting the ship's boats away, but *U-435* surfaced and fired another torpedo, which entered No. 4 hold, causing the ship to settle by the stern, raising her bows high into the air. Those who managed to get into the two boats were left at sea for four days. Many aboard were badly scalded and all had completely insufficient clothing. On one boat, seven men died during the first night. Frostbite and hypothermia set in, and there was nothing to drink as the water aboard froze solid. The survivors picked up late on 2 April had to be lifted out of their boat by slings as they were too weak to climb, but they were fortunate, as their rescuing Soviet minesweeper later ran down the other lifeboat with nine men left aboard, although some survived until picked up. Out of sixty-six men aboard the *Induna*, just twenty-four survived, and of these, eighteen lost limbs.

As the *Trinidad* entered the Kola Inlet, the destroyer *Effingham* was torpedoed and sunk, also by *U-435*.

PQ13 brought home the reality of the Arctic convoys and the cost of keeping the Soviet Union supplied. Some 30,000 tons of desperately needed merchant shipping was lost, along with more than a quarter of the ships. Despite Admiralty attempts to dismiss these losses as 'stragglers', the fact remains that at least two groups of ships had attempted to re-form themselves and one to the east of the convoy route had lost two ships steaming towards Russia without any escort at all. The distant escort was more of an escort on paper than in reality. It could have been used to support and replace the troubled *Trinidad*, it could have used its destroyers and aircraft to find, round up and protect the stragglers. As it was, it was little more than a waste of fuel and resources.

Meanwhile, the *Silja*, which had been so much trouble, was found later on 30 March by *Oribi* and taken in tow by the minesweeper *Harrier* so that she too eventually reached Kola safely.

Far less fortunate were the other two whalecatchers, *Sulla* and *Sumba*. It is generally believed that *Sulla* was sunk on 1 April by *U-436*. The fate of *Sumba* has been widely disputed, although many believe that she capsized after gathering too great a weight of ice on her superstructure.

On a brighter note, between them QP9 and PQ13 had shot down several German aircraft, sunk two U-boats and a German destroyer. These losses and those earlier during the two battles of Narvik, were gradually making the Germans more and more reluctant to use their surface fleet, and especially the heavy units, instead relying on air power and the U-boat. The importance of naval aviation, especially carrier-borne aviation, had occurred to them, but despite the order to convert two ships and resume work on the one carrier under construction, the will to pursue this to the end was clearly lacking – one just has to look at the efforts of the American shipbuilding industry in converting Cleveland-class cruisers to light aircraft carriers, and of building substantial numbers of auxiliary or escort carriers both for their own use and that of the Royal Navy, while at the *same time* building up a massive fleet of Essex-class fleet carriers to see just what could be done. Germany lacked America's shipbuilding industry and manpower, but failed even to make a proportionate response.

Two of the merchant ships also carried a substantial number of naval personnel, taken off by warships before their ships reached Soviet territory, whose purpose has been something of a mystery. It does seem that an ever-increasing number of British personnel had to be based in the Soviet Union to speed the turn-round of both merchant ships and warships. Port facilities at Murmansk were poor, and were not the best at Archangel even when it was open, and despite the brutal and demanding nature of the Soviet regime, very little coordination existed to enhance the throughput of cargo and the refuelling of ships, the responsibility for which lay primarily in British hands. Ships needed to carry sufficient supplies for the return trip. In fact, the anchorage at Vaenga Bay was crowded with British ships while ashore a Russian airstrip was used by RAF personnel to prepare the Hawker Hurricane fighters being sent to the Soviet Union. This was an exposed position and anchors frequently lost their grip. Basically the Soviet attitude was one of suspicion and obstruction. The lack of suitable cranes in the Soviet ports meant that heavy lift ships were earmarked by the Ministry of War Transport in London to speed the discharge of cargoes. These were essential for the discharge of armoured vehicles, especially tanks, and their crews often spent as long in Russia as the Royal Navy personnel posted there in the naval shore parties.

Even when the Russians were prepared to help, they were hindered by their own country's backwardness. Hospital facilities were primitive, a major concern when convoys arrived with men wounded and others, especially survivors plucked from the sea, suffering from exposure. The late arrival of the damaged *Trinidad* was not simply a setback for the convoy escort programme, it also meant that here was a ship whose sick bay could not be used.

One of the lessons that was becoming clear by this time, as German operations against the convoys intensified, was that warships needed to stay close to the convoys rather than being distracted from this duty by the temptation to chase and attack the enemy's warships and U-boats. Once warships had dashed off for the greater glory and excitement of 'beating up' the enemy, the merchantmen were left exposed, and so too were those on the minor escort vessels, even if the escorts were successful and returned unscathed. There was also the problem of fuel and ammunition expended in chasing the enemy.

Had they had more ships available, and more fuel, the Germans could have done much at first by tempting escorts away and then leaving the convoys defenceless against the U-boats.

Chapter 10

The Threat of
the *Tirpitz*

The two most impressive German warships were the sisters *Bismarck* and *Tirpitz*. These battleships had an official net displacement of around 43,000 tons and a full load displacement of around 48,000 tons, although a post-war United States Navy assessment put the latter figure at closer to 50,000 tons. A broad beam ensured that they had the stability to act as an effective gun platform in the open seas and three screws gave them a maximum speed of 30 knots. Heavily armoured, these ships had two twin 38-cm (approximately 15-inch) turrets forward and another two aft. Their reconnaissance aircraft were four single-engined Arado Ar196 monoplane floatplanes, capable of flying at almost 200mph. Each had a complement of 2,200 men, including the admiral's staff and war correspondents.

Bismarck's active career was very brief indeed, being sunk on 27 May 1941, during her maiden sortie into the Atlantic. The operation was not completely one-sided as during the long chase by the Royal Navy, the British battle-cruiser *Hood* was blown out of the water by a shell believed to have come from *Bismarck*'s escort, the heavy cruiser *Prinz Eugen*.

Having lost two major ships so early in the war, with the *panzerschiff Admiral Graf Spee* lost to three British cruisers in December 1939, Hitler became extremely nervous about allowing the few major units of the *Kriegsmarine* anywhere near British warships. He was especially worried about carrier-borne aircraft, even though his own *Luftwaffe* had inflicted serious damage on the aircraft carrier *Illustrious* in January 1941 and, later that year, her sister ship *Formidable*. So it was that the only time the *Tirpitz* fired her guns in anger was when they were used to bombard shore installations at Spitzbergen, the Norwegian island on which the Russians had long-standing coal mining rights.

Nevertheless, the threat of the *Tirpitz* was so real and her proximity to the convoy route so close that the ship's destruction became almost an obsession with the Admiralty, and indeed the entire British War Cabinet. While the Fleet Air Arm had by this stage established a good reputation for sinking enemy warships, with the attacks on the *Konigsberg* and the Italian fleet at Taranto, as well as assistance in the sinking of the *Bismarck* and at the Battle of Matapan, the destruction of the *Tirpitz* was to be far more difficult. The ship was usually anchored in a Norwegian fjord, whose steep sides precluded the type of torpedo-bomber attack that had worked so well against heavily armoured battleships. Dive-bombing had sunk the light cruiser *Konigsberg*, but could only damage a battleship, with bombs often bouncing off armour plating. The high mountains surrounding the fjord and its steep sides meant that level bombing tended to be from too great an altitude, and in any case, the Fleet Air Arm lacked aircraft capable of delivering a large enough bomb, while the ship was for part of the time beyond the range of RAF heavy bombers – but this was to change.

Sink the *Tirpitz*!

The first attempt to sink the *Tirpitz* was in March 1942 using aircraft from HMS *Victorious*, but this was beaten off by a combination of heavy AA fire and German fighters.

It was clear that the destruction of the *Tirpitz* would require exceptional measures, and the Royal Navy, sometimes considered conservative, was in fact well prepared for this. The service had not neglected specialized craft once war started, and had captured Italian human torpedoes, known in British naval circles as 'chariots'. It had developed a one-man submarine, the 'Welman', which proved impractical, but had then gone on to develop the midget submarine. British midget submarines were known as 'X-craft' and had a four-man crew. One or two members of the crew had to leave the craft in wet suits with breathing apparatus to place explosive charges on the target, rather than, as with Axis midget submarines, carrying torpedoes.

The first serious attempt to sink the *Tirpitz* was in October 1942, using two-man human torpedoes. It was a failure because the two chariots slung under a fishing boat broke loose in bad weather close to the target.

It was to be almost a year before a further attack could be made. The second attempt used X-craft, but the operation was not without its problems. On the morning of 22 September, 1943, *X6* ran aground in the Kaafjord, then broke free and surfaced after hitting a rock, but although she dived again, her gyro was out of action and the periscope barely usable. She then ran into a net, surfaced, and was fired at and had hand-grenades thrown at her by members of the battleship's crew before she could escape. Lieutenant Donald Cameron in *X6* then went astern, and in doing so his hydroplanes struck the side of the *Tirpitz* and dropped his charges. He then scuttled *X6* and ordered his crew into the water, where they were picked up by one of the battleship's picket boats.

Earlier, *X7*, commanded by Lieutenant Basil Place, snagged a mine hawser. Place had to leave the submarine and crawl along the casing before using his feet to disentangle the hawser. He then had to push the mine away with his feet several times before the submarine was free. It was then *X7*'s turn to get caught in a torpedo net surrounding the *Tirpitz*. In attempting to go astern to escape, Place also surfaced. He dived quickly, but found that *X7* was stuck at 95 feet. Further manoeuvring allowed the X-craft to rise, but this time Place found himself inside the net less than a hundred feet from the *Tirpitz*. He placed his charges, but continually became stuck in nets as he attempted to escape.

At 08.12, three minutes early, the charges exploded, knocking Cameron, who was aboard awaiting interrogation, off his feet. The explosions also blew *X7* clear of the nets, but by this time she was uncontrollable and surfaced, where she came under heavy fire from the Germans. Place gave the order to abandon ship, but only himself and one other survived, with the other two crew members killed by machine-gun fire. Meanwhile, panic had swept through the *Tirpitz*'s gunners and they fired indiscriminately, killing 120 German personnel, many of them in other ships and at shore installations.

Unusually, Place and Cameron were each awarded the Victoria Cross while still German prisoners of war. The damage to the *Tirpitz* was considerable, and she was out of action for several months.

There were to be no less than twenty-two air attacks on the *Tirpitz*. One of them had some success. Operation Tungsten was mounted on 3 April 1944 using aircraft from *Furious* and *Victorious* and three escort carriers, *Emperor*, *Pursuer* and *Searcher*. The larger carriers carried Fairey Barracudas for dive-bombing and torpedo-dropping, while the escorts carried a mixture of Grumman Wildcats and Hellcats and Vought Corsairs to provide fighter cover. A more effective aircraft than the Albacore, the Barracuda was another attempt to replace the Swordfish, and around 2,600 were built, even though it was described by some as a 'maintenance nightmare', and also had the unfortunate reputation of occasionally diving into the ground.

The target was difficult, and not just because of the terrain. The Germans had installed a smoke pipeline around the shores of the fjord and simply had to turn on a tap to fill the area with smoke. There were also smoke pots around the ship. It was estimated that it could take just eight minutes to fill the whole fjord with smoke.

Given the difficult location, the raid needed to be conducted in daylight, and a dawn raid was decided upon to give the attackers at least the cover of darkness while on their way to the target. The aircrew were woken at 01.30, having been briefed that this was to be a very dangerous operation and that heavy casualties must be expected.

The first strike aircraft were flown off at 04.30, flying just above sea level to evade enemy radar, before climbing to 8,000 feet to cross the snow-covered mountains. They arrived over the ship at 05.30. Sub-Lieutenant John Herrald recalled:

As I looked at this hill, it fell below us slowly, and then with a sudden surge we were over the top. There below us lay the *Tirpitz* in the exact place we had been told to look for her. Suddenly the leader shouted over the intercom: 'Attention fighters! Anti-flak! Over, over!' and as he said that he was slowly doing a half-roll and going down to the target. We peeled off and dived down behind him. While we were going down on our attack, the fighter squadrons were strafing the anti-aircraft positions and ships. They supported us with everything they had got, no risk seemed too great for them to take.

I had the nose of my aircraft pointing just below the funnel of the *Tirpitz*. I could see the fighters raking her decks, and for a few seconds I lived in a world which just contained my aircraft and the *Tirpitz*. I kept her nose glued to that point of the ship. I gazed at my altimeter and saw that I had a thousand feet to go until I got to my bombing height. In the few seconds that followed I could see the details of the ship; the swastika

96

painted on her funnel, the faces of the ack-ack crews glaring up at us, and, a great sight, the leader's bombs bursting on the turrets.[1]

He dropped his bombs as he pulled out of his dive and started to weave to avoid enemy flak as he climbed away.

A second wave of aircraft appeared an hour later, fully expecting a hot welcome from the Germans, but they could still see the ship through a smokescreen produced by canisters placed around the fjord, while the smoke made it difficult for the AA gunners to see the attacking aircraft. The attack succeeded in inflicting further damage on the warship, resulting in a large oil leak. The two air attacks combined put her out of action for another three months. In fact, fifteen bombs had hit the ship, and with the fighters strafing the upper deck and superstructure, the attacks left 122 dead and a further 316 wounded, including the ship's commanding officer. Three Barracudas were lost, one fighter suffered an accident and another had to ditch.

The Heavy Bombers Take Their Turn

It was now the turn of the Royal Air Force, but even for the Avro Lancaster, probably the best heavy bomber in the war in Europe, the operation presented a formidable challenge. The return flight was around 3,000 miles. The question of whether or not it would be possible was solved by the commanding officer of the selected squadron, the famous 617 'Dam Busters' Squadron, Wing Commander J. B. 'Willie' Tait, who had three aircraft fully fuelled and loaded with the correct weight of bombs and sent off with his least experienced crews to fly around Great Britain, a distance equal to the flight to and from the target. The least experienced crews were chosen because their performance would dictate the maximum range. Another aircraft was sent off with half fuel to represent an empty aircraft. Once the aircraft landed, their performance was assessed. The target was just beyond range.

The solution soon occurred to Tait's superior, Air Vice Marshal the Honourable Ralph Cochrane. The attack could be mounted from the Soviet Union, using an airfield at Yagodnik, on an island in the Dvina River, some 20 miles from Archangel. More important, it was just 600 miles from the Altenfjord.

'Fly to Yagodnik from northern Scotland with your bombs,' said Cochrane. 'Refuel there, do the job, return to Yagodnik to refuel again and come home.'

In the event, two squadrons were sent, with No. 9 Squadron accompanying 617, while two Consolidated Liberator bombers carried ground crew and spares. The force flew from their base at Scampton in Lincolnshire to RAF Lossiemouth in northern Scotland and, on 10 September 1944, took off for Russia, carrying their 12,000-lb Tallboy bombs and so much fuel that the aircraft were a ton over-weight. The flight itself was not without its problems, as being so far north the magnetic compasses failed to work properly, and the navigators were forced to use sextants. This was fine for a 20 knot ship, but unsatisfactory in an aircraft flying at more than ten times that speed. Clear visibility enabled them to use landmarks. The flight took more than twelve hours, made worse by anxiety towards the end as they were unable to pick up a signal from the radio beacon at Yagodnik because it was transmitting on another frequency. It was only by luck that aircraft descending through very low cloud found the river and made their way to the airfield. Just eleven Lancasters and the two Liberators made it successfully to the airfield, but fortunately the 'missing' aircraft were soon found at other Russian airfields, including four that found their way to an airfield on another island in the same river. Even so, six aircraft from the two squadrons were written off because they had landed on marshes or ground that was too soft.

While the scattered aircraft were flown to Yagodnik, the operation was delayed for three days because of heavy rain. It was not until 15 September that the weather cleared, and a weather reconnaissance aircraft returned with the report that the skies over the Altenfjord were also clear. The waiting crews were ready, and engines were quickly started. Soon twenty-eight Lancasters from Nos 9 and 617 squadrons were in the air, keeping radio silence and flying low over the wave tops to ensure that the enemy could not detect them until the last few minutes of the attack. Just 90 miles from the target, the aircraft were forced to climb over mountains, but as Altenfjord came into view ahead of the leading aircraft, they could see the first of the smoke coming from the smoke pots. One Lancaster crew member estimated that there must have been a hundred of them. Then the flak started. As the hull disappeared under the smoke, bomb-aimers tried to keep their sights on the mastheads, but then these too disappeared.

All of them lost their marks in the last minute or two before the bombs were dropped, and as their aircraft shot upwards with the release of the bombs, many hoped that theirs had hit the target. Flickers seen through the white smoke followed by a plume of black smoke showed that the bombs were exploding, but the realists guessed that these were their bombs striking the side of the fjord. A few kept their bombs and made a second run, while some returned to Yagodnik with their bombs, hoping for a second attempt later, but the rain returned. One aircraft failed to return, having drifted off course and crashed into a mountain. One bomb-aimer believed that he had seen a bomb from the aircraft in front of him hit the ship, and some time after their return, a message was received from a Norwegian source that she had in fact been hit – and the 12,000-lb Tallboy bomb had blown a large hole in the forward deck.

The damage was serious enough for the ship to be moved south to Tromso for repairs, 200 miles further south and shortening the return trip from Lossiemouth by 400 miles, bringing the ship within range. Even so, overloaded fuel tanks would be needed to give the aircraft an extra 300 gallons. Unable to use the bomb bays that would be filled by the Tallboys, they hunted for tanks that had once been used in Wellingtons and could be slid inside the fuselage. As preparations for the attack were being made, reports came in that at least twenty and perhaps as many as thirty *Luftwaffe* fighter aircraft had been moved to the airfield at Bardufoss, close to Tromso, doubtless to provide air cover for the *Tirpitz*. Accuracy meant that the attack would have to be made by day with the aircraft operating in a loose gaggle rather than in a tight formation in which they could cover each other. To save weight, there would be no mid-upper gunners. The fear was that sending aircraft on such a mission would be tantamount to suicide.

Once again, the squadron had to wait for a break in the weather. They were sent north to Lossiemouth, while in London arguments started over whether the aircraft should carry Tallboys or 2,000-lb armour piercing bombs. Those with first hand experience knew that the 2,000-lb bombs would not work. A senior officer slid the memorandum advocating the armour-piercing bombs into his in-tray, saying that he would look into it the following day!

The aircraft took off in the early hours of 12 November, hoping to be over Tromso by dawn, flying at 1,000 feet over the sea. As they climbed towards Tromso, German radar picked them up and the air gunners closed up over their guns as they reached 14,000 feet. Then they saw the ship ahead and below, like a large elongated spider amidst the web of her torpedo nets. The AA gunners aboard the *Tirpitz* were the first to open fire. The bomber crews waited for the smokescreen to start, but the Germans had still to prime the smoke pots that had only just been moved down from the Altenfjord.

As the aircraft dropped their bombs one by one, wheeling as the massive 6 ton weight was released, they watched anxiously for fighters. A yellow flash on the foredeck told of a bomb hitting the ship, then a bomb hit the shore before two more in close succession struck her, one by the bridge on the starboard side and one abaft the smoke-stack, while others hit the sea only feet from the ship. Then, through the smoke from the fires came a flash and a plume of steam 500 feet high as a magazine exploded. As 617 Squadron's Lancasters throbbed away from the scene, No. 9 Squadron's aircraft followed and aimed their bombs into the smoke. Despite their fears, there were no signs of fighters, and as the last aircraft turned for Lossiemouth, they were able to look back. As the smoke cleared, they could see the *Tirpitz* start to list.

For the bomber crews, the flight home was anything but an anti-climax. Tait, the squadron commander, lost his artificial horizon and then, in a state of exhaustion, had to find a diversionary airfield as bad weather closed Lossiemouth. He eventually landed at a small airfield that was home to a Coastal Command torpedo-bomber squadron. When he eventually did get to Lossiemouth, by road, the reconnaissance report was coming in, followed soon by confirmation from a Norwegian agent that the great ship had capsized. She took with her 1,204 members of her crew. Despite frantic rescue efforts, including cutting holes in the hull, the bodies of many of the dead crew members remained there until the war ended.

The *Tirpitz* no longer presented a threat, but one Royal Navy officer had the bad grace to claim that she had still not been sunk as her hull was out of the water!

Note:

1. Imperial War Museum Sound Archive, Accession No. 2508.

Chapter 11

Hard Pounding

It was soon clear that the Arctic convoys were to receive the full attention of the Germans. Unlike the Atlantic convoys, beyond the range of German aircraft for most of the distance, the Arctic convoys were within range of airfields in Norway. Already, PQ13 had marked a change in the operation of the Arctic convoys. They now had to be fought through. In fact, three convoys stand out as being of significant importance, PQ13, the first to encounter serious opposition, PQ17, famous for being scattered by the Admiralty and then mauled by the Germans, and PQ18, the first to have an escort carrier, and in this case bringing both fighter and anti-submarine aircraft to the fray.

The problem was that, from this time on, the hours of daylight were to increase to the extent that in high summer only a brief period of twilight was interspersed between one day and the next. Tovey wanted the convoys suspended in high summer; Churchill insisted that they continue. Tovey asked the Soviet Union to increase anti-submarine patrols in the Barents Sea and ensure that additional destroyers were present for the final leg of the convoy route, but his request was honoured more often in the breach than in the fulfilment. This left Tovey with increasing recourse to the ships of Western Approaches Command, itself under pressure as the Battle of the Atlantic remained at its height.

The next convoy, PQ14, was to have a heavier close escort, although still without its own air cover. As a distant escort, the heavy cruiser *Norfolk* would patrol south-west of Bear Island, while heavy cover would come from the battleships *King George V* and *Duke of York*, with the aircraft carrier *Victorious* again, and another heavy cruiser, *Kent*, as well as eight destroyers. The close or local escort consisted initially of a destroyer, augmented by two minesweepers and two anti-submarine trawlers. This took the convoy as far as a rendezvous point on 11 April, 120 miles south by south-west of Jan Mayen Island, where the cruiser *Edinburgh*, with Rear Admiral S. S. Bonham-Carter, waited with six destroyers, four corvettes and two trawlers, *Lord Austin* and *Lord Middleton*.

The convoy itself consisted of twenty-five merchantmen, of which eleven were British, including the commodore's ship, *Empire Howard*. Ten were American, with just two Soviet, another Dutch and a Greek-owned but Panamanian-flagged ship. These ships left Reykjavik on 8 April 1942, having earlier sailed from Oban on the west coast of Scotland. Once again, a synchronized departure was attempted with QP10 leaving Murmansk on 10 April with the vessels from PQ12 and some of those from PQ13 that had managed to discharge their cargoes in time. This time, many of the ships were loaded with Russian timber, one of the few items that the Soviet Union could provide in return for British war aid.

On the night of 10/11 April the convoy ran into thick ice, and its difficulties were compounded by thick fog that made it difficult for ships to extricate themselves. No less than sixteen ships were separated from the main body of the convoy, many of them badly damaged, as were the two minesweepers, which were forced to return to Hvalfjord on 13 April with many of the damaged merchant ships, although another six continued until they met QP10 and returned to Iceland with that convoy. The convoy was thus in one night reduced to eight ships. The tanker *Hopemount* was badly damaged, with her propeller having been in contact with an ice growler, and a hole in her forepeak. However, her cargo was a vital 12,000 tons of boiler and diesel oil and lubricants, intended for British warships based in the northern Soviet Union. Her mission was to replace the tanker already at Vaenga, whose supplies were all but exhausted.

The lack of air cover was felt desperately on 15 April, when shortly after daybreak a Blohm und Voss Bv138 flying boat found the convoy and remained with it until a Focke-Wulf Fw200 Condor took over. It was not until late in the day that an attack came from Junkers Ju88s of KG30, but little damage was done. The following day the convoy suffered almost constant attacks from U-boats and the *Luftwaffe*, with the Ju88s making high-level and torpedo bombing attacks. The torpedoes from the U-boats could be so clearly seen in the clear water that 'you could see the two red and white bands on the torpedoes. They passed right across the bow ...'.

Even so, the only casualty was the loss of the convoy commodore's ship *Empire Howard*, sunk on 16 April by torpedoes from *U-403*. The first torpedo hit the boiler room and the second the engine room, killing all of those on watch below, before a third hit the after holds that contained ammunition, which exploded, breaking the ship in two. A deck cargo of army lorries fell over her port side and into the sea. Despite this, it is believed that as many as forty of her ship's company of fifty-five survived to jump into the sea. However, tragedy struck as the anti-submarine trawler *Northern Wave* depth charged the submarine. The percussive effects of the explosions were intensified by the water, killing and maiming many of those who had previously jumped. Just eighteen survived to be dragged aboard the trawler *Lord Middleton*, and of these, half died from their injuries. Among those who died in the water was Captain E. Rees, RNR, the commodore, although the ship's master, Captain Downie, survived. The role of commodore now passed to the vice commodore, Captain W. H. Lawrence, master of the *Briarwood*.

On 17 April, the two convoys crossed paths and two Soviet destroyers transferred from QP10 to PQ14. Renewed air attacks started as early as 05.00, but one of the aircraft was shot down by *Briarwood*'s DEMS gunners, and later the destroyer *Bulldog* claimed to have sunk a U-boat as the U-boat's torpedoes failed to find the mark while the convoy zigzagged. The following day at 02.00, three enemy destroyers, which had five days earlier attempted to attack QP10 without success, were sighted, but as *Edinburgh* steamed towards them, they turned and headed back to port. Dense fog then protected the convoy, but those aboard had to resist the temptation to fire when they heard aircraft rumbling overhead for fear of giving away their position. The convoy was then joined by the four minesweepers that had escorted QP10 clear of the Kola Inlet, and arrived there on 19 April in a strong gale.

Hopemount soon took over her duties as oiler for the British warships, and as she became lighter and rose higher in the water, her damaged bow and stern became visible. The bow plates were repaired, after a fashion, with the plates drawn together with long bolts. The propeller was surrounded by wooden scaffolding on which canvas was hung to contain the heat from an enormous blow lamp so that it could be repaired by Russian dockyard workers who displayed more energy than skill. Once heated, the propeller blades were beaten back into shape, or something resembling it. It was never quite right again, and the ship used to vibrate at certain revolutions, but she would be able to steam home.

The ships were by this time also subjected to aerial attack by the *Luftwaffe* while discharging their cargo and waiting for the next homebound convoy. QP10 had endured a far less happy voyage than PQ14, with four ships totalling 24,481 tons lost to air and U-boat attack, although six aircraft were shot down and another damaged. Several ships were lost to German air attack, with *Luftwaffe* bases sometimes as little as 25 miles away.

Life in Russian Ports

The situation for ships while turning around at a Russian port was not helped as the local people were often prone to stealing from those they could board, being especially keen on finding food, clothing and bedding. The Soviet Union provided guards for the quaysides, while Royal Navy and Royal Marine personnel mounted guard on the ships, especially the crippled *Trinidad*, allowed the all too rare privilege of a Russian dry dock. On one occasion, a group of workmen emerged through a hole in the ship's side with stores stolen from the ship. The British guards fired warning shots over their heads. Typical of the Soviet reaction was the arrival the next day of a political commissar herding a group of children whom, he claimed, were the thieves, adding that it was 'most regrettable that the British should have opened fire on small helpless children'.

In an attempt to resolve the situation, refuse from the cruiser was accompanied by small morsels of food when it was dumped on the side of the dry dock. Food and refuse were also raided by the Russian workers. Eventually, the damaged refrigerators were emptied and although the meat they contained was by this time unfit for human consumption, this too was stolen at night, even though the Russian guards shot an elderly worker attempting to escape with a carcass. Even a pot of jam was worth a Soviet bullet for the man attempting to steal it.

In an attempt to establish some goodwill, parties were sent ashore where they found the locals friendly, but begging them for chocolate and cigarettes. When supplies ran out, the attitude changed, and the visitors were subjected to insults, including 'Fuck you, Jack!' On the other hand, an empty shed was used to provide a concert by a Red Army choir, while there were competitive Anglo-Russian drinking bouts and *Trinidad*'s ship's company provided a return concert party for the Russians.

Ships of the period, and for many years after the war, could not discharge waste while in dry dock, and most dry docks were equipped with latrine blocks with crude wooden planking with holes sawn and running water underneath – a form of mass sanitation that encouraged many youngsters to light cotton waste and send it floating towards the exposed buttocks and hanging genitalia of their shipmates. Murmansk and Archangel could not even provide this amenity – holes had to be cut in the ice!

Conditions aboard those merchantmen unfortunate enough to have been frozen in Archangel for the winter, waiting for the late spring thaw, were harsh, especially as fuel supplies ran low and so too did stocks of food. One British seaman recalled:

> Our only occupation was keeping the ship clear of ice and snow ... It was seldom possible to bath. All the toilets were frozen up ... One's WC was a bucket of snow up on deck.
>
> Scabies became a nuisance and added to our cocktail of complaints. Eventually we had our water rationed and we used to go with our buckets and obtain a supply of warm red water for our ablutions.

Such was the strain and monotony of these conditions that men could, and did, go mad. Food was another problem. The seaman continued:

> Our daily food became steadily worse and almost uneatable. The poor cook became our worst enemy so that every mealtime he used to disappear from the galley and take refuge in his room. As we ran out of stores we replenished from ashore.

Not that there was much to obtain from ashore, although on one occasion the Russians supplied four yak carcasses, which as one British seamen noted, was probably generous given their own straitened circumstances.

So limited were Soviet facilities, that *Trinidad*'s Walrus was unshipped and flown to the Soviet seaplane base at Gryaznaya so that its crew could maintain patrols over the Barent's Sea.

British organization was not above criticism. HMS *Edinburgh* carried steel plates to assist in the repair of *Trinidad*, as well as a Commander Constructor from the Royal Corps of Naval Constructors, but the crippled cruiser's crew were also hoping for food and treats and, perhaps most of all, post from home. Instead they found that someone had sent boots and briefcases! The real problem was not simply the lack of sheet steel, but the need for internal stiffening, for which the Russians could only offer timber. A raiding party was sent to dismantle a redundant railway line, while another party distracted the Russian guards with chocolate and cigarettes.

Trinidad's Traumas

Trinidad arrived a cripple on 30 March, but left on 13 May! Her place on escort duties was taken by another cruiser, HMS *Liverpool*, escorted by two destroyers. The departure of *Trinidad* just before midnight on 13 May was to enable her to steam to Iceland and on to the United States for permanent repairs, accompanied by four destroyers, although two of these were the badly damaged *Foresight* and *Forester*. It was considered more important to get the cruiser to the United States than to cover the next pairing of inward/outward convoys, although the same thought did not seem to have occurred to the Russians, with just three Hawker Hurricanes providing air cover instead of the six expected, and none of the Petlyakov Pe-3 fighters. British precautions were far more thorough. Rear Admiral Burrough was with the cruisers *Kent*, *Liverpool*, *Nigeria* and *Norfolk* accompanied by four destroyers west of Bear Island, while Tovey himself in *Duke of York* was accompanied by *Victorious*, *London*, and the USS *Tuscaloosa* and *Washington* with eleven destroyers to the south-west, all to keep the *Admiral Scheer* from leaving port at Narvik. *Trinidad* worked up to 20 knots, but at daylight on 14 May, still only a hundred miles out, the *Luftwaffe* started to mount continuous reconnaissance patrols. It was clear that an aerial attack could not be long delayed, while U-boats had already been detected. Indeed, ashore in Norway at Banak, Ju88s of KG30 were being prepared for a bombing mission, as were He111s of KG26 at Bardufoss, but with torpedoes.

At 21.00, the cruiser's radar detected enemy aircraft coming from the south and south-south-east in waves at 15, 30, and 40 miles, then another wave at 60 miles. At 22.00, the first attack was made by

Ju88s dive-bombing the cruiser as she took evasive action. There were many misses, but no direct hits on the cruiser or her escorting destroyers. At 22.37, He111s came in low over the waves, interrupting the dive-bombing attack, but these were rebuffed by intense AA fire, especially from the destroyers. An attack by a further eight He111s followed, but although they dropped their torpedoes, Captain Saunders successfully combed them. However, as she turned to port to avoid the last three torpedoes, a solitary Ju88 dived out of the cloud and dropped four bombs before the AA guns could be redirected skywards. The first bomb missed, but blew up under the bridge to port, tearing off temporary steel plating and sending water into the ship just below 'B' turret, flooding the magazine. The second went through the Admiral's sea cabin and rattled through several mess decks to explode in the stokers' and petty officers' mess decks, tearing a massive gash in the port side. The final two bombs were near misses, but so near that they inflicted damage to the temporary repairs and the sea flooded into the ship. It was small consolation that the starboard AA gunners had caught the Ju88 and sent it burning into the sea.

Burning and taking in water, Captain Saunders continued to fight his ship, which despite listing to starboard, continued at 20 knots. The second bomb had caught many survivors from the Polish submarine *Jastzrab* and from merchant vessels whose escape was hindered by the fact that the cruiser's Walrus amphibian was burning fiercely in its hangar. The crew of 'B' turret escaped by crawling along the tops of their gun barrels, but most of those below decks handling ammunition were killed. Further forward, beneath 'A' turret, escape hatches had jammed trapping men below decks until their comrades realized their predicament and were able to release them, albeit into spaces by this time also on fire. Ready use ammunition stored close to the AA armament began to explode in the heat. Flooding of the port side reduced the list, but at a cost of allowing the bows to sink further. Even as the decision was taken to abandon ship, further torpedo-bombing runs were made against the ship, but the continued intensive AA barrage warded off further hits. At 23.30 the attackers drew away and the cruiser's speed was reduced to stop fanning the flames, which were being forced up the superstructure making the bridge untenable. The crew started to abandon ship while her escorting destroyers closed in to provide anti-submarine cover and take off survivors.

First to take off survivors was *Matchless*, with most of her intake being the wounded. *Forester* was next, also taking some of the cruiser's Oerlikons, and was followed by *Foresight*. *Somali* was last, taking the remainder of those able to leave. She was saved by the two-man crew of an aft AA mounting who spotted a lone Heinkel He111 that was approaching on the cruiser's port quarter. The German aircraft was shot down as it turned and launched its torpedo. Meanwhile, one of the ship's engineering officers, Lieutenant J. G. Boddy, had gone below looking for any remaining members of his division, for which action he was awarded a posthumous Albert Medal. Once aboard *Somali*, Rear Admiral Bonham-Carter ordered *Matchless* to sink the cruiser, sending three torpedoes into her starboard side and hastening her end at 01.20 on 15 May 1942, as the survivors aboard the destroyers watched.

The battered force of four destroyers withdrew westwards to find that they were being approached by Rear Admiral Burrough's cruisers, *Nigeria*, *Kent*, *Liverpool* and *Norfolk*. Even so, the combined force, while 350 miles off the coast of Norway, was attacked by twenty-five Ju88s, although not sustaining further damage. An indication of the strength of German air power in the area can be judged by the fact that on 15 May, the day that saw *Trinidad* condemned to the deep, Junkers Ju87 Stuka dive-bombers had raided Murmansk, damaging the American merchantman *Yaka* and also a Soviet submarine.

Bonham-Carter mentioned to some of the survivors that he regarded himself as something of a Jonah, having had five ships sunk from under him. Nevertheless, he also had the moral courage to point out what was becoming obvious to him, Tovey and Pound. He wrote to the Commander-in-Chief Home Fleet:

> We in the Navy are paid to do this sort of job, but it is beginning to ask too much of the men of the Merchant Navy. We may be able to avoid bombs or torpedoes with our speed, a six or eight knot ship has not this advantage.

The situation had changed by this time. Despite repeated requests by Tovey to suspend the convoys during the long summer days, the order was given that they must continue, and even if Churchill had hesitated for one minute, in the United States Roosevelt was also of the opinion that the Soviet Union must be supported at all costs. Not

1. The Winter War between the Soviet Union and Finland gave an early indication of
   Stalin's intentions. The Finnish armed forces were heavily outnumbered and short of
   heavy weapons, but they were well-trained and had the right equipment for Arctic
   warfare. Here is a Finnish ski patrol waiting for Russian troops. *(IWM Q55566)*

2. The scene at Narvik after the Second Battle of Narvik, 13 April 1940, an unlucky
   day for the German Navy. *(IWM A25)*

3. The Norwegian campaign saw operations in poor weather, and this image of a slush-covered flight deck aboard HMS *Furious* would be recognized by many on other carriers sent to Arctic waters.

4. Even life aboard a cruiser could be uncomfortable, and the Great War-vintage *Cairo*, seen here at Narvik, was compared unfavourably by one of her ratings with later ships. *(IWM N331)*

5. The Norwegian campaign started well for the Royal Navy, but ended with the disastrous loss of one of just six operational aircraft carriers left in the Royal Navy by May 1940, HMS *Glorious*. This was taken the day before she was sunk by the German battle-cruisers *Scharnhorst* and *Gneisenau*.

6. The German invasion of the Soviet Union, Operation Barbarossa, caught the Red Army and Air Force unprepared. Russian pilots often resorted to desperate measures, as this Heinkel He111 shows, with a wing that has been 'chewed' by the propeller of a Russian fighter. *(IWM HU39684)*

7. Destroyers were not always ideal for convoy duties in very heavy seas with their narrow beam, and could not always exploit their speed. Here HMS *Echo* leads her sister, *Eclipse*, out of an Icelandic fjord.
(*IWM A8089*)

8. Far better suited to convoy escort duties were the sloops. This is the Free French manned *Aconit*, leaving Hvalfjord in Iceland before escorting a convoy. *(IWM A7310)*

9. The Fairey Swordfish was the mainstay of the air cover for the convoys once escort carriers appeared on the scene. While appearing to be obsolete, these aircraft performed well, and had the advantage that they could loiter on anti-submarine patrols more successfully than seemingly more modern aircraft.

10. Before the advent of the escort carrier, a number of convoys had the limited 'one throw' fighter protection of a CAM-ship, with a single Hawker Hurricane fighter to be flown off, and then ditched. This is the *Empire Tide* at Hvalfjord in 1942.   *(IWM A10115)*

11. Among the aircraft encountered by the convoys were the dreaded Junkers Ju87 Stuka dive-bombers and, although considered obsolete by the time Barbarossa started, they could be very effective and accurate. *(IWM HU58529)*

12. Distant or heavy cover for the convoys included at least one battleship and, whenever possible, an aircraft carrier as well. This is *Victorious*, one of the Royal Navy's new, fast, armoured carriers, at Iceland, just before the raid on Petsamo.

13. Close or ocean escort before escort carriers made their appearance would be nothing heavier than a cruiser. This is HMS *Scylla*, with her crew attempting to clear the forecastle of ice. Even armament could be affected by ice. *(IWM A15365)*

14. If Swordfish found a submarine, they could depth charge it as it dived. Later, rocket
    projectiles were available for this. Eventually, Swordfish were fitted with radar,
    mainly to detect surface vessels or surfaced submarines, but at short range a
    periscope could be detected. *(IWM H17567)*

15. The first escort carrier to appear on an Arctic convoy was HMS *Avenger* with
    PQ18, bringing both Hurricane fighters and Swordfish anti-submarine aircraft to
    convoy protection. Here six Hurricanes are ranged on the carrier's flight deck.
    (IWM FL1268)

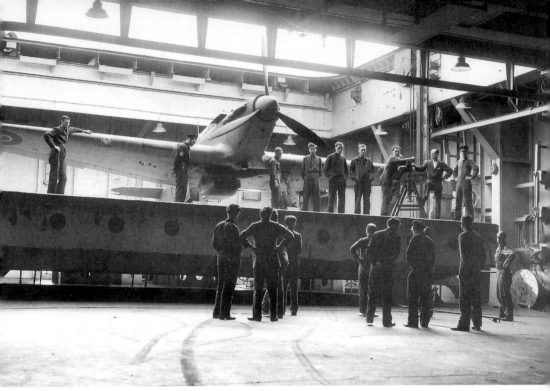

16. Without folding wings, there was a limit to the number of Sea Hurricanes that could be carried on a carrier, but the aircraft was a considerable boost to a convoy's survival rate. *(IWM A10982)*

17. Sadly, even an escort carrier could not provide a guarantee of absolute protection. This is an ammunition ship blowing up, in this case taking her attacking aircraft with her. The sole survivor was a steward blown off the upper deck. *(IWM A12275)*

18. Escort carriers often did more than simply support their aircraft, as they were often called upon to refuel smaller escorts. Here is HMS *Honeysuckle*, one of the famous Flower-class frigates, being refuelled by *Trumpeter* in a very icy Kola Inlet. *(IWM A28203)*

19. The big fear for the Royal Navy was that the German battleship *Tirpitz* would put to sea from her Norwegian base and wreak havoc on the convoys. These are Fairey Barracuda dive-bombers on their way to attack the ship. *(FAAM CAMP/266)*

20. The raid got through, as this photograph of the oil slick surrounding the ship shows, but was not successful enough as she remained afloat. The aircraft simply could not carry heavy enough bombs to sink the *Tirpitz*. *(FAAM CAMP/568)*

21. The three men who were determined to fight the convoys through, although probably with scant knowledge or understanding of the hardships involved, included the American President Franklin Roosevelt. *(IWM NYP12886)*

22. Joseph Stalin was ungracious and unappreciative, often leaving the Western Allies with the impression that he might cede territory in return for an armistice. Stalin had no appreciation of naval matters. *(IWM HU10180)*

23. Caught between the growing power of the United States and the ambitions of the Soviet leader was the British wartime Prime Minister, Winston Churchill.
(IWM MH26392)

24. If aerial attack could not destroy the *Tirpitz*, then other means had to be tried, but an attempt with a two-man human torpedo, or 'chariot', failed due to bad weather.
(IWM A22111)

25. More successful were midget submarines or X-craft, with their four-man crews, but even these resulted in the capture of the men concerned, with another two killed.
(IWM A21698)

26. The cruiser HMS *Belfast* played an important role in the Battle of the North Cape, and is seen here steaming off Iceland. (IWM A15530)

27. Realizing that something larger was needed, the Castle-class was a larger corvette than the Flower-class, and was reclassified later as a frigate when this type of ship was reintroduced to the Royal Navy. This is *Leeds Castle*. *(IWM A25732)*

28. Aid to the Soviet Union included the battleship HMS *Royal Sovereign,* transferred in 1944 along with eight of the ex-United States Navy Town-class destroyers and four submarines. This is the battleship shortly after the handover. *(IWM A23816)*

29. At first the Admiralty was convinced that American welded construction would be unsatisfactory in Artic waters, so a number of British converted escort carriers were introduced, including HMS *Vindex*. Here she has Fairey Swordfish ranged on her flight deck.   *(FAAM CARRIER V/25)*

SAINT
VALENTINE'S
DAY
1945.

The single-engined Stringbag
Has flown for quite a time,
Its prehistoric silhouette
Is known in every clime.
How different the 88,
With fuselage so slim—
A monoplane with motors two;
Don't make mistakes with him!

Yet what a metamorphosis
A bit of action brings,
When Junkers fly at 80 knots
And grow some second wings:
And Stringbags (clearly Nazified)
And Wildcat sixes too
Become the targets of all guns
Whilst 88's fly through....

The leopard cannot change his spots,
Nor I (alas!) change mine:
Remember this, and I'll be pleased
To be your Valentine.

30. Aircraft recognition was a definite weakness for the Alllies throughout the war years. This 'Valentine Card' was an attempt to drive home the difference between the single-engined biplane Swordfish and the twin-engined monoplane Ju88 after one naval airman had become tired of being shot at by the ships he was trying to protect! *(via Lord Kilbracken)*

only did the convoys now routinely include American merchant ships, the United States Navy had also committed a squadron consisting of the battleship USS *Washington*, with her 16-in guns, the aircraft carrier *Wasp*, two heavy cruisers *Tuscaloosa* and *Wichita*, and six destroyers, commanded by Rear Admiral R. C. Griffen, which were attached to the Royal Navy's Home Fleet.

In an attempt to remove the threat presented by German major surface units, on 31 March, thirty-three Handley Page Halifax heavy bombers of No. 4 Group, RAF Bomber Command, had been sent to bomb the *Tirpitz*, but most failed to find the target in bad weather and five were shot down, with another seven lost when the attack was repeated on 28 and 29 April. The problems encountered were the difficulty of finding the ship in a narrow Norwegian fjord, compounded by a heavy AA barrage and an intense smokescreen. Nevertheless, the bombs used were inadequate for the task, too small to provide a worthwhile 'mine' effect through a near miss, and more likely to break up or bounce off on striking the battleship's armoured decks or gun turrets.

Evolving Strategy

The Allies were not on their own in looking for solutions. The Germans decided that torpedo-bombers were more likely to be successful in attacking ships at sea than the level bombers and dive-bombers used so far. The *Kriegsmarine* had Heinkel He115 seaplanes, but these were slow and elderly, designed more for reconnaissance duties off battleships and cruisers and hampered by the drag of their floats. Rivalry between the *Kriegsmarine* and the *Luftwaffe*, driven by Goering's dislike of his naval opposite number Admiral Raeder, was overcome by Hitler's intervention. The *Luftwaffe* was to make available Heinkel He111 bombers capable of carrying two torpedoes apiece, while further trials showed that the Junkers Ju88 was also capable of delivering torpedoes. On 1 May, the first aircraft were available at Bardufoss. For the Germans, the U-boat was also by this time the tool of most significance in maritime warfare, driven to a great extent by Hitler's obsession in harbouring both literally and figuratively his major surface units, doubtless influenced by the early loss of the *Graf Spee* and then the *Bismarck*, which gave his senior naval officers no confidence at all and engendered an approach that was always risk-adverse.

Meanwhile, Soviet air and naval forces had been barely effective, with Red Air Force bombing of German air bases insufficient to make any impact on the air/sea war, or indeed in the *Luftwaffe*'s support for German ground forces in Russia. Despite laying mines off Petsamo and attacks on German coastal convoys by Soviet submarines, aided by similar attacks from British submarines, the Germans had also managed to lay mines to frustrate Allied shipping, while the approaches to the Kola Inlet and the Gourlo, the entrance to the White Sea, became happy hunting grounds for the U-boat packs. At no time did the Soviet Navy take its share of the responsibility for a convoy. Such escorts as were sent out only steamed with the convoy for a short distance before arriving or after leaving, and so often even these failed to coordinate properly with the close escort, but instead went their own way, possibly simply to demonstrate that they were their own masters.

PQ15/QP11

The conflicting demands of the North Atlantic and Arctic convoys, plus the fact that Egypt and India were being served by convoys taking the long route via the Cape of Good Hope and, for Egypt, the Suez Canal, meant that the strain on both merchant and naval tonnage was becoming acute. The United States entering the war was a help, but that country came with its own commitments, supporting American forces as they prepared to begin the long fight back across the Pacific, ensuring that links between the United States and Australia were not harmed, and also supplying the Soviet Union via the South Atlantic, the Cape of Good Hope, the Indian Ocean and Iran.

For the convoy organizers, the presence of German heavy units in Norway was a threat that could not be ignored. In this context, it remains surprising that heavy units of the Royal Navy and United States Navy were kept so distant from the convoys, in contrast to the Mediterranean where fleet carriers and battleships were part and parcel of the convoy escort, and paid the price.

With the decision to include air-dropped torpedoes in the German weapons inventory, the Arctic convoy war took a turn for the worse as far as the Allies were concerned.

The next convoy to Russia, PQ15, left Reykjavik on 26 April 1942. This was another large convoy and included in its twenty-five ships were two ice-breakers. The commodore was Captain H. J. Anchor, RNR, aboard the *Boatavon*. Apart from the ice-breakers, other innovations included a catapult-armed merchant ship, a CAM-ship, the *Empire Morn*, with a single Hawker Hurricane fighter that would have to be ditched after its one chance of providing air cover for the convoy. The second Hurricane aboard was in a crate and would be assembled at the end of the voyage and put on the catapult ready for use on the homeward QP convoy ... provided that the pilot from the original aircraft had been saved. Of possibly greater use was the presence of an AA cruiser, HMS *Ulster Queen*, in effect a small armed merchant cruiser having been a Belfast Steamship Company packet boat on the Liverpool–Belfast route, with six 4-in high-angle AA guns, four twin 2-pdr AA guns and ten 20-mm Oerlikons. She would be placed in the centre of the convoy. Finally, an S-class submarine, HMS *Sturgeon*, was to accompany the convoy as far as 5 degrees east. Although there were Allied submarines in the area, their patrol line had to be pulled back to 150 miles off the Norwegian coast because of increased aerial reconnaissance activity during the long summer hours of daylight, making time for recharging batteries difficult to find.

The close escort included four Halcyon-class ocean minesweepers with the senior officer of the escort, Captain J. F. H. Crombie, aboard one of these, HMS *Bramble*, and six destroyers. This was augmented by Force Q, in reality the destroyer *Ledbury* and the Royal Fleet Auxiliary oiler *Grey Ranger*, all of which were joined on 30 April by the cruisers *London* and *Nigeria*, with the latter flying the flag of Rear Admiral H. M. Burrough.

Once again, distant cover included Tovey's flagship, *King George V*, and the carrier *Victorious*, although this time the cruiser strength was augmented by two American ships, *Wichita* and *Tuscaloosa*, as well as the British *Kenya*. Accompanying this force was the battleship *Washington*, in which Rear Admiral R. C. Griffen, USN, flew his flag. The overall screen of ten destroyers included four from the United States Navy. The work of the distant escort was to be marred by an accident on 1 May, when the escort was zigzagging and ran into fog. Tovey ordered the zigzagging to stop, but the order was not received aboard the destroyer *Punjabi*, which ran under the bows of the *King George V* and was immediately cut in half. As had happened before, many of her casualties occurred as the stern sank and her depth charges exploded killing men already in the water and further damaging the battleship. It was little short of a miracle that the forward section floated for forty minutes and allowed 206 men to be saved.

When Vice Admiral A. T. B. Curteis arrived on the *Duke of York* the following day, Tovey transferred his flag to the newer ship, sending *KGV*, as she was affectionately known in the Royal Navy, to Scapa and then on to Liverpool for repairs, while Curteis also returned to Scapa in the elderly *Nelson*.

For the first time, American merchantmen were in the majority for the convoy itself, with no fewer than fifteen ships. The British contingent was for the first time in the minority, with just seven ships, plus one from Panama. Completing the convoy were a Canadian ice-breaker on delivery to the Soviet Union and a Russian ice-breaker.

At first the convoy enjoyed good fortune, for it was not until it was 250 miles south-west of Bear Island late on 30 April that it was spotted by a patrolling Fw200 Condor. In part, its good fortune was due to low cloud that also brought snow showers. There were a number of U-boat alerts, however, and almost twenty-four hours after the first aircraft sighted the convoy, six Ju88s appeared and made a half-hearted attack, with the leading aircraft shot down by AA fire from the cruiser *London*.

That same day, 1 May, saw Force Q waiting to refuel the escort on QP11, southbound, while *London* and *Nigeria* were also to join the convoy from Russia. It was from QP11 when it approached the following morning that PQ15 learnt of the appearance of German torpedo-bombers, as well as German destroyers and the inevitable U-boats. The winter ice was also slow to retreat.

As if the German threat was not enough, the Polish submarine *Jastrzab* was detected by the minesweeper *Seagull* and the destroyer *St Albans* and depth charged, then gunned once she surfaced and before she was recognized as being friendly. Casualties included two Royal Navy signals ratings serving aboard and three members of her own crew killed, with six others, including her commanding officer and his British liaison officer, wounded. Damaged beyond repair, the former American submarine had to be sunk by gunfire. The Polish submarine was off course, but such occurrences were not unknown because of the difficulty of obtaining accurate compass readings in Arctic waters.

QP11 had in fact suffered heavily at the hands of the enemy. Consisting of thirteen merchantmen, it was an unlucky number that departed Kola on 28 April. They had left Kola with the escort enhanced by four ocean minesweepers and two Soviet destroyers. The close escort was led by Commander M. Richmond aboard the destroyer *Bulldog*, accompanied by five other destroyers, four Flower-class corvettes and an anti-submarine trawler. Operating close to the convoy was the cruiser *Edinburgh*. The corvettes were to stick with the convoy at all costs, and the destroyers were to place themselves between the convoy and any emerging German threat.

Soviet air cover was also expected to be provided for the convoy, but this was not available on 29 April when the convoy was spotted by a German reconnaissance aircraft. At 04.30 the following day, signals were picked up from *U-88*, which was forced by the escorts to dive when she was discovered on the surface astern of the convoy. Later, the convoy changed course to avoid a U-boat spotted on the surface ahead of it. As the day progressed, U-boat contacts were made repeatedly, keeping the escorts steaming at high speed and deploying depth charges, albeit without sinking any U-boats although they may well have kept the pack at bay. At 17.30, the locally-based escort turned back to the Kola Inlet.

'Indescribable conditions. First of all on the afternoon watch, lovely bright sunshine, turned to heavy overcast,' David Walker, a signals rating aboard HMS *Bulldog*, remembers. 'Conditions were treacherous, night and day, with ice flying around. Icicles hung everywhere – on the ship's stays there was ice. Ships being torpedoed, and all of a sudden they just went up.'[1]

Fortunately, things were much better down below, assuming that the ship was undamaged, of course.

'Pretty good inside,' recalls David Walker. 'On our mess deck, we had a little stove that kept us warm. We couldn't take off our clothes in case we suddenly had to go to action stations.'[2]

As night fell, Rear Admiral Bonham-Carter aboard *Edinburgh* had his ship taken 15 miles ahead of the convoy, hoping to detect U-boats on the surface and, steaming at 19 knots without a destroyer screen, depending on his ship's speed to keep her out of trouble. His optimism was ill-placed as *U-436* and *U-456* were ahead of him waiting patiently for QP11. The asdic operator had detected a U-boat's presence before the attack but was told to ignore it. *U-436* fired no less than four torpedoes at the cruiser, all of which missed, but at 16.15 two from *U-456* struck her on the starboard side, one blasting its way into the forward boiler room, which quickly flooded, while the second blew the stern off, blowing away the rudder and the two inner screws. The ship started to roll to starboard, but *U-456* had no torpedoes left to finish the job, and frantic attempts to save the ship were being made aboard by damage control parties while navigating and engine room personnel attempted to turn her on the two outboard screws and return to Murmansk. Two British and two Soviet destroyers made haste to stand by the crippled cruiser, while the Germans intercepted her radio signals and decided that the order forbidding operation by surface forces to conserve fuel could in this case be ignored. 'Admiral Arctic', *Konteradmiral* (Rear Admiral) Schmundt sent his three destroyers, the *Hermann Schoemann*, Z24 and Z25, from Kirkenes at 01.00 on 1 May with orders to sink the British cruiser.

At 05.40 on 1 May, the first aerial torpedo attack against an Arctic convoy was mounted by six Ju88s while the convoy was heading west, parallel to the edge of the ice and 150 miles off Bear Island. This first attack was unsuccessful. While the aerial attack was in progress, *Amazon* forced a surfaced U-boat to dive. As on the previous day, the convoy started to make repeated changes of course to avoid the U-boats. It was at 13.45 that one of the corvettes detected the three German destroyers on her radar, followed shortly afterwards by a sighting from the Town-class destroyer *Beverley*. The destroyers were ordered to form on *Bulldog* and make smoke, while the convoy with the corvettes and armed trawler turned away, making a further turn later as a U-boat was sighted. At 14.07, the destroyers on both sides opened fire and loosed torpedoes, none of which hit, and after a brief and completely inconclusive engagement, the German destroyers turned away after inflicting some damage to *Amazon*. Meanwhile, a torpedo from a destroyer, or more probably a U-boat, had sunk a straggler, the Soviet freighter *Tsiolkovsky*, and a trawler was sent back to pick up survivors. The damage to *Amazon* also involved casualties.

'We were attacked by four German destroyers,' recalled David Walker, aboard HMS *Bulldog*. 'Always remember that *Amazon*, second in the line behind us, was hit on the bridge, her captain had his head blown off. We managed to beat them off.'[3]

This brought the German destroyers back to the attack, and a fresh engagement commenced at 14.40, which lasted for five minutes. The British destroyers were now caught between guarding the convoy, which was making its way slowly through an ice field, and roaming free to counter the Germans. The senior officer escort decided that the Germans wanted to break up the destroyer screen slowly, then roam freely through the convoy which was becoming widely spaced out and more difficult to defend as it struggled through the ice. At 16.00, the Germans reappeared yet again, and this time a longer engagement ensued, lasting for ten minutes during which *Bulldog* suffered some superficial damage. A further engagement occurred at 16.58 that lasted for seven minutes without either side scoring a hit. Yet another attack came at 17.40, with nothing more than near misses in six minutes of frantic combat. On this occasion, the British destroyers gave chase until the Germans disappeared into the smoke and fog. Commander Richmond in charge of the escort hung around for three hours until he finally decided that the destroyers were gone for good and rejoined the convoy, with his destroyers warding off two U-boats as the convoy reassembled.

On 2 May the pressure was maintained, with the destroyers attacking a suspected U-boat without obtaining a confirmed kill, and later a solitary aircraft ran in to make an unsuccessful torpedo attack. As the convoys passed, an He115 seaplane armed with a torpedo appeared, but failed to do anything other than circle at a safe distance.

Meanwhile, the situation aboard *Edinburgh* was bleak indeed. There was additional pressure on the crew because she was carrying 5 tons of Soviet gold bullion intended for the United States in part payment for the aid being shipped to the Soviet Union. The admiral had accepted full responsibility for the fate of his ship, but once order was restored and the damaged areas sealed off, she was able to steam at 8 knots, despite her bow being down in the water. Aboard, without heat or light, the situation was grim, and despite it being May, her deck and upperworks were covered in ice, while the quarterdeck was severely damaged by the torpedo that had cut off her stern. The cruiser could not be steered and four valiant attempts by the destroyer *Forester* to put a line aboard to take the cruiser's anchor chain so that she could provide steering were unsuccessful as the cruiser's crew slipped on the ice-encrusted deck. Eventually, after breaking off to attack a surfaced U-boat, a line was passed through the destroyer's bull-ring and *Forester* was at last able to keep the cruiser on course, but her speed had dropped to just 3 knots. When at 06.00 on 1 May the Soviet destroyers announced that they were short of fuel and had to leave, the tow was dropped and the two

British destroyers were ordered instead to provide a U-boat screen. Later, on learning of the destroyer engagement, Bonham-Carter ordered the destroyers to 'take every opportunity to defeat the enemy without taking undue risks to themselves'.

Ashore in Russia, Admiral Bevan organized a Soviet patrol vessel to stand by *Edinburgh*, and later a tug and minesweepers joined at around midnight on 1/2 May. While the situation appeared hopeful by 06.30 on 2 May, despite the non-return of the two Soviet destroyers, the three German destroyers finally put in another appearance, using a snowstorm to hide their approach. An oil slick from the cruiser provided guidance as they sought their prey. The British destroyers turned to face the Germans as they emerged from the snowstorm, led by the *Hermann Schoemann*, while the other two German ships struggled to find the cruiser. Tows were cast off as Bonham-Carter sought not to pull the other ships into danger, and *Edinburgh* moved out of control, turning three times in forty minutes, making her a difficult target, but also making accurate fire from her remaining 'B' turret difficult. Against the odds, a salvo hit the *Hermann Schoemann*, destroying her engines and leaving her without power. At 06.50 *Forester* engaged Z24, and was making a torpedo attack when three 5.9-in shells from Z25 struck her, damaging 'X'-gun and having a devastating impact on 'B'-gun, the bridge and the boiler room, with her commanding officer killed immediately. As *Foresight*, which had been struggling to sink the *Hermann Schoemann*, turned to the aid of her sister ship, she received the full force of fire from the surviving German destroyers and was brought to a halt when one of her boilers was knocked out of action by a salvo of four shells.

Unknown to Z25, a salvo of torpedoes fired by her at long range struck the stricken *Edinburgh* at 07.02 on the port side, bursting through so fiercely that she was almost open from side to side and in danger of breaking in two. She rolled over from her starboard list, righted herself, and then started a fresh list to port. Destroyers came alongside to rescue the wounded and Merchant Navy personnel – survivors from ships sunk on the outward convoy – and the order was given to abandon ship. Preoccupied with the rescue of personnel from the *Hermann Schoemann* and having crippled two British destroyers, the Germans remained unaware of the eventual sinking of the *Edinburgh* until U-456 returned to base after having trailed the cruiser during her long and fruitless struggle to the Kola Inlet.

Further attempts by the German destroyers to finish the work on their British opponents were fought off, and after *Z25* had been hit in the radio room, they eventually moved away. Some survivors from the *Hermann Schoemann* who had been left in rafts were picked up by *U-88*.

The weather remained bad, with mist and ice, but in the early hours of 3 May, six Heinkel He111s flew in at wave top height, prompting a rapid and effective response from the convoy's AA gunners, who blew two aircraft out of the sky and so damaged a third that it crashed. Despite this splendid response, the commodore's ship, *Boatavon*, was one of three ships torpedoed and sunk, losing 15,800 tons of shipping in just one attack, leaving the escorts to pick up 137 survivors. An attack by Ju88s shortly before midnight that same day damaged the armed trawler *Cape Palliser*, but it was some consolation that one of the aircraft was shot down.

Notes:

1. Imperial War Museum Sound Archive, Accession No. 23186.
2. Ibid.
3. Ibid.

Chapter 12

Changing Tactics

Stalin simply assumed that his allies had sufficient ships, whether warships or merchantmen, to pursue the war. He cared little about the problems faced by the United States in the Pacific, after all the Soviet Union was not at war with Japan, and on one occasion pointed out that at one stage some ninety merchantmen were stuck either in Iceland or in the United States. He little appreciated the threat presented by the *Tirpitz*, and if lesser forces had already wreaked havoc on the convoys, that was due to British, and possibly also American, shortcomings.

On the other hand, perhaps Franklin Roosevelt, the American president, also knew little about naval matters? As for Churchill, he was not only squeezed between his two Allies, heavily dependent upon American aid and fearful of the consequences of a deal between the Soviet Union and Nazi Germany, but he also knew that the ultimate American war aim was to emerge as what would now be described as a global superpower. The end of British dominance was all too clear, and it was clear that Canada was increasingly looking towards the United States rather than the mother country, even if the transfer of allegiance of Australia and New Zealand was not so apparent. The irony was that while the UK was bankrupt, indebted to the dominions and the United States, it was adding to its precarious financial condition by subsidizing the Soviet Union.

Churchill's reaction can best be summed up in his own words:

The Russians are in heavy action and will expect us to run the risk and pay the price entailed by our contribution ... The operation is justified if half gets through. Failure on our part to make the attempt would weaken our influence with both our major allies.

With so much pressure on the British, Convoy PQ16 could not be smaller than the largest so far. Yet, Iceland was not a safe base. Ships could be, and were, attacked while in Iceland. German agents existed there and the Allied presence was resented by the local population. It was just one such German agent who reported the departure of PQ16, which was accompanied by no less than thirty-six merchantmen when it left Hvalfjord on 21 May 1942, with Commodore N. H. Gale, RNR, as convoy commodore aboard the SS *Ocean Voice*.

Once again the convoy had a CAM-ship, the *Empire Lawrence*. A heavy lift ship, the *Empire Elgar*, was also present among the eight British ships, outnumbered by the nineteen-strong American contingent. There were just five Soviet merchantmen. Despite the size of the convoy, the initial close escort was weak, with an ocean-going minesweeper accompanied by just four armed trawlers, one of which had to turn back unable to match even the slow speed of the convoy. On 23 May a more substantial escort appeared in the form of the AA ship *Alynbank*, a converted merchantman and former Bank Line cargo-liner, accompanied by four corvettes. Once again two submarines travelled with the convoy, the *Seawolf* and the large ocean-going *Trident*, and Force Q was also present with the oiler *Black Ranger* and a destroyer. That same day, Rear Admiral Burrough left Seidisfjord in the cruiser *Nigeria* with a screen of three destroyers, as well as another five destroyers, for the close escort. Once again he was ready to take on a combative role when the enemy threatened, while the corvettes remained close to the convoy. The three cruisers *Kent*, *Liverpool* and *Norfolk*, sailed later from Hvalfjord.

Aboard HMS *Ashanti*, commanded by the senior officer escort Commander Richard Onslow, was a small party of RAF radio operators who were German-speakers. Their ability to listen in to the orders given to the *Luftwaffe* aircrew, and even the chatter between the pilots while still on the ground at Bardufoss and Banak, was to prove invaluable in the days ahead.

The perceived threat on this occasion was less the German destroyers, which had been so mauled by the close escort to PQ15, but more the heavy cruiser *Admiral Scheer*, stationed at Narvik and joined on 26 May by the pocket battleship *Lutzow*, the destroyer *Hans Lody* and the torpedo-boat *T7*, as well as the fleet oiler *Dithmarschen*. The German classification of torpedo-boat should not be confused with the smaller and faster E-boats that so beset the British with problems in the English Channel and the southern North Sea, but instead this was in effect a small destroyer. That the Germans themselves were not overly confident even before their bitter experiences with their major fleet units early in the war can be judged by the fact that, before war broke out, the *Lutzow* was originally going to be called *Deutschland*, but someone clearly thought of the impact on national morale of a ship of that name being lost!

Just in case the *Tirpitz* did venture out, Admiral Tovey was aboard the battleship *Duke of York* accompanied by Rear Admiral Griffen in the battleship *Washington*, while the cruiser escort comprised HMS *London* and the USS *Wichita*, as well as the carrier *Victorious*, with nine British and four American destroyers, all operating as part of the heavy or distant escort. The Allied submarine screen off Norway comprised five British and three Soviet boats. The Red Air Force promised a 200 bomber attack on German airfields in Norway, but as so often happened, this came to nought. PQ16 had been fought through before the air operation started, and just twenty aircraft were committed. Truly, the Royal Navy was paying the price of carrier aircraft having been neglected between the wars, for fast armoured carriers with aircraft such as the capable Grumman Avenger could have done much to carry the war to the German airfields.

The balancing convoy, QP12 left Kola on Thursday 21 May. As usual, four of the Royal Navy's locally-based minesweepers took the convoy to sea while two Soviet destroyers were to augment the initial escort. The British destroyer force comprised the *Inglefield*, in which the senior officer escort, Captain Percy Todd, was present, and five others, supported by four armed trawlers and both the AA cruiser *Ulster Queen* and the CAM-ship *Empire Morn*, which had not launched even its original Hurricane on the outward voyage. There were fifteen merchant ships.

The initial progress of QP12 was good, as poor visibility kept German air activity to a minimum. It was not until late morning on 25 May that the convoy was spotted by the *Luftwaffe*. In sequence, a Focke-Wulf Fw200 Condor, a Blohm und Voss Bv138 flying boat and two Junkers Ju88s appeared over the convoy. *Boadicea* was the pick-up ship for the Hurricane, and as conditions were good it was decided to launch the aircraft from the catapult on the *Empire Morn*. This was always a finely judged decision, for apart from the risk to the pilot, no one could ever be sure that the best opportunity was being taken until it was too late, and either the aircraft had been expended leaving the convoy to face aerial assault without the benefit of fighter cover or, more usually, the aircraft had remained unused.

On this occasion, Flying Officer John Kendal, RAFVR, almost immediately found that he had lost radio contact with his fighter direction officer, Sub-Lieutenant P. G. Mallett aboard the CAM-ship. He had also lost sight of his preferred target, the Bv138, in cloud, so chose to chase after a Ju88 instead. Despite the high speed of the German aircraft, he managed to catch it and shoot it down. By this time, having flown at maximum speed the entire length of the convoy, Kendal's Hurricane was short of fuel and he prepared to ditch. He found *Boadicea* easily enough, but she was near low cloud and a rainstorm. Mallett radioed that he should try an escort to the rear of the convoy, but could not get confirmation from Kendal, whose radio was broken. Kendal seemed to have received the message as he headed for *Badsworth*, and then climbed above to get a safe height from which to bale out. He disappeared into the low cloud and his engine was heard to cut out. His aircraft then appeared, diving into the sea, followed by Kendal, whose parachute did not begin to open until he was 50 feet above the water – too late. He hit the water before the canopy of the parachute was fully opened. Kendal was promptly picked up by the destroyer, who signalled *Empire Morn* that he had incurred serious injuries; he died within the next ten minutes.

Kendal's take-off may well have driven the Bv138 away. Certainly QP12 continued its progress and for the rest of the voyage remained unmolested, arriving in Iceland on 29 May, minus one ship that had not kept up, had fallen behind and eventually returned to Kola.

The two convoys passed on 25 May, some three hours after Kendal's death. PQ16 had been ploughing through fog for the previous day. In fog, attempts were made to maintain direction by ships sounding their course and speed in Morse on their sirens. At about 05.00 on 25 May, visibility began to improve, and shortly afterwards the cruisers and destroyers joined the convoy. This was to be the last period of peace and calm for the next six days.

At 06.00 an Fw200 Condor appeared and was greeted by a heavy AA barrage, while the ships in the convoy started to zigzag. This, though, had to be stopped whenever they ran into a fog bank for fear of a collision. The destroyers also took the opportunity to refuel from the *Black Ranger* once the aircraft had left, and managed to complete this by noon, allowing the oiler and her escort to leave the convoy. The southbound convoy, QP12, was sighted at 14.00 and reported having spotted a U-boat earlier in the day. At 15.00, the lookouts aboard a destroyer spotted a U-boat to starboard, and she turned towards it opening fire, forcing it to crash-dive, before starting a depth charge attack, but contact was quickly lost and the destroyer returned to her allotted position in the screen. Later, another Blohm und Voss Bv138 flying boat appeared, keeping careful watch on the convoy.

The first attack came at 19.10, by which time the sky was perfectly clear. Nineteen He111 bombers swept in from the south, and the *Empire Lawrence* launched her Hurricane flown by Pilot Officer Hay. Hay quickly shot down an He111, setting it on fire, and damaged a second aircraft before his own aircraft was hit, believed to have been by AA fire from an American merchantman. Wounded in the legs, Hay nevertheless managed to bale out and was rescued by the destroyer *Volunteer*. Strangely, the CAM-ship had a second fighter pilot, a member of the Royal Canadian Air Force, no doubt in case the first pilot was lost on the outbound convoy!

Having been disrupted in their attack, the surviving He111s nevertheless pressed on to make a torpedo attack, which was completely unsuccessful. They were followed by six Ju88s, which dive-bombed the convoy, with near misses being almost as effective as direct hits. *Hyderabad* was shaken by a near miss, while the American freighter *Carlton* was so shaken that her main steam supply pipe between the boiler and the engine was fractured. The trawler *Northern Spray* was assigned to tow her back to Iceland, which, incredibly, both ships reached safely. A further attack by twelve Ju88s rounded off the day. During the three attacks, AA fire had accounted for two *Luftwaffe* aircraft.

The convoy had nevertheless been fortunate in that it had missed a U-boat wolf-pack while fighting off the *Luftwaffe* – the question then arises as to whether communication between the *Luftwaffe* and *Kriegsmarine* was as good as it should have been. Did the *Luftwaffe* let the U-boats know that it had spotted the convoy, or could it have done so? After all, at least one U-boat had surfaced during the day. That night, drifting ice gave those aboard the ships a noisy and restless time.

At 3.05 on 26 May, *U-703* torpedoed the *Syros*, an American merchantman at the rear of the seventh of the nine column convoy.

Nine members of her ship's company were lost, but the survivors were picked up by the destroyer *Hazard* and the trawler *Lady Madeleine*. Two other U-boats, *U-436* and *U-591*, had also fired torpedoes at a merchantman and at a destroyer *Ashanti*, but missed. This put Burrough in a dilemma as he was all too well aware of the vulnerability of a cruiser following the loss of *Trinidad* and *Edinburgh*. He decided that he had no option but to take his ships and their destroyer screen away to join QP12, steaming at 20 knots, generally believed to be fast enough to avoid all but a lucky torpedo hit from ahead. This made sense in improving the survival chances of the cruiser squadron, but it withdrew from the convoy a significant proportion of its AA fire, and also left those aboard the merchantmen and the smaller escorts feeling vulnerable once again. Part of the problem was that most of the remaining escort vessels lacked heavy high-angle AA weapons and the older ships had to wait until their light AA armament could be brought into use.

The convoy had seen the last of the U-boats, although no one aboard the ships was to know that until much later, but on 26 May, it was to face a further day of aerial attack. The first attack was again by a mixed force of Ju88s and He111s, and attacks continued at intervals throughout the day until the last attack at 18.00, when seven He111 torpedo-bombers and eleven Ju88s attempted to strike, but retired in the face of a fierce AA barrage. Despite the repeated attempts by the Germans, no serious damage was suffered that day. At 03.20 the following morning, doubtless expecting to find the defences less alert, another attack occurred, but again without inflicting damage.

The strain of operating under almost continual air attack is wearing, even in warmer climates. Doing so in the Arctic wearing bulky clothing and having sweat freeze on the face is still worse. Men grabbed food and sleep as and when they could. The provision of food could be difficult as on some ships the stewards were preoccupied with handling the ammunition supply. Men went to sleep in their clothes so that they could be ready at a moment's notice and back at action stations. The presence of radar did at least help, allowing some warning of impending attack and allowing men to stand down, however briefly. The mixture of bombing and torpedo attacks placed extra strain on the defences, as the former came in high and the latter came in low, so it was a finely judged decision as to whether the AA defences should aim at one or the other.

The convoy then met heavy pack ice that forced it to turn towards the south-east, towards the North Cape and the *Luftwaffe* base at Banak. By mid-morning on 27 May, the convoy was once again heading due east, and met a succession of attacks with He111s and Ju88s coming in waves, the latter making good use of a film of stratus at around 1,500 feet that made it difficult to see the diving aircraft until it was almost too late. There were more than one hundred attacks that day.

At around midday the Russian merchantmen *Starii Bolshevik*, carrying a cargo of vehicles and explosives, was set on fire forward by a bomb. Her crew began to fight the blaze but ready-use ammunition by the gun on the ship's forecastle exploded and the gun fell through the deck. As she dropped astern, the destroyer *Martin* sent her ship's boat with a surgeon-lieutenant to provide assistance, even though the Russian ship was now the centre of attention for the bombers and the water around her was erupting with near misses. The young surgeon-lieutenant, R. Ransome-Wallis was able to rescue three badly wounded Russian sailors whom he brought back to his ship and operated on. Assistance from a French corvette saw the fire aboard the *Starii Bolshevik* brought under control and the ship eventually rejoined the convoy.

A classic example of just how much damage a near miss could do was suffered by the Polish-manned destroyer *Garland*. A stick of four bombs fell into the water, and as they exploded they splattered her hull with splinters and put out of action her 'A' and 'B' guns and one of her Oerlikon AA weapons, as well as knocking out the forward boiler room, bringing down her radio aerials and igniting smoke floats on her deck. Of her crew, twenty-five men were dead and forty-three wounded. A trawler had to run alongside to act as a communication link between the Polish ship and the escort leader.

Two American ships were among those hit by a further attack at 13.10. The cargo ship *Alomar* was hit by two bombs, and within five minutes the *Mormacsul* was set on fire. Both ships fell astern quickly and a corvette was ordered to stand by, but both sank within twenty minutes. Three Ju88s in a V formation then fell on the *Empire Lawrence*, with bombs entering No. 2 hold before one exploded, and the ship started to take on water and list to port. As she lost way, she was attacked again, with four bombs hitting the engine room, Nos 4 and 5 holds and her magazine, which exploded. The ship split apart just as a trawler drew alongside to offer assistance. The lifeboats were already loaded and the men were simply waiting for the ship to lose way before lowering them – always a wise precaution – but the explosion blew the port boat to pieces, killing many of those aboard, and blew the starboard boat clear. As the ship sank, the *Luftwaffe* began strafing the wreckage, a completely unnecessary act as the ship was clearly destroyed, but her DEMS gunners stayed at their posts. Her master, Captain H. S. Darkins, who was burning the confidential code books, was lost with his ship. It was left to a trawler and a corvette to pick up survivors. The CAM-ship's Hurricane had already seen action, otherwise it would have been wasted, but the ship also took 5,000 tons of supplies down with her.

Meanwhile, two other ships had also been badly damaged by near misses. One of these, the American cargo ship *City of Joliet*, was so badly shaken that she was abandoned, although her crew later went back on board. Ultimately their efforts were to be in vain as she sank early the next day, 28 May. The *Empire Baffin* was also damaged, although not so seriously. The attacks continued while *Martin* was taking badly wounded survivors off an armed trawler, with eight Ju88s encouraging a speedy transfer of the victims. The situation eased considerably as the convoy turned to the north-north-east as the ice permitted.

At around 20.00 that evening, a further attack was pressed home. This time the victim was the *Empire Purcell*, crippled by a stick of four bombs, with two exploding in the No. 2 hold and another two exploding alongside, with the bunker collapsing and coal cascading into the stokehold, while water flooded into the engine room from fractured valves. The cargo was mainly ammunition, so the order was given to abandon ship, but the frozen davits allowed one boat to fall into the sea, killing six men outright with two more dying shortly afterwards, but others trapped under the capsized lifeboat were rescued by Able Seaman William Thomson. The master, Captain Stephenson, and three of his officers eventually left the ship in the other lifeboat, just before she blew up.

The same attack included a number of torpedo-bombing He111s, one of which dropped its torpedoes at extreme range towards the *Lowther Castle*, and both struck the port side, bursting into No. 2 hold and setting the cargo on fire, as well as wrecking the steering. The ship quickly settled bows first and the order was given to abandon ship, but one of the lifeboats was badly handled and once again fell into the water, although in this case the only fatality was the ship's master. As she fell astern, other aircraft bombed and strafed her, but once abandoned, with her survivors picked up by the corvette *Honeysuckle*, she burnt for a further eight hours before blowing up.

The convoy commodore's ship, the *Ocean Voice*, had a large hole blown in her hull by the forward hold, just above the water-line, and caught fire. There was little wind at the time and only a low swell, so the fire was extinguished and the ship continued her course. However, the fire had damaged the bridge sufficiently for the commodore to transfer leadership of the convoy to the vice-commodore, Captain J. T. Hair, master of the *Empire Selwyn*.

The merchantmen were not the only victims during this terrible ordeal. The Polish-manned *Garland* took so much damage that she was ordered out of the escort and told to make her own way to Kola.

While performing sterling work in rescuing survivors, a new task was given to the corvettes, that of transferring ammunition to ships that were running low. Some of the newer weapons on the American merchantmen were not maintaining a high rate of fire, and these had a surplus of ammunition, while ships that had been putting up a heavy rate of AA fire, including the warships, were running dangerously low.

The casualty rates continued to climb. There were men with burns and scalds, others had suffered severe frostbite, and many had both. One man with his leg broken in six places, and doubtless other injuries as well, died in *Martin*'s sick bay. Another in the same sick bay had a broken back. One required brain surgery. The crew set about the grim task of burying the dead at sea.

At 21.30 on the 28 May, the attacks started again. By this time, three Soviet destroyers had ventured out to help the convoy home and reinforce its depleted escort. They put up an impressive display of AA fire that helped to ensure that this attack was ineffective, as was an attack made early the following morning. Late on Friday 29 May, the convoy escort was joined by the ocean minesweepers of the 1st Minesweeping Flotilla from Kola.

Not all of the convoy was destined for Murmansk, as six ships were destined for Archangel which had reopened after its long winter closure. Captain Crombie in *Bramble* was to take six merchant ships into the White Sea and on to Archangel, and to help with this extra leg he selected *Martin* and the AA ship *Alynbank*. While the

Archangel detachment was still in sight of the main convoy, shortly before midnight, thirty-three Ju88s attacked, with eighteen heading for the main convoy and the remainder for the Archangel ships. The attack was beaten off. This was the last attack endured by the ships heading for the Gourlo and the White Sea, but the Murmansk ships were less lucky, with three attacks on 30 May, although no ships were hit and two aircraft were shot down. Soviet Hurricanes provided air cover after 13.00 that day and at 16.00 the convoy entered the Kola Inlet.

Later that day, Crombie and the Archangel ships proceeded through the White Sea headed by the ice-breaker *Stalin* towards the estuary of the River Dvina, and the slow forty hour crawl through the ice to Archangel. As they steamed through the narrow channel cut by the ice-breaker, they were apparently easy targets and were bombed by Ju87 Stuka dive-bombers. However, these bombers were driven off by heavy AA fire.

All in all, PQ16 had brought 321 tanks to the Soviet Union, although another 147 had been lost *en passage*. There were also 124 aircraft and 2,507 vehicles.

Even with the loss of a number of merchantmen, the convoy was still considered to be a success, as up to half the ships were expected to be lost. This was extravagance with scarce ships and even scarcer men. The 'success' was recognized by an order directly from King George VI to 'splice the mainbrace', that is provide an extra ration of rum for those aboard the warships.

More effective recognition of what was needed came from Commander Richard Onslow, the senior officer escort. He reported that the convoys needed increased AA capabilities and air cover, noting that the CAM-ships were extremely limited in what they could provide. The answer was, of course, an escort carrier. He also noted that the use of the escorts to rescue survivors distracted them from providing anti-submarine and AA cover, so dedicated rescue ships were necessary. Also needed were fire-fighting tugs to help the crews of those ships that had caught fire, or to enable ships that had broken down to remain with the convoy. Most importantly of all was the shortage of ammunition, with little or no replenishment available at Vaenga.

Sadly, although Onslow's recommendations were to be adopted, this did not happen until convoy PQ18, and in the meantime, PQ17 had to be run through to the Soviet Union.

Soviet Ports

The situation in the two main Russian ports used by the convoys was dire. Neglect and bomb damage ensured that berths were unusable and wharves had collapsed. The Royal Navy's escort vessels were in such demand that many did not even wait for a return convoy, but responded to orders that sent them elsewhere. The merchant vessels had no option but to wait until their cargoes could be unloaded, and found that the Russians were incapable of handling the cargo that did arrive, despite Stalin's incessant demands for more. A warmer reception was given to the naval personnel and Merchant Navy officers because of the Soviet preoccupation with uniforms, but most Merchant Navy ratings did not wear uniform and so were treated with disdain and as of no account by the Russians.

The Royal Navy built up extensive base facilities at Murmansk, occupied by Naval Party NP100, and Archangel, the home of Naval Party NP200, both of which included a small American contingent. The liaison with the Soviet Union demanded a full admiral's presence in Moscow, but the role of Senior British Naval Officer North Russia, SBNONR, was that of a rear admiral, initially R. H. Bevan, then E. R. Archer, and then J. Egerton. At first the post was based at Murmansk, but it was not until 1943 that close liaison was possible and the post moved to the Soviet naval base at Polyarnoe, this despite the fact that one of the SBNONR's duties was liaison with Admiral Golovko, commander of the Northern Fleet. Other duties included the organization of the QP series of convoys, as well as the allocation of berths for incoming convoys, or anchorages for those ships waiting for a berth, and assessing the order of priorities for discharging cargo. NP100 also monitored German signals traffic. Senior British Naval Officers with the rank of commander were also based at Murmansk and at Vaenga, which also had a hospital and a camp for survivors. NP200 only came into existence while Archangel was open and able to handle cargo.

Officially, the personnel in the naval parties were there for nine months at a time, but Soviet bureaucracy demanded that they have visas, an unusual aspect of the relationship since service personnel do not normally even need passports. The harshness of Soviet life, especially in their own armed forces, was reflected in an inability to understand why British personnel posted to the Soviet Union needed relieving, and so visas were often extended and men found their stay

128

prolonged as a result, while the Russians ignored requests for fresh visas for relief personnel.

Initially, the Russians refused to allow British ships to use Polyarnoe, and only the necessity of having assistance with minesweeping and then in supporting the submarine fleet allowed this rule to be relaxed. In addition to the flotilla of ocean minesweepers under his command, SBNONR also had the trawler *Chiltern*, which had arrived as part of the escort for PQ12 and PQ14, and then PQ15, after which she stayed and became the fleet tender at Polyarnoe. A launch would have been better for this work, but the ship bringing it, the British cargo vessel *Earlston*, was sunk on 5 July 1942 as part of convoy PQ17.

Robert Towersey, who was flag lieutenant to Rear Admiral Archer, recalled:

> The Russian people are charming, it is the system that is the problem. Anybody who was exceedingly friendly we knew to be suspect. Political commissars [and] the NKVD [predecessor of the KGB] were everywhere ... it was almost impossible to make a telephone call without hearing the tapper talking to his mates or music playing.

It was not only telephone calls that were interfered with, as at first mail was also affected until the British circumvented this by ensuring that mail for personnel posted to the Soviet Union went in diplomatic bags.

Relationships with the Russians were difficult on a professional level. Anyone who seemed to be too close to the British was immediately transferred elsewhere as they were suspect, even dancing partners provided at the Red Navy Club at Polyarnoe. There was never much to do ashore. 'Went ashore once, but couldn't find anywhere to go. Nobody could speak English and we couldn't speak Russian. Only ashore for a couple of hours then back on board,' David Walker recalled.[1]

Movement was difficult as the Russians placed guards at the gangway to every ship and at points around the ports, and given the general poor relations and language barriers, the opportunity for misunderstanding and frustration was considerable. Papers were constantly being examined, and if anything was considered to be out of order, passage was refused. Occasionally, people did manage to get further ashore than the confines of the port or the adjoining town, itself holding little to attract the visitor. One watch ashore managed to reach the airfield at Gryaznaya and found new Hawker Hurricanes of the latest mark abandoned and unused, rather than the Mark 1 aircraft considered suitable for the CAM-ships (perhaps naturally enough, as they were disposable). In the cockpits, tags hung showing that the aircraft had been passed as airworthy, with the date and the initials of the company test pilot. Other aircraft had clearly suffered damage due to heavy and careless handling. One naval officer complained that the Russians never seemed to repair anything.

'Always thought that the Russians did not give the British or the Americans credit for the enormous help they gave,' remarked Henry Granlund, a British naval officer. 'The Russian people were never told about the help being given. Even tanks, for example, were always repainted immediately they arrived so that their origins could not be seen.'[2]

Notes:

1. Imperial War Museum Sound Archive, Accession No. 23186.
2. Imperial War Museum Sound Archive, Accession No. 8836.

Chapter 13

Convoy is to Scatter

Perhaps it would have been better if Convoy PQ16 had suffered more greatly, as the lower-than-feared losses gave the Allied leadership renewed and ill-deserved confidence in their ability to support the Soviet war effort. Typical of this was the telegram sent to Stalin from Churchill after PQ16's safe arrival:

> We are resolved to fight our way through to you with the maximum amount of war materials. On account of *Tirpitz* and other enemy surface ships at Trondheim, the passage of every convoy has become a serious fleet operation. We shall continue to do our utmost.

The build-up of the British presence in northern Russia was continuing, with Consolidated Catalina flying boats of RAF Coastal Command's 210 and 240 squadrons designated for operations in support of the Norwegian Resistance movement, and there were plans for torpedo-bombers to be based there as well. Five Catalinas at a time were based in Russia, and patrols included keeping a watch on the Altenfjord, near the North Cape. As discussed earlier, this was a favourite lair for the *Tirpitz*, as the steep sides of the narrow fjord made bombing difficult and torpedo-bombing impossible. Meanwhile, the German naval build-up also continued, with *Tirpitz* and *Admiral Hipper* expected at Trondheim, and *Admiral Scheer* and *Lutzow* at Narvik.

The Royal Navy expected these ships to be brought out to destroy the convoys – it was inconceivable to men of the 'big gun' navy that such precious assets should lie wasted, especially while the German Army was being pushed back by Soviet forces. It took some time for the message to get through that the real threats to the convoys came from below the sea and above it, from U-boats and from aircraft, rather than from battleships and heavy cruisers. It was also true that many senior officers relished the idea of a major fleet engagement, and this was especially the case later on when Admiral Sir Andrew Browne Cunningham, 'ABC' to his men, took over as First Sea Lord. This man had spent his time as Commander-in-Chief Mediterranean Fleet looking for such an engagement with the Italian Navy, who were almost as keen as the Germans to disappoint him.

The British strategic assessment was that the situation was entirely in Germany's favour, with naval forces operating close to their bases and supported by land-based aircraft and a screen of U-boats. In the event of the Germans sallying forth, the Home Fleet plan was for the unfortunate convoy to sail to the west to longitude 10 degrees east, hopefully to lure the Germans on to the guns of the Home Fleet that would be beyond any effective German aerial attack. Tovey hoped that the Germans would give chase, but realized that they might well suspect his intentions and return to harbour, or instead opt to hang around off the coast waiting for the convoy to return to its course, during which time they could be prey for the Allied submarines off the Norwegian coast.

Poor Morale

On the other hand, there were many in the merchantmen and the convoy escorts who had started to wonder whether they were being used as bait to attract the German ships out to battle with the Royal Navy.

The Admiralty did not agree with Tovey's logic, and instead proposed that in such circumstances any convoy should scatter. The logic was that many ships spread across the ocean would be far more difficult for the Germans to track down than a concentrated group of ships. Tovey's view was that this would be 'sheer bloody murder', not least because in keeping together there was a degree of unity that boosted strength, since the merchantmen had shown themselves increasingly competent at contributing to the convoys' AA defences, and also improved morale. In the end a compromise was agreed. The Home Fleet would give its usual distant or heavy cover, while the cruiser squadron would provide a supplementary escort as far as 10 degrees east, but would be allowed to proceed beyond Bear Island to a point no further east than 25 degrees if the convoy was threatened by 'the presence of a force which the cruiser force could fight'. In

132

other words, the cruisers could face German cruisers and destroyers, but not battleships or battle-cruisers, or (as previously mentioned) what the British press termed 'pocket battleships' (*panzerschiffs*, armoured ships), but which the Germans had by this time reclassified as heavy cruisers. Tovey's alternative suggestion that the convoy should be split in two was also rejected, largely because the Admiralty was caught between American irritation that supplies were building up and Soviet anger that their demands were not being met. There were other problems. Some of the ships waiting in Iceland for the next convoy had been troubled by indiscipline. The rapid expansion of the merchant fleets created by the war and the loss of so many experienced men to the navies, as reservists were called up, had meant that many of those manning the ships lacked experience of life at sea, while others saw no reason why they should risk life and limb for what they saw as a British war. Idleness contributes greatly to indiscipline, and life for the merchant seamen was a dreary round of visits to unattractive locations, with too much time spent cooped up in ships that were overcrowded, given the presence of the AA gunners, and in between there was the stress and strain of fighting the convoys through, and if they were not fighting the Germans or waiting for them to attack, it was usually because the weather was so bad!

Poor motivation was not confined to the merchant seamen, but also affected the Royal Navy. Henry Granlund, a naval officer who sailed with the convoys recalled:

> Sometimes people were late back from leave. If there wasn't a good excuse, they appeared before the first lieutenant or the commanding officer and for a serious offence they could be given cells. To some, fourteen days in cells were better than the conditions on the Russian convoys.[1]

Nevertheless, while most simply did their duty and prayed for survival, there were other attitudes as well, again according to Henry Granlund: 'Many people regarded them as a challenge, and some people even enjoyed them.'[2]

The Admiralty did not want to see the loss of further ships having already lost *Trinidad* and *Edinburgh* in Arctic waters. Given the scale of losses in the Far East and the Mediterranean, this was understandable. On the other hand, the presence of such ships had a deterrent effect on the Germans and a comfort factor for those with the convoys.

Unlucky QP13

In planning for PQ17, a larger than usual escort was arranged and again rescue ships were to be provided as well as a dummy convoy. Quite how a dummy convoy could be provided given the shortage of merchant ships is another question, but in fact the 'dummy' turned out to be more of a dummy raiding force than a convoy. The distant cover would include the United States Navy's Task Force 99 under Rear Admiral Griffen, while Rear Admiral Louis 'Turtle' Hamilton would command the First Cruiser Squadron sailing with PQ17. Tovey would also have his new second-in-command, Vice Admiral Sir Bruce Fraser. Hamilton was an advocate of naval air power, and one of those, also present in the United States Navy, who believed that air power should be used to keep the seas open rather than bombing German cities.

The dummy convoy was known as Operation ES, and consisted of minelayers and four colliers escorted by two cruisers, *Curacao* and *Sirius*, five destroyers and a number of armed trawlers. Doubtless colliers were chosen as such ships were more likely to have been available given that the normal heavy British coastal traffic along the east coast was suspended after the fall of the Low Countries as it was too exposed to attack by German aircraft and light forces. ES sailed from Scapa two days after PQ17 and headed towards the Norwegian Sea to give the impression that it was making for southern Norway on a raiding or mine-laying mission. It remained undetected by German reconnaissance, even when repeated a week later, and was nothing more than a waste of time and fuel, keeping scarce ships away from more productive duties.

Meanwhile, a telex message from German naval headquarters to the local commander at Narvik on 14 June was intercepted by Swedish intelligence and the information passed to the British Naval Attaché in Stockholm, Captain Henry Denham. This revealed details of operation *Rosselsprung*, 'The Knight's Move', which comprised the German plans to destroy the next convoy. It made it clear that aerial reconnaissance was to locate the convoy before it reached Jan Mayen, and that this would lead to air attacks from bases in northern Norway. The heavy cruisers and six destroyers would move to Altenfjord while *Tirpitz* and *Admiral Hipper* would move to Narvik. Warships would commence operations once the convoy reached 5 degrees east. Once the convoy reached the meridian of Bear Island, there would be coordinated attacks by aircraft, surface vessels and U-boats. In short, the complete and devastating destruction of an entire convoy, using surface vessels that could achieve as much in a few hours as a U-boat wolf-pack could achieve in as many days. The more adventurous and confident approach being planned could have owed much to the replacement of the unwell *Vizeadmiral* Otto Ciliax aboard the *Tirpitz* by *Vizeadmiral* Otto Schniewind, who was anxious that his battle group should conduct offensive operations. A further sign of the change in attitude was the allocation of 15,000 tons of bunker oil. The Germans had also built-up their air strength in Norway, and while this included additional He115 seaplane torpedo-bombers, the real significance lay in additional He111s and Ju88s, and thirty Ju87 Stuka dive-bombers. Reconnaissance strength was also boosted.

The one advantage that the Royal Navy held was its possession of naval air power, and even the limited capabilities of the British naval aircraft of the day had undermined confidence to a degree perhaps not appreciated outside Germany. Obsolescent Swordfish biplanes had not only crippled the Italian battle fleet at Taranto, they had contributed to the loss of the *Bismarck*, sister ship to the *Tirpitz*, the previous year. Blackburn Skua fighter/dive-bombers had sunk the cruiser *Konigsberg* during the Norwegian campaign of 1940. Even the fighters, the slow and lumbering Fairey Fulmar, had had an impact. The head of the German Navy, *Grossadmiral* (Grand Admiral) Erich Raeder, was keen to show what his service could do, and so win the Führer's favour, but he hesitated to send his ships to sea without strong assurances of support from the *Luftwaffe*. The two heavy cruisers, *Lutzow* and *Admiral Scheer*, with a maximum speed of just 28 knots, were regarded as being especially vulnerable, and, after all, their sister, *Graf Spee*, had been destroyed by a heavy cruiser and two light cruisers.

Three U-boats were sent to patrol off Iceland, keeping watch for Allied shipping movements. During the period 15–23 June, eight U-boats were dispatched to a patrol area off Jan Mayen to wait for the next convoy.

Nevertheless, caution was still the watchword, even at the very top. Raeder approached Hitler with his plans for the Knight's Move, seeking full *Luftwaffe* support, since only the Führer himself could ensure that this would happen. Hitler agreed, but on condition that the major fleet units were not to venture out to sea until any aircraft carrier had been dealt with by the *Luftwaffe*. Disappointed, Raeder did at least manage to persuade Hitler that the ships could go to sea if carrier-borne aircraft were out of range. Hitler reluctantly agreed, but the plan could still only go ahead subject to his approval. Once again, the Führer system was stifling initiative, while locally, communications between operational units of the two armed services involved remained patchy.

Tovey took the Home Fleet to sea to provide the distant or heavy escort, flying his flag in the battleship *Duke of York*. His deputy Vice Admiral Fraser was aboard the aircraft carrier *Victorious*, with Rear Admiral Burrough aboard the cruiser *Nigeria*, joined by the heavy cruiser *Cumberland*, while Rear Admiral Griffen was aboard the battleship USS *Washington*. An anti-submarine screen of a dozen British and American destroyers completed the force.

The Home Fleet then indulged in the wasteful farce that was Operation ES by steaming eastwards as if it was covering the decoy convoy. Only afterwards could Tovey take his force to patrol an area where it could offer some support to the convoy. Among Tovey's problems was the ailing First Sea Lord, Dudley Pound. He was interfering in Tovey's decisions, using the fact that the Admiralty could have more up-to-date information due to the Ultra decrypts to reserve much of the decision-making to himself. It was clear that the Admiralty expected to control the convoy from a distance.

PQ17 left Hvalfjord on 27 June 1942, and like PQ16 before it, consisted of thirty-six merchantmen, most of them American, under the command of Commodore Dowding in the *River Afton*. It also had two fleet oilers, one of them comprising Force Q with its escorting destroyer. The convoy carried 150,000 tons of stores and general cargo, as well as 594 tanks, 4,246 military vehicles and 297 aircraft.

On 26 June, the reciprocal convoy QP13 had left Archangel, and on 28 June it was augmented by vessels from Murmansk, giving it a total of thirty-five merchantmen, making it the largest southbound convoy so far. It was under the command of Commodore N. H. Gale in *Empire Selwyn*, with Commander P. Todd as senior officer escort in the destroyer *Inglefield*. Once the usual Kola-based minesweepers and the Soviet destroyers had departed, there were five destroyers, including the Polish-manned *Garland* (with some of the survivors from *Edinburgh* who had volunteered to fill the gaps in her ship's company left by the casualties of her outward passage), the AA ship *Alynbank*, four corvettes, two ocean minesweepers and two trawlers, while the submarine *Trident* was to stay with the convoy until 1 July. *Inglefield* and another destroyer had run through from Scapa with spare parts and much needed ammunition for the other ships of the escort.

Initially, the weather was poor, despite the time of year, but even so the convoy was noted by the Germans on 30 June and 2 July. On 2 July, PQ17 and QP13 passed, and Force Q, the oiler and destroyer, switched from PQ17 to QP13.

On 3 July, three of the destroyers were detached on direct orders from the Admiralty to conduct a sweep looking for the *Tirpitz*, known to be missing from her moorings. The following day, QP13 was divided, again on Admiralty orders, with nineteen ships, including the *Empire Selwyn* with Commodore Gale aboard, directed to Loch Ewe in Scotland, while the remaining sixteen, mainly American, maintained their course for Hvalfjord with Captain J. Hiss, master of the *American Robin*, as commodore. The destroyers *Inglefield* and *Intrepid* went to Iceland, although they left the convoy on 7 July, early in the morning, to refuel at Seidisfjord, but the convoy still had two minesweepers, a French corvette and both trawlers.

The Loch Ewe contingent arrived safely. The Iceland-bound ships were navigating by dead reckoning, not having had a chance to take an astronomical fix for three days due to the heavy overcast. Commander Cubison, the senior officer aboard the minesweeper *Niger*, estimated from soundings taken at 20.00 that the convoy was north-east of Straumness, the north-west tip of Iceland, and ordered the convoy to move from five columns to two so that it could pass between Straumness and a British minefield. He then left the convoy and pushed ahead to make a landfall. Two hours later, the radar showed 'land' at a distance of one mile and the ship signalled that the course should be altered to the west, but the land shown on the radar was a large iceberg. It took just forty minutes for *Niger* to steam into the British minefield and blow up, with a heavy loss of life. Cubison realized his mistake in time to signal to Hiss that the convoy should resume its earlier course, but he was too late. Within minutes, five ships were sunk by mines and another ship badly damaged. Confusion reigned as those aboard the merchant ships thought that they were being attacked by U-boats.

The surviving warships had charts showing the minefield, and once he had established his position, Lieutenant Biggs commanding *Hussar*, and *Lieutenant de Vaisseau* Bergeret of the *Rosalys* entered the minefield, with the British ship leading the remaining merchantmen to safety while the French corvette spent more than six hours searching for survivors and succeeded in rescuing 179 men.

The fault for this mishap lay firmly with the Admiralty. Captain Hiss had no opportunity for a thorough briefing either for himself or to pass on information to the other masters. *Niger*'s radar was simply not good enough for navigation in such conditions.

The Knight's Move

PQ17 meanwhile had been reduced to thirty-five ships when an American ship ran aground off Iceland, and despite a trawler and a tug being sent to her aid, the ship was left behind. Most of PQ17's ships were intended for Archangel, with just eight for Murmansk as the latter port had been bombed so heavily that it had had to suspend operations for a period. The ice cap had receded further than usual for the time of year, allowing the convoy to keep well to the west and pass north of Bear Island. Nevertheless, while still in the Denmark Strait heavy ice was encountered and another American ship was too badly damaged to continue, and her repeated radioed requests for help doubtless helped to provide the Germans with the position of the convoy. Next, one of the naval auxiliaries, the oiler *Grey Ranger*, intended to act as a fuel ship in Russia, also struck a growler which split her bows wide open. She too was forced to turn back, but it was decided that she should swap places with the *Aldersdale*, the other fleet oiler, and that her fuel should be used to top up the escort vessels.

As usual, the initial escort from Iceland had been light, consisting of just three minesweepers and four trawlers when the convoy left Hvalfjord, but on 30 June the ocean escort arrived. This was led by Commander J. E. Broome in the destroyer *Keppel*, one of eight destroyers and three corvettes, two AA ships converted from fruit carriers, and two submarines, escorting the convoy, while another destroyer and the tanker *Aldersdale* comprised Force Q. There was also a solitary CAM-ship, *Empire Tide*.

Broome immediately ordered the anti-submarine trawlers to position themselves at the four corners of the convoy box and put the AA ships within the outer columns of the convoy. He also placed the better armed Liberty ships at the edges of the convoy. His intention was to produce an effective mix of anti-submarine and AA capability at key points around the convoy to provide the best possible protection.

Rear Admiral Louis 'Turtle' Hamilton had been present when Broome had briefed the convoy masters at Hvalfjord. His four cruisers, led by his flagship *London*, were to provide heavy support for the convoy. The other cruisers were *Norfolk* and the American ships *Tuscaloosa* and *Wichita*, supported by one British and two American destroyers. While the masters had been briefed on what to do in the event of air attack, within his squadron Hamilton made it clear that while the primary objective was to get PQ17 to the Soviet Union, a subsidiary objective was to try to draw out the heavy units of the *Kriegsmarine*, not for the cruisers to engage these, but instead to shadow them and report their position to the Home Fleet.

The cruiser squadron was the last to leave Iceland, sailing on 1 July, their superior speed making it easy for them to catch the slow moving convoy, proceeding at just 8 knots. The weather at the outset was good, and on 1 July while the Allied Cruiser Squadron was catching up, the escorts took the opportunity to refuel. At midday, the first U-boats were sighted and chased off, but this caused radio silence to be broken and confirmed to the Germans once again the convoy's position. Two U-boats, *U-255* and *U-408* now maintained contact with the convoy's progress, while *U-334* and *U-456* were directed to join them. Another six U-boats were directed further east to form a wolf-pack or patrol line. The U-boats were assisted by a Blohm und Voss Bv138 reconnaissance flying boat which arrived at 14.00 and started to transmit homing signals for the U-boats. Alarm spread through the convoy when capital ships were spotted silhouetted against the horizon, but on investigation by a trawler, these proved to be the Home Fleet.

After Force Q had left on 2 July to join QP13, the number of aircraft keeping PQ17 under observation rose to three. Later that afternoon, the convoy was forced to wheel to avoid torpedoes believed to have come from *U-456*, which was counter-attacked by three destroyers and a corvette, but without success. One of the British cruisers in Hamilton's squadron sent a Walrus over the convoy. At 18.00, the USS *Rowan*, an American destroyer escorting the Allied cruisers, approached the convoy to refuel from the *Aldersdale*, and as she did so nine He115 seaplanes made a half-hearted torpedo attack on the AA ship *Pozarica*, until confronted by her heavy AA fire to which *Rowan* also made a contribution, shooting down one aircraft, which crash-landed in the water. The Germans were not without nerve, however, as one of the other aircraft landed and rescued the crew from the downed aircraft! Mercifully, fog then descended and the convoy was able to change course to the east, towards Bear Island, unnoticed by the *Luftwaffe*.

The following day started with a number of U-boat scares, which kept the escorts busy as the convoy passed in and out of fog banks. While tracking down U-boats doubtless kept them at bay, it also meant that fuel and in some cases depth charges were being used at a considerable rate. With Hamilton and his cruisers steering a parallel course some 40 miles to the north, the convoy continued to be kept under close observation by a Walrus, at this time from HMS *London*. Hamilton's own theory at this time was that the *Tirpitz* and *Admiral Hipper* would be sent after QP13 in an attempt to draw the Home Fleet away, leaving PQ17 for *Lutzow* and *Admiral Scheer*. Doubtless with the Battle of the River Plate in mind, Hamilton believed that his orders gave him scope to engage these two German ships. There was an exchange of fire between the Walrus and the Bv138 later when the former landed close to *Keppel* with a message from Hamilton for Broome, advising the senior officer, escort, SO(E) that the ice-edge had receded considerably to the north and that the convoy should change course to the north increasing the distance between it and the *Luftwaffe* base at Banak, but Broome, the SO(E), did not take the convoy as far north as Hamilton suggested, anxious to continue pressing eastwards.

The situation was complicated at this time by poor weather over Norway that prevented effective aerial reconnaissance. No one on the British side was aware that the *Lutzow*, *Scheer* and six destroyers had left their base at Narvik under the command of *Vizeadmiral* Oskar Kummetz, but they were convinced that *Vizeadmiral* Otto Schniewind had taken the *Tirpitz* from Trondheim with *Hipper*, four destroyers and two large ocean-going torpedo-boats. Nevertheless, the more northerly of these two forces, that from Narvik, soon ran into trouble, with the *Lutzow* running aground as she emerged from the Ofotfjord in fog, while further south three of Schniewind's destroyers hit uncharted rocks, although two replacements were with him when he took the *Tirpitz* and *Hipper* into the Altenfjord.

Aware of the movements of the *Tirpitz* group, Hamilton was then shadowed by German aircraft and sent his Walrus off on a reconnaissance sortie, but the aircraft hit fog and then ran out of fuel, having to make a forced landing and be taken in tow by a trawler. As the aircraft had jettisoned its depth charges prior to landing – a measure that was always recommended, especially for landings in the open sea in case the aircraft sank and the escaping crew were killed as the depth charges hit their pre-set depth – two of the escorts thought they were being attacked and opened fire. Meanwhile, the fog that had made life so difficult for the Walrus closed in over the convoy so that the German reconnaissance aircraft lost track of it, and when it did begin to lift, the fog then settled at a convenient mast height – poor for aerial reconnaissance, but reassuring for station-keeping.

Once again information came from intelligence sources in Sweden about German intentions, which were that the convoy would be attacked between longitudes 15 and 30 east, and this was passed on by the Admiralty early on 4 July when the convoy was almost exactly midway between these two points. With the movement of the German ships, it seemed that a combined heavy force was preparing to attack.

PQ17 was by this time some 60 miles north of Bear Island, when a lookout aboard the AA ship *Palomares* heard the sound of aircraft engines overhead, and as the fog thinned those aboard saw a Heinkel He111 diving to launch its torpedo. Too late, the ships AA defences opened up while six blasts were given on her siren to warn those around the ship that she was about to take evasive action. The torpedo missed *Palomares*, but continued on to hit the American merchantman *Christopher Newport*, a Liberty ship carrying 10,000 tons of munitions, despite one of the gunners aboard calmly taking aim and striking the torpedo with his .30 machine-guns. Exploding in the engine room, the torpedo killed an engineer and two greasers, while the ship lost power and started to swing round out of control, forcing the rest of the convoy to have to change course to steer around her – unwelcome fireworks with which to celebrate Independence Day! The rescue ship *Zamalek* was soon alongside and took aboard forty-seven survivors, many of whom had time to dress in their best clothes and bring with them small arms and personal possessions. While the *Aldersdale* offered to tow the stricken merchantman, the delay in setting up a tow would have left both

141

ships and any others at the scene exposed, and so Broome ordered the submarine *P614* to torpedo the *Christopher Newport*, but two torpedoes from the submarine and then depth charges from the corvette *Dianella* failed to deliver the desired *coup de grâce*, leaving the job to *U-457* later.

Set against this loss was the signal from the Admiralty to Hamilton allowing him the discretion of taking his cruisers beyond 25 degrees east. Unaware of the full picture, Tovey later signalled Hamilton, warning him not to enter the Barents Sea unless he could be certain that he would not encounter the *Tirpitz*. Hamilton decided to take his cruisers further south. Only then did he discover that the convoy was 30 miles further south than he had expected it to be, as a result of Broome's decision to press on to the east. He eventually took his ships to a position 12 miles ahead of the convoy and at 16.45 ordered Broome to change course to the north-east. The convoy obeyed, but in the meantime it was under observation by both the *Luftwaffe*, who had decided that the anti-submarine aircraft flown from the USS *Wichita* had come from an aircraft carrier, and the commanding officer of *U-457*, shadowing the convoy, who reported that the cruiser squadron included a battleship. Combined, these two reports misled the Germans into believing that the Home Fleet was much closer than was the case, when in fact it was 350 miles away from the convoy. The result was that the German surface ships would not sail because Hitler had insisted on any aircraft carrier being put out of action first. Meanwhile, the other U-boats were homing in on *U-457* and PQ17.

The first of the assembled U-boats to attack was *U-88*, which had lain low and quiet while the first escorts steamed by, and then risen to periscope depth amidst the convoy and fired salvoes of torpedoes from bow and stern tubes, none of which found a target. A formation of He115s also headed for the convoy, but failed to get beyond the convoy's air defences. Despite the increased threat, the Cruiser Squadron's destroyer screen started to fall back towards the convoy to refuel from the *Aldersdale* in a flat calm sea. At 19.30, the American *Wainwright* was preparing to start replenishment when a stick of bombs exploded on her port bow, persuading her commanding officer, Captain D. P. Moon to postpone refuelling and position his ship abeam of *Keppel* ready for the expected air attack.

Radar returns were good in the calm conditions, and at 20.20 the duty radar operators aboard the *Palomares* detected a low-level attack, always giving shorter warning than a high-level attack. Upwards of twenty-five He111s of KG26 and a number of torpedo-carrying Ju88s of KG30 flew straight into the convoy, attacking from astern. The *Wainwright*, which had complete freedom of action at this time, turned to starboard and raced past the convoy towards the German aircraft, turning her beam on to give the largest number of AA weapons a chance to bear on the attackers, and opened fire giving an effective long-range barrage that effectively turned back the first wave. One He111 was shot down, and even though it released its torpedoes, they failed to find a target. The second wave was more determined. The leading He111 dropped a bomb on the surfaced *P614*, and despite being on fire from the intense AA barrage, released its torpedo to sink the British merchantman *Navarino*. Her lifeboats were lowered so hurriedly that they slipped in the davits, tipped their unfortunate occupants into the cold water and were nearly mown down by the ship that followed. The aircraft then struck the water and those aboard a passing merchantman could see the crew being burnt alive as the aircraft sank. Then the aircraft that followed dropped a torpedo that struck the American merchantman *William Hooper*, and exploded the boiler. The cruisers then arrived to lend their contribution to the AA barrage, but the attack began to falter, although the British destroyer *Offa* claimed a Heinkel. Several ships narrowly missed torpedoes, while shots from the American *Hoosier* detonated a torpedo warhead. Less fortunate was the Soviet tanker *Azerbaijan*, which was hit by a torpedo and exploded in a sheet of flame, but survived largely because she was carrying linseed oil rather than fuel oil. Equally unfortunate were those aboard the *Empire Tide* and *Ironclad*, which suffered damage from AA gunners forgetting the injunction to be careful about hitting other convoy ships when firing at low-flying aircraft.

In the aftermath of the attack, the rescue ships moved in and the escorts were ordered to set about sinking both the *Navarino* and the *William Hooper*, which they failed to do before moving on. But the *Azerbaijan* astonished everybody as with her largely female crew she steamed on at 9 knots, although one boatload of crew members had actually reached the water and pulled away. After being rescued by the *Zamalek*, the tanker's master refused to accept their return as they were deserters! Surprisingly, despite at least seven U-boats being present, they had not intervened, failing to attack the convoy when everyone was preoccupied with the air attack.

Aircraft were in the air from the cruisers, with the Walrus from *Norfolk* looking for icebergs while the Vought Kingfisher from *Tuscaloosa* was looking for U-boats, but the Admiralty was now warning that heavy surface units were at sea. Broome ordered the Hurricane from *Empire Tide* to be launched in order to shoot down the Bv138 shadowing the convoy. He also contacted the two accompanying submarines, one of which signalled back that if heavy enemy surface units attacked, he intended to remain on the surface, receiving the reply from Broome, 'So do I.' A further line of defence was from the Allied submarines, with six Soviet boats watching the Norwegian coast between Vanna and the North Cape, and eight British boats and one Free French further out to sea, augmented by the two submarines that had accompanied the convoy.

Convoy is to Scatter

At 21.11, the Admiralty signalled both Hamilton and Tovey: 'Cruiser force to withdraw to westward at high speed.' The clear impression was given, following early warnings about the proximity of enemy surface units, that the *Tirpitz* was at sea. The next signal, at 21.23, was addressed to both officers and also to Broome: 'Owing to threat from surface ships convoy is to disperse and proceed to Russian ports.' Then at 21.36, to the same three recipients, added emphasis was given to the previous signal with the unambiguous words: 'Convoy is to scatter.'

The Admiralty was convinced that the *Tirpitz* was at sea. Reconnaissance flights had been interrupted by an accident to an RAF Catalina flying boat, despite a member of the naval staff maintaining that there was no indication that the ship was at sea. A complete communications silence from the Germans could not be enforced once major fleet units had gone to sea as the U-boat commanders would have had to be warned that friendly surface vessels were at sea. On the other hand, signals traffic had already indicated a strong U-boat presence that threatened the cruisers.

The problem was that the Admiralty believed that it alone had possession of all the facts, and to be fair, the First Sea Lord, Pound, also felt that it would be unfair to place the full burden of absolute responsibility on the shoulders of Commander Broome once Hamilton had left with his cruisers. Dispersal was Pound's solution, his second-in-command, the Vice Chief of the Naval Staff, Vice Admiral

Sir Henry Moore, believed that this would take too long, and that the quicker the ships dispersed, the safer. When Pound stated that by 'dispersal', he meant 'scatter', the further signal was sent to ensure that this was understood.

While everyone involved at the Admiralty was acting with the best of intentions, albeit they placed a higher value on their own major ships than on the merchantmen in the convoy, they were seemingly unaware of the nature of running a convoy through to northern Russia. As the convoys proceeded, they were channelled into an increasingly narrow funnel between the southern edge of the Arctic ice-cap and the Norwegian coast, making the final stages the most hazardous, caught between proximity to German airfields and the ice, a northern Scylla and Charybis. It was also the case that the merchantmen in a convoy were always ordered to keep station, not to straggle and that survival lay in operating as a unit, for mutual protection and, if the worst came to the worst, rescue.

The signal gave both Hamilton and Broome problems. Hamilton had no option but to set course westwards, but he delayed for thirty minutes in the hope that *Norfolk* would be able to recover her Walrus, but without success, so he turned the cruiser squadron round and continued on his way. This had the embarrassing result that the merchantmen and close escort could see the heaviest ships available deserting them, racing past the convoy at high speed.

Broome also hesitated, but for a different reason, since he knew that the merchantmen would be vulnerable on their own. At 22.15 he ordered the hoisting of the signal to scatter. This meant that the convoy had to separate fanwise, with each column steering a course outwards at 10 degrees more than its inner neighbour. Individual ships then steered away from their closest neighbour and increased to best speed, the maximum speed of which the individual ship was capable given the weather conditions. While this was happening, the ships in the centre column maintained station, then finally they too scattered, with the odd numbers moving out to starboard, the even numbers to port. Heading the centre column was the *River Afton*, with the convoy commodore, who signalled that he did not understand the order, forcing Broome to take his destroyer, HMS *Keppel*, alongside to repeat the order through a megaphone. He then apologized for having to leave the convoy. As for the destroyers, Broome decided that his destroyers should come together as a cohesive fighting force, while the other warships made their own way to Russian ports.

145

The scatter signal caught some of the ships at an awkward moment, with the destroyer *Somali* in the middle of refuelling from *Aldersdale*, and having to stop abruptly so as to rejoin Hamilton's squadron, fortunately heading in the destroyer's direction.

Tovey believed that scattering the convoy would result in 'sheer bloody murder', while Broome expected 'a shambles' and a 'bloody business'. Both were to be proved right. Worse was to follow when they heard from the Admiralty early the following morning that enemy ships were simply presumed to be north of Tromso, but that it was uncertain whether or not they were at sea at all.

Happy Hunting for the Germans

Around midnight, *U-456* was the first to report the withdrawal of the cruisers, and later this was one of several U-boats to report merchant ships heading in unexpected directions, which was soon confirmed by aerial reconnaissance. Early on 5 July, *U-334* tried to torpedo the *Navarino*, but the ship sank before the torpedoes could reach it. *U-334* then disposed of the *William Hooper*. *Konteradmiral* (Rear Admiral) Hubert Schmundt, 'Admiral Arctic', lost no time in ordering his U-boats into action against the merchant vessels, while KG30's He111s were getting ready at Banak. Elsewhere, on learning of the convoy scattering, senior officers pressed for the *Rosselsprung* operation to be activated, but Raeder refused. When aerial reconnaissance showed the Home Fleet heading north-east, the major surface units were ordered to be ready to go to sea while Raeder approached Hitler for his approval, which was given. A battle group led by the *Tirpitz* with *Hipper* and *Scheer* slipped out to sea with a screen of seven destroyers and two ocean-going torpedo-boats. Shortly after leaving Norway, the Soviet submarine *K-21* spotted *Tirpitz* (every Allied submarine commander's dream) and fired her torpedoes, but without success. For his part, Raeder then sent a signal to Schniewind implying caution by stating that 'partial success' would be more important than 'total victory involving major expenditure of time'. The battle group was spotted by the British submarine *Unshaken* and then by an RAF Catalina flying boat before the Germans eventually lost their nerve and recalled the ships to port, to the dismay of those aboard who felt embarrassed at sitting in port while the rest of the armed forces were involved in increasingly intensive warfare. When *Vizeadmiral* Oskar Kummetz proposed that *Scheer* should return to sea on her own, he was refused.

It was left to *Kapitän* Wagner, Chief of Naval Operations, to sum up the situation: 'Every operation by our surface forces has been hampered by the Führer's desire to avoid losses and reverses at all costs.'

Meanwhile, the remaining British warships, without a convoy to escort, had formed themselves into small groups. The AA ship *Palomares* had recovered the Walrus from *Norfolk* and taken it in tow, while her commanding officer had ordered two minesweepers to accompany him. The two submarines and *Daniella* remained together, while another three corvettes set off eastwards to Russia. The other AA ship, *Pozarica*, under the command of Acting Captain E. Lawford, attempted to gather a few merchant ships together and escort them, but was told not to do so as the order to scatter had come from the Admiralty and left no grounds for any other action. Nevertheless, *Pozarica* then gathered together the three corvettes and joined them heading east. The actions of the AA ships were controversial, with many aboard the corvettes feeling that their duty lay with the merchant ships, but how they could have done much to protect these once the convoy had scattered is unclear. Instead, the corvettes at least had a chance to protect the precious AA ships, and in turn benefit from their heavy AA firepower. In fact, Captain Lawford allowed the commanding officer of *Poppy* to take his ship and return to do what he could for the convoy. Lawford also took the rescue ship *Rathlin* under his wing. When four American merchantmen gathered around the *Palomares* on 5 July, the group was discovered at 13.00 by a Bv138 flying boat and the naval vessels then left them, heading for the Matochkin Strait.

Nevertheless, some protected grouping did take place. One such was with the anti-submarine trawler *Ayrshire*, whose commanding officer was not enthusiastic about abandoning the convoy. He headed towards the edge of the ice to get as far away as possible from the Germans, gathering up as he did so the American *Ironclad* and then the Panamanian *Troubador*, with her cargo of coal, some of which was donated to the trawler. The following morning, the group expanded yet again with the inclusion of the American *Silver Sword*, and the four ships edged into the ice, where Lieutenant Leo Gradwell, RNVR, ordered all engines to be stopped and fires damped while he sent his deputy to confer with the masters of the three merchantmen.

They decided to use the guns of some tanks stowed on the deck of one of the ships as a makeshift armament. The *Troubador* had drums of white paint as well as coal among her cargo, and the crews of all four ships set to hastily painting their ships white, so that they merged with the background and were invisible to reconnoitring aircraft. Gradwell had decided that they should lie low and wait until the action was over.

Not every ship was so lucky with the pack ice. The elderly American merchantman *Pankraft* had suffered near misses in a bombing attack and the steam pipes between the boilers and the engine had ruptured. As her boats pulled away, a Ju88 strafed the ship with incendiary shells and set the ship on fire. They were later to be discovered and rescued by the corvette *Lotus*, who nearly blew herself out of the water as she intended to sink the *Pankraft* with close-range gunfire, and was only prevented from doing so in time by the merchantman's master! In fact, the *Pankraft* burnt for some time, being spotted by the *Olopana* (of whom we shall learn more later) on 6 July, but not blowing up until 06.00 on 7 July.

Faced with a patrolling Focke-Wulf Fw200, some members of the crew of the *Alcoa Ranger* considered surrender, but while some waited at boat stations ready to leave the ship, the aircraft seemed to lose interest and flew away. At 10.30 on 5 July the Liberty ship *Samuel Chase*, the crew took to the boats, being convinced that a U-boat was tailing them and expecting to be torpedoed when the U-boat dived. After waiting for two hours, during which time nothing happened, they reboarded their ship and continued on their way.

By this time, a number of ships had been attacked by U-boats. *U-703* had already made two unsuccessful attacks on the *Empire Byron*, but a fifth torpedo fired from a stern tube struck the engine room, badly damaging the ship and sending her deck cargo of army lorries flying into the air. A sixth torpedo missed the stricken ship, but by this time she was sinking stern first taking eighteen of her crew with her. An American ship sent an SOS on her behalf, but failed to give the position. The survivors took to the lifeboats only to find that *U-703* surfaced alongside them. Fortunately, the ship's master had ordered his officers to take off their epaulettes from their greatcoats and none of them were taken aboard as a prisoner, but the U-boat commander did take an army officer, an instructor taking passage to teach the Red Army how to handle the new Churchill tanks. Some photographs were taken, some basic supplies given to the men in the boats, who were berated by one German officer for helping the Russians.

Also unlucky was the American cargo ship *Carlton*, which was hit by two torpedoes shortly after 10.15, with a third racing through the ship's lifeboats and rafts. Three men were killed in the engine room. Again the U-boat *U-88* surfaced, although this time simply to take details of the ship. Nevertheless, over the next couple of hours in what seemed like an all too rare act of compassion, a succession of flying boats flew out, landed in the calm sea and rescued all but seventeen of the ship's company, who had erected a sail and set off for the nearest part of Russia. The reason for the German concern soon became clear when it was discovered that they were used for propaganda, with claims that the ship had been sunk by a British submarine because she was steaming in a southerly direction. For the crew, reality set in when they finally finished up in Stalag Marlag-Milag Nord, near the port of Bremen.

That afternoon, the four American merchantmen that had been briefly escorted by the *Palomares* group were caught by *U-88* and Ju88s at around the same time, 15.00, helped by homing signals sent by a Bv138. The Ju88s attacked and sank the *Fairfield City*, but another ship, the *Daniel Morgan*, was able to take cover as fog descended. However, shortly afterwards a succession of attacks eventually resulted in her hull being split open. The *Daniel Morgan* lost four men as she sank, with her end hastened by two torpedoes fired by *U-88*. The survivors, who told the commander of *U-88* that the ship had carried food and leather instead of tanks and steel, were later picked up by the Soviet tanker *Donbass*.

Another informal grouping steaming north-east included the British merchantmen *Bolton Castle* and *Olopana*, the American *Washington*, which was already damaged by a number of near misses, and the Dutch *Paulus Potter*, although the elderly *Olopana* fell astern. At around 17.00 a Ju88 dived on *Washington*, but the aircraft's bombs missed, leaving it to strafe the ship out of frustration. Shortly after 17.30, several more Ju88s arrived and bombed the ship, wrecking the steering gear and so damaging the hull that she started to take on water. Her master ordered the crew into the lifeboats fearful that the explosives in one of her holds might explode.

A similar fate awaited the *Bolton Castle* when a bomb fell into No. 2 hold and started progressive explosions among the cargo of bombs stacked there, with the explosions and fire creating a heat so

149

intense that the hull started to melt. Once again yet another crew took to the boats, although the ship did not explode, she simply sank. The *Paulus Potter* suffered a similar fate, but remained afloat to allow a U-boat to eventually give the *coup de grâce*.

The Ju88s had earlier attempted to attack the *Olopana*, which had fooled them into thinking that she had been hit by using smoke floats and getting her crew to prepare to abandon ship. She was now in a position to rescue the crews of her former companions, but discovered that none of them wanted to be rescued. They were all making their own arrangements to sail to Russian territory, in one case as much as 400 miles away, with one master explaining that his men felt safer in the lifeboats.

As KG30's three squadrons of Junkers Ju88s quartered the area seeking lone merchant ships to attack, *U-88* was one of three submarines to find the American merchantman *Honomu*, with a mixed cargo of steel, munitions, tanks and food. This was the nature of submarine warfare, as none of the U-boat commanders was aware of the intentions or exact position of the others until the attack started. *U-456* fired the first torpedo, which struck the ship by her No. 4 hold, causing her to start sinking, and then a second torpedo fired by either *U-456* or *U-334*, struck near No. 4 hold. Together the torpedoes killed nineteen of the crew and the second persuaded the surviving crew members that she should be abandoned. The two U-boats then surfaced and were joined by *U-88*. Having drawn first blood, it was *U-456* who took the ship's master prisoner and gave the thirty-six survivors in the boats some provisions. The U-boats then moved off under diesel power on the surface, showing their confidence that Allied intervention was unlikely.

A far harder target was the British cargo ship *Earlston*, which first evaded an air-dropped torpedo and then found that she was being tailed by a U-boat in white camouflage. Her master increased the ship's speed to the maximum, and ordered all of his firemen to be on watch in the stokehold, reducing the speed differential between the hunted and the hunter. Meanwhile, the embarked members of the Maritime Regiment of Artillery fired at the U-boat, eventually forcing her to dive and lose her speed advantage. Nevertheless, in the circumstances, even the gallant *Earlston*'s luck was due to run out. First, a flight of Ju88s found her, and despite the heavy AA fire that kept them from landing a direct hit, a near miss exploded close to the engine room, shifting the engines on their mountings and fracturing the steam pipework. Her master ordered the ship to be abandoned as she was carrying explosives. As the boats pulled away, three U-boats surfaced and one of them, *U-334*, fired a salvo of torpedoes at the stricken ship, one of them hitting No. 2 hold in which explosives were carried and, with a massive explosion, she split in two. The large steam launch needed for harbour duties at Polyarnoe by the Royal Navy contingent was sent flying into the sea, the far heavier tanks went with the ship to the seabed. The Norwegian master of the *Earlston* was taken prisoner by *U-334*, which remained on the surface with the other two U-boats until persuaded to dive by strafing Ju88s who mistook them for British submarines!

The American *Peter Kerr* was another of those ships steaming south, and at first she too was lucky as she was missed by torpedoes dropped from no less than seven He115s over a period of two hours while her master zigzagged his ship and altered her engine speed. At 17.00 her luck ran out as four Ju88s attacked at high level and beyond the range of her AA fire. No less than three dozen bombs rained down, of which just three hit the ship while others were near misses that proved almost as damaging. The *Peter Kerr*'s steering was disabled and her forward holds and radio room were on fire, with water flooding in forward. The crew quickly abandoned ship and as they pulled away, they too were to see their ship blow up.

At about the same time the convoy commodore's ship, the *River Afton*, was hit by a torpedo from *U-703* which immediately knocked out her engine room, but also a lifeboat. A second torpedo struck the boiler room and destroyed a second lifeboat, killing many of the men in it and blowing others into the sea. The survivors were left with a small dinghy and Carley floats as they abandoned ship, while a third torpedo sped the sinking vessel on her way. As survivors clutched rafts and floats, the dinghy capsized, with at least one man drowning in his heavy clothing. The ship's master and a naval officer taking passage to the Soviet Union righted the dinghy, and then used a briefcase to bale out. They were eventually rescued by the corvette *Lotus* later that day.

Another of the groupings included the fleet tanker *Aldersdale*, which was heading for Novaya Zemlya (twin islands divided by the Matochkin Strait), and on the way soon found herself with the *Ocean Freedom*, the rescue ship *Zaafaran* and the minesweeper *Salamander*. *Zaafaran* was, like the *Zamalek*, a captured German ship built for the Pharaonic Mail Line, and seized by the British on the outbreak of war. They were both managed by the General Steam Navigation Company, which had operated cross-Channel services and day trip-per operations on the Thames, as well as having a cargo fleet serving near Continental ports. That fateful afternoon of 5 July, four Ju88 bombers found the four ships and went into the attack. The heavy AA fire of the combined group of ships forced three of the aircraft to abandon their attacks, but the fourth put a stick of bombs across the *Aldersdale*'s stern, the position of the engine room on a tanker. The tanker stopped and started to ship water. *Salamander* came alongside to rescue the crew of the *Aldersdale*, but as the ship refused to sink, plans were laid to tow her. The engineer was then given five minutes to see if he could restart the engines, but this was impossible. As the attack turned on the other ships and *Salamander*'s support was needed, it was decided that the best course of action was to sink the ship, but this proved difficult. The first close-range shot by *Salamander* only saw her own guard-rail shot away. Then the breech block fell out of her single 4-in gun. A decision was taken to leave the tanker to her fate.

Zaafaran was in trouble. Her engines had been put out of action by near misses from a Ju88, and those aboard had started to abandon ship. Aboard *Zamalek*, *Zaafaran*'s plight could be seen, and a signal was sent to *Palomares*, the AA ship, to send the anti-submarine ships to pick up survivors. The ocean minesweeper *Britomart*, was immediately dispatched, but before she could reach the stricken *Zaafaran*, *Zamalek* arrived and picked up the crew and passengers, all survivors of an earlier sinking, with just one unaccounted for. A fresh grouping now emerged, consisting of *Ocean Freedom*, *Zamalek*, HMS *Britomart*, *Halcyon*, *Palomares* and *Salamander*. Elsewhere, the *Pozarica* group lost the rescue ship *Rathlin* as she could not keep up.

Ironically, the U-boats were drawn clear of the area on 6 July to allow the *Rosselsprung* operation to go ahead, while Tovey and Pound considered whether the Home Fleet should be sent east to cut off the *Tirpitz* and destroy her before she could return to base. But the Germans were already returning, and the Home Fleet was eventually moved south to Scapa Flow. Eventually, the submarines were allowed out again, and *Konteradmiral* Hubert Schmundt, Admiral Arctic, was able to plan a fresh wolf-pack, sending freshly refuelled and rearmed boats to the approaches to the White Sea. Almost unscathed, KG30 still had its Ju88s ready to return to the attack. Novaya Zemlya seemed to be the sole hope of the convoy ships, hoping that Soviet defences would shelter them. So many ships were headed in that direction that it almost seemed that the survivors of the convoy would re-form, but to the cynics the strait was nicknamed 'Funk Creek'.

The situation by this time was that seven ships were strung out along the edge of the ice, including the *Olopana* and the CAM-ship *Empire Tide*, making their way through ice floes and growlers, taking what cover and comfort they could from sea smoke and fog banks. Even so, an Fw200 Condor had spotted them and directed the U-boats to the area.

Late afternoon on 6 July, the American merchantman *John Witherspoon* spotted a surfaced U-boat and opened fire, forcing the submarine to dive, but at 16.30, *U-255* fired a spread of four torpedoes, one of which struck the cargo ship, with the loss of one of her crew. The U-boat surfaced among the survivors, and the crew provided cigarettes, water and cognac as they questioned and filmed them, then a fifth torpedo was fired, breaking the *John Witherspoon* in two so that she sank almost immediately. Unable to identify the master to take him prisoner, the final act of the U-boat was for its commanding officer to indicate the direction of land before diving.

Some ships relied on speed to make their landfall, and one of these was the American cargo liner *Pan Atlantic*, capable of 12 knots – fast for a cargo ship at the time. Well away from most of the other ships, the master believed that he had a good chance of reaching Cape Kanin. In fact, the *Pan Atlantic* was being chased by two U-boats, *U-88* and *U-703*, but just as they were moving in to attack at 06.00 on 6 July, a solitary Ju88 dived down towards the ship, dropping a bomb into one of the holds filled with cordite, and in an instant, the bows had been blown off the ship, sinking her in just three minutes. She took twenty-six men with her.

Not as fast, the Russian tanker *Donbass* was more successful, reaching Molotovsk on 9 July after successfully fending off an attack by a Ju88, which was damaged by the ship's gunners, who now included a number of Americans.

First to arrive at Novaya Zemlya on 6 July, was *Britomart*, sent on ahead to make contact with the Russian residents at Lagerni. Given the closed nature of Soviet society, and despite the war and the Soviet Union's desperate situation, non-Russian ships could not turn up at any port and expect a warm welcome. It had to be explained that the

Allied vessels were simply looking for a safe haven. That afternoon, *Britomart* was joined by *Palomares*, still with *Norfolk*'s Walrus in tow, two other minesweepers, *Halcyon* and *Salamander*, the rescue ship *Zamalek* and the *Ocean Freedom*. It says much for the reliability of the Walrus that, despite several days under tow in the open ocean and cold (even in July), once refuelled it was able to make an ice reconnaissance flight and report back that the Kara Sea was effectively impassable because of ice. This was part of the problem of having Murmansk all but closed due to the bomb damage suffered earlier, since the port would have been accessible. The first group of ships were soon joined by *Pozarica*, *Poppy* and *La Malouine*; the ships were anchored so that their guns could point at the entrance to the strait, although with nothing better than 4-in, they would have been hard-pressed had the Germans arrived. Now able to reconstitute the convoy, *La Malouine* was sent to round up stragglers, and succeeded in finding four merchantmen, directing them to the strait as the weather began to close in. These were not the only arrivals as they were soon joined by *Lotus* with the survivors from the *Pankraft*, and then three armed trawlers arrived at dawn the following day. Another arrival early on 7 July was the corvette *Daniella*. After refuelling, she returned to sea to search for survivors.

The German aircraft appeared not to notice the growing number of ships at Lagerni, concentrating on finding solitary merchantmen at sea. They did find the *Aldersdale*, and she was eventually sunk by *U-457* at 07.00 on 7 July, after the fuel-starved Germans rejected as impractical, towing her to a Norwegian port. Another ship to be discovered at this time was the *Hartlebury*, a British cargo vessel commanded by Captain Stephenson, Vice Commodore of PQ17, which was found by *U-355* late in the afternoon of 7 July. The U-boat fired three torpedoes, far too many at one time for such a target, and broke the ship's back. Attempts to launch lifeboats and life-rafts were chaotic and resulted in further loss of life as the ship continued under way. Two more torpedoes were fired into the rapidly sinking ship, killing one man who had scrambled back on board after being dragged along by a lifeboat still attached to the ship, while her master died as a result of injuries received when he dived off the stern of the ship – the last man to leave.

As the survivors huddled together in a swamped lifeboat, *U-355* surfaced and demanded to have the merchantman's master. Photographs were taken and the submariners demanded to know why they were helping the Communists, before handing over bread and schnapps. Only four of the twenty men in the lifeboat survived. Worst affected in these sinkings were the stokers, who had been working below in intense heat and wore only the minimum of clothing. Unable to don warm clothes in the time taken to escape, they soon perished in the intense cold. Aboard one raft, out of fourteen men just five survived. On another raft, all nine men survived, helped by a can of whale oil which they rubbed into their feet to stave off hypothermia. The survivors from the *Hartlebury* eventually ended up on the American *Winston Salem*, which had run aground on Novaya Zemlya.

Another U-boat, *U-255*, was still hunting at this time, and discovered the rescue ship *Rathlin* and the American merchantman *Bellingham*. Two torpedoes were fired at the cargo ship, but one missed and the other failed to explode, although it hit the ship. Both ships managed to get away before any further torpedoes could be fired, but then *U-255* found the *Alcoa Ranger* steaming south, and fired a single torpedo into the American ship. The torpedo entered a forward hold and as water started to flood in, the ship started to settle by the bows. The submarine surfaced, briefly interrogated the crew, by now in the ship's boats, and then pumped shells into the ship since *U-255*'s torpedo tubes were empty. As she headed south on the surface, *U-255* was spotted by the CAM-ship *Empire Tide*, which eventually sought refuge in Miller Bay. Meanwhile, *Olopana* was still plodding on, despite the crew being exhausted and stressed by the events of the past few days. While her master wanted to seek refuge in a suitable bay, he also became aware that his ship was being shadowed by a U-boat, in fact *U-255*, by now with her torpedo tubes reloaded. Instead of finding somewhere to rest his crew, *Olopana*'s master decided to press on. Very early on 8 July, *U-255* finally managed to get ahead of the cargo ship and fired a torpedo which exploded into the engine room, killing three men on watch. The impact threw a gunner and a seaman overboard and wrecked the starboard lifeboat. *U-255* surfaced and once again used her gun to complete the job, but the cargo ship's radio operator got off a distress signal which encouraged the submarine to leave the scene. Meanwhile, the port lifeboat was lowered so quickly that it was swamped when it hit the water, leaving most of the crew to escape using rafts.

The two ships that had escaped *U-255* – *Rathlin* and *Bellingham* – were discovered by a patrolling Fw200 Condor at 02.30 on 8 July.

Unusually, the aircraft then decided to attack rather than call other aircraft in to do the job, but it ran into the combined fire of both ships and the two outer engines were set on fire. It dropped its bombs and blew up a tank containing ammonia on *Bellingham*'s deck, before crashing into the sea. Despite being damaged and having wounded men aboard, the *Bellingham* and *Rathlin* continued their voyage and both arrived safely at Archangel on 9 July.

The Germans were now congratulating themselves on virtually wiping out an entire convoy, and it was left to *U-88*'s commanding officer, Heino Bohmann, who had been present at so much of the destruction, to inject some realism into the debate over how many ships had been sunk, realizing that many ships had passed either undetected or had survived attack.

The Convoy Returns

On 7 July, Commodore Dowding set about the task of re-establishing the convoy, anxious to move on especially as his two AA ship commanding officers were convinced that their present haven could just as easily become a trap. Many of the masters of the merchant vessels took an opposing opinion, feeling confident that the combined AA armament of the convoy and its escorts would be a guarantee against aerial attack, and hoping for heavy units of the Home Fleet or the Soviet Navy to provide support before PQ17 resumed its course. Yet, ships at anchor presented a far easier target from the air than ships on the move. As they were at the extreme limit of radio range for contact with the Admiralty, full authority devolved on to the local commanders.

At 19.00 on 7 July, Dowding aboard *Lotus* led the remnants of PQ17 out of the Matochkin Strait. It was a clear, frosty evening to start with, but they soon ran into fog and the American merchantman *Benjamin Harrison* returned to the strait. Worse was to come, for Schmundt had found just enough time to deploy a cordon of U-boats between the ice pack and the coast, and the conditions meant that the ships were being driven into a funnel with little scope for slipping past.

There were six U-boats waiting for the convoy, *U-255*, *U-457* and *U-703* were from the original force, reinforced by *U-251*, *U-376* and *U-408*, while the hardworking *U-88* and *U-355* were returning to base, short of fuel and torpedoes.

As 8 July dragged on, first the fog and then, from 16.30 onwards, the ice pack hindered progress and broke up the orderly formation of the 'convoy', by this time just four merchant ships. The rescue ship *Zamalek* got stuck on a submerged ice-ridge, and it was some hours before she could be freed. It was then discovered that she had developed a leak in the accident. *Zamalek* and the merchantmen took on board survivors as and when they found them.

Mid-morning on 9 July, the convoy was sighted by a U-boat, and during the afternoon and early evening, other boats homed in on the sighting. A depth charge attack followed on *U-376*, but this was unsuccessful. The corvettes remained close to the merchantmen and the AA ships, too short of fuel to spend time chasing submarines, but the convoy was once again divided in two, with the groups about 40 or more miles apart. Indeed, the overall direction was back towards Norway because of the ice.

Forty Ju88s of KG30 appeared over the convoy, waiting for the opportunity to attack. Then a formation of five dived down, and afterwards aircraft appeared from different directions, making evasion difficult. Near misses by three bombs damaged the hull plates of the *Hoosier* and fractured her steam pipes, so that she gradually lost way, taking on water but settling on an even keel. The boats were lowered and the survivors quickly picked up. *Poppy* forced *U-255* to remain at a distance. It might have been possible to salvage the ship, towing her to safety, but the fuel shortage was too acute and the need to keep as many ships together as possible meant that she had to be sunk. However, after an unsuccessful attempt at sinking her by gunfire simply left the ship in flames, it was down to *U-376* to sink her later.

Both the AA ships were by this time desperately short of ammunition, but the Ju88s continued to attack in waves as the day progressed. A plea for Soviet fighter cover was ignored.

At around 02.00 on 10 July, more near misses damaged the hull of the Panamanian *El Capitan*. Two hours later, a near miss on the *Zamalek* caused a panic among the Russian 'deserters' from the tanker *Azerbaijan*. This time they started to launch a Carley float and were only discouraged by a burst of machine-gun fire from the bridge. Nevertheless, the ship gradually lost way, and she fell behind the convoy. No other ship came to her aid, and so the combined engineering teams of the two rescue ships had to return to the engine room, which was in darkness, replace light bulbs, bandage fractured oil and steam pipes, and get the engines going again. Within an hour she was making 10 knots, but taking on water as her rivets had been strained.

As the remaining ships neared the Russian coast, instead of Soviet fighter cover they were attacked again by a solitary Ju88, and once again near misses proved fatal for a ship. *El Capitan* finally lost way as her cooling water intake valves were shattered and water started to flood into the engine room, quickly quenching the flames under the boilers, while oil pipes also burst. The trawler *Lord Austin* came alongside and took off the crew and the survivors from the *John Witherspoon*. As the ship began to sink slowly, once again it was left to a U-boat, *U-251,* to send her to the bottom.

The ships reached the anchorage off Iokanka shortly after noon on 10 July, with the battered *Zamalek* having regained her position. At last, two Soviet destroyers finally appeared and led the Allied ships into the Gourlo, the strait leading to the White Sea, then left them to proceed through the White Sea to the River Dvina. At 16.00 on 11 July, the *Zamalek* was at the quay at Archangel. One insane seaman rescued from a casualty of the convoy jumped overboard, while the seamen from the *Azerbaijan* left under armed guard for a Gulag.

The other group of surviving ships consisted of just two merchantmen, *Ocean Freedom* and *Samuel Chase,* escorted by the corvette *Lotus,* ocean minesweepers *Britmart* and *Halcyon,* and two trawlers. Once again, as they headed for Cape Kanin, there was no sign of Soviet assistance. This small group was attacked for ninety minutes by sixteen Ju88s from Banak and aircraft from Petsamo starting at 11.00 on 11 July. As before, near misses forced *Samuel Chase* to lose way, forcing *Halcyon* to take the ship in tow while a trawler provided anti-submarine support. *Britomart* and *Northern Gem* stuck with *Ocean Freedom,* which then suffered a near miss which damaged her but did not stop her. Later in the day Soviet Hawker Hurricanes and Petlyakov Pe-2 fighters appeared, chasing the Ju88s away.

These ships were followed by *U-255* almost to the Gourlo, but at last it turned away, and on its homeward passage discovered the abandoned *Paulus Potter,* which was boarded in case the ship could be salvaged, but the engine room was flooded. Instead the submariners managed to help themselves to choice items of food from the ship and, more valuable still, found confidential papers in a weighted case that had not been thrown overboard in the confusion as the ship was abandoned.

The corvette *Daniella* was at sea on 8 July looking for survivors, and during the next eight days the corvette found no less than sixty-one survivors, and much wreckage.

Meanwhile, the armed trawler *Ayrshire* had left the ice with its three charges at 21.00 on 6 July. The four vessels hugged the edge of the ice and made a slow passage, until very early on 9 July they reached a fjord on the northern island of Novaya Zemlya. After coaling from *Troubador*, the ships then steamed down the coast until they reached the Matochkin Strait, but *Ayrshire* and *Ironclad* then ran aground, with the former losing her asdic dome. Both ships were abandoned without further serious damage. On learning from the Russians at Lagerni of the departure of the other ships and of boatloads of survivors to the south, *Ayrshire* left the merchantmen at anchor and went searching, finding thirty-four men in three boats from the *Fairfield City*, who were picked up and taken to a Russian hospital on Novaya Zemlya. *Ayrshire* then discovered the merchantman *Benjamin Harrison* at anchor. Lieutenant Leo Gradwell advised Archangel of his position and waited for further orders. Unknown to him, some miles to the south (also at Novaya Zemlya) lay the CAM-ship *Empire Tide*, whose master also contacted Archangel.

Others reached Novaya Zemlya by their own efforts, and these included ten survivors from the *Olopana*, who had earlier seen the *Zamalek* in fog, but had not themselves been seen by the rescue ship or by two corvettes later. On reaching the Russian islands, they scrambled ashore and broke up their raft to make a fire while two members of the party went to a lighthouse seeking help. The lighthouse was unmanned, but it did give them a vantage point from where they could see the *Winston Salem*, which had beached and was sheltering survivors from the *Hartlebury*. The *Winston Salem* was spotted later by a Russian Catalina flying boat that was evacuating a wounded gunner from the *Empire Tide*.

Eventually two Russian ships arrived – the armed trawler *Kerov* and the ice-breaker *Murman* – and they attempted to tow the *Winston Salem* off the beach, but without success. At this time the *Azerbaijan* also arrived safely at Novaya Zemlya. Meanwhile, the Catalina had spotted survivors from several ships in boats, including the *Bolton Castle*, *Carlton* and *Olopana*, while a Russian coaster found others, including more from the *Olopana*, and a number from other ships including *Alcoa Ranger*, *Washington* and *Paulus Potter*, who were transferred to the *Empire Tide*, which soon had almost

159

130 men aboard. The coaster also brought supplies from the now abandoned *Winston Salem* and a number of other boats to the *Empire Tide*, in the belief that all this would be useful for the voyage across the White Sea. While pleas were sent out for assistance from the British naval representatives in northern Russia, a Ju88 appeared over the *Empire Tide*, but disappeared as the ship's Hurricane fighter was prepared for launching.

It was not until 22 July that the seaworthy ships at Novaya Zemlya were able to move, with a reinforced escort and with the arrival at last of two Soviet destroyers. The surviving ships finally reached Archangel on 24 July. The *Winston Salem* was finally refloated after her fuel oil had been pumped out to make her lighter, and she too reached Archangel on 28 July.

Not everyone reached Russia. The *Carlton*'s boat, spotted and waved to by a Catalina on 10 July remained at sea until 19 July when *U-376* appeared and provided some provisions taken from the *Hoosier*. Yet that same day, one of the men in the boat froze to death. They eventually made landfall after nineteen days at sea in an open 32 foot boat, and found themselves in German-occupied Norway, ending up in Stalag Marlag-Milag Nord near Bremen.

There had been little liaison between the Allies and the Soviet authorities. Misunderstandings continued even after the ships reached Archangel, with the Walrus from HMS *Norfolk*, towed in by *Palomares*, put on a railway flat car by Russians who insisted that it was part of the consignment. The Russians refused to believe that the convoy had ever included thirty-six merchantmen, while Stalin angrily cabled Churchill on 16 August: 'Has the British navy no sense of glory?'

The statistics were devastating. Twenty-four ships out of thirty-six had been lost, with the numbers evenly divided between eight ships sunk by U-boats – eight by aircraft, and another eight damaged by aircraft and finished off by U-boats, more than 142,000 tons of shipping altogether. The war effort had lost 430 tanks and 210 bombers, as well as 3,350 vehicles and almost 100,000 tons of ammunition. In the circumstances, it was perhaps surprising that just 153 lives were lost.

Despite these losses, the Soviet Ambassador in London, Ivan Maisky, became very angry when told that the Admiralty would not send any further convoys to north Russia until the dark night returned. Pound also upset the Russians when he said that nothing could be done until the Soviet Union could provide better air cover.

The Russians for their part criticized the order to withdraw the cruisers. Meanwhile, ashore in the Soviet Union, the survivors fretted, wanting to know just when PQ18 would come, for without that convoy's safe arrival there could be no convoy home. This situation was bad enough for the naval personnel and the army gunners, and for those amputees who knew that they would never go to sea again, but for the able-bodied British Merchant Navy personnel there was another reason for wanting to get home; their pay had stopped as soon as their ship had been sunk.

Notes:

1. Imperial War Museum Sound Archive, Accession No. 8836.
2. Ibid.

Chapter 14

The Escort Carrier Arrives

In the wake of the disaster that was PQ17, a number of measures were immediately put in place. Some of these were more or less routine, such as the despatch of four destroyers to Archangel loaded with ammunition and replacement AA gun barrels, as well as interpreters in an attempt to improve liaison with the Russians – all of which arrived on 24 July 1942. Then on 13 August, the American cruiser *Tuscaloosa* sailed. She was escorted by two American and one British destroyer, carrying RAF ground crew and equipment, as well as spares, for two squadrons of Hampden bombers destined to be based in northern Russia, along with photo-reconnaissance Spitfires and a squadron of Coastal Command Catalina flying boats. Also included in the cargo carried by the second group of warships was a demountable medical centre and hospital unit, with appropriate medical supplies, but while the Soviets took the medical supplies, they rejected the hospital that would have done so much to improve the lot of Allied seamen in need of attention on reaching a Russian port.

Survivors from PQ17 were brought back to the UK aboard the three American ships plus three British destroyers, including *Onslaught*, which had sailed outward with the Americans, *Marne* and *Martin*. As a result of Ultra intelligence, the three British destroyers discovered the German minelayer *Ulm* off Bear Island, and while the two M-class ships shelled the minelayer, *Onslaught* sent three torpedoes towards the *Ulm*. The third torpedo went straight into the mine magazine, which exploded, but despite the massive explosion, the commanding officer and fifty-nine of the ship's company survived.

The despatch of the Hampden bombers was unfortunate. Already obsolescent at this stage of the war, several were shot down in transit

162

by the Germans and by the Russians. One of those shot down by the Germans came down over Norway, and as bad luck would have it, contained details of the defence of the next pair of convoys, PQ18 and QP14. Doubtless because PQ18 was to have an escort carrier, plans were laid to attack the convoy with a combination of *Luftwaffe* bombing and U-boats, but QP14 was to be the target for the *Admiral Scheer*, with the cruisers *Admiral Hipper* and *Koln*, and a supporting screen of destroyers. The German surface force moved to the Altenfjord on 1 September.

PQ18 was the first Arctic convoy to have an escort carrier, with the American-built HMS *Avenger*. The carrier had three radar-equipped Swordfish from 825 Squadron for anti-submarine duties as well as six Sea Hurricanes, with another six dismantled and stowed beneath the hangar deck in a hold, for fighter defence. The fighter aircraft were drawn from 802 and 883 squadrons. Another Sea Hurricane was aboard the CAM-ship, *Empire Morn*. The convoy escort also included the cruiser *Scylla*, two destroyers, two AA ships converted from merchant vessels, four corvettes, four anti-submarine trawlers, three minesweepers and two submarines. Once again there was a rescue ship, but just one as three American minesweepers being delivered to the Soviet Union also acted in this role.

While the convoy had gained an escort carrier, the Home Fleet had lost its fleet carrier, *Victorious*, which needed a refit after suffering damage while escorting the convoy Operation Pedestal to Malta in August. Also missing were the American ships, transferred to the Pacific. Tovey also made other changes to the distant escort. This time he would remain aboard *King George V* at Scapa Flow where he could have constant telephone communication with the Admiralty, while his deputy, Vice Admiral Sir Bruce Fraser went to sea in the battleship *Anson*. The strong destroyer escort afforded PQ16 would be repeated to protect both PQ18 and QP14. This meant allowing the destroyers to leave the close escort to the corvettes, trawlers, AA ships and minesweepers if the situation warranted it, with freedom of action to make a sweep looking for U-boats or German surface units. Nevertheless, to save fuel, the officer in command of the destroyers, Rear Admiral Robert Burnett, aboard the light cruiser *Scylla*, ordered that no U-boat hunt by the destroyers was to exceed ninety minutes. Not only would the convoy have the support of Force Q with its fleet oiler, but this time there would be two of them. Force P, with two tankers and four destroyers was deployed ahead of the convoy to Spitzbergen, while a re-supply operation for the Norwegian garrison there was also linked with these forces.

Once again, Iceland was the main rendezvous. Even getting to Iceland was difficult. Seas were so rough that a Sea Hurricane was swept off *Avenger*'s deck, and the steel ropes securing aircraft in the hangar failed to stop them breaking loose, crashing into one another and into the sides of the hangar. Fused 500-lb bombs stored in the lift-well broke loose and had to be captured by laying down duffle coats with rope ties, these ties being quickly secured as soon as a bomb rolled on to the coats! The ship suffered engine problems due to fuel contamination. Even remote Iceland was still not completely safe, for here the carrier was discovered and bombed by a Focke-Wulf Fw200 Condor long-range maritime reconnaissance aircraft, which dropped a stick of bombs close to the ship, but without inflicting any damage.

The engine problems meant that the convoy, already spotted by a U-boat while on passage to Iceland from Scotland, had to sail without the carrier, and on 8 September, the convoy was discovered by another Condor. Low overcast cloud then protected the convoy from German aircraft until 12 September, when a Blohm und Voss Bv138 flying boat dropped through the clouds. By this time *Avenger* had caught up with the convoy and was able to launch a flight of four Sea Hurricanes, but not in time to catch the German aircraft before it disappeared.

The Swordfish were extremely vulnerable on the Arctic convoys. This meant that the fighters were not simply concerned with protecting the ships from aerial attack, they also had to cover the Swordfish, which could have fallen prey to many German aircraft. At 04.00 on 9 September, the Sea Hurricanes were scrambled after Swordfish on anti-submarine patrol were discovered by another two *Luftwaffe* aircraft, a Bv138 flying boat and a Junkers Ju88 reconnaissance aircraft, but again, these disappeared into the low cloud before the fighters could reach them. Another Swordfish role revealed exactly what the *Luftwaffe* was up to, and on one occasion, PQ18's Swordfish reported that Bv138s were dropping mines ahead of the ships.

PQ18 was repeatedly attacked from the air, requiring the ships to make mass turns and to put up heavy AA fire, all of which made life for the returning Swordfish crews very interesting. Ditching in the sea was never anything to be considered lightly, but in Arctic waters, survival time could be very short indeed. The Sea Hurricanes attempted to keep a constant combat air patrol, CAP, over the convoy, with each aircraft spending twenty-five minutes in the air before landing to refuel. In such circumstances, keeping a constant watch over the Swordfish as well was almost impossible.

On 14 September, the first Swordfish of the day found *U-589* on the surface, but she dived leaving the Swordfish to mark the spot with a smoke flare. Once the aircraft had gone, the submarine surfaced and continued charging her batteries. Alerted by the Swordfish, the destroyer *Onslow* raced to the scene. Once again *U-589* dived, but the destroyer attacked with depth charges and destroyed her. This led the Germans, so far not accustomed to a convoy having its own air cover and aerial reconnaissance, to change their tactics. Reconnaissance Bv138s and Ju88s were sent to intimidate the Swordfish, forcing them back onto the convoy, until the Germans were driven away by heavy AA fire. The Swordfish would then venture out, only to be found and driven back again.

Later that day, another attack by Ju88s was detected by the duty Swordfish. This time *Avenger* herself was the target, moving at her maximum 17 knots. The Sea Hurricanes broke up the attack, and no ships were lost, but eleven Ju88s were shot down, again mainly by AA fire. Further attacks that day saw another German aircraft shot down, without any losses to the convoy. In a final attack, three of the four patrolling Hurricanes were shot down by friendly fire, although all three pilots were saved. In this attack, *Avenger*'s commanding officer, Commander Colthurst, successfully managed to comb torpedoes dropped by the Germans. A bomb dropped by a German pilot, who flew exceptionally low to ensure that he did not miss the target, hit the ammunition ship *Mary Luckenbach*, which blew up, taking her attacker with her. The sole survivor from the ammunition ship was a steward taking the master a cup of coffee, who was blown off the upper deck by the explosion and found himself a half mile down the convoy.

Not all of the rescues were left to the rescue ships. At the height of the battle for PQ18, the destroyer *Offa* saw a cargo ship, *Macbeth*, hit by two torpedoes and beginning to sink with her cargo of tanks and other war materials. *Offa*'s commanding officer, Alastair Ewing, took his ship alongside *Macbeth* and, at the cost of some guard-rails and stanchions, enabled all of the merchantman's sailors to jump aboard before she sank.

The next day, the remaining Sea Hurricanes and the Swordfish were again in the air, with the former breaking up further attacks. It was not until 16 September that the Swordfish were relieved of their patrolling by shore-based RAF Consolidated Catalina flying boats of No. 210 Squadron operating from Russia. The break was short-lived. Later that day the convoy passed the homeward convoy, QP14, with the survivors of the ill-fated PQ17, and *Avenger*, with her aircraft and some of the other escorts transferred to this convoy. The interval had been used by the ship's air engineering team to assemble five Sea Hurricanes, more than replacing the four lost on the outward convoy. All in all, the Sea Hurricanes had accounted for a total of five enemy aircraft and damaged seventeen others out of a total of forty-four enemy aircraft shot down. It was fortunate that the three Fairey Swordfish remained serviceable as no replacement aircraft were carried.

During the convoy, *Avenger*'s commanding officer, Commander Colthurst, changed the operational pattern for the Sea Hurricanes in an attempt to get the maximum benefit from his small force, having a single aircraft in the air most of the time rather than having all of his aircraft, or none of them, airborne at the same time.

One Sea Hurricane pilot was lucky to be snatched from the sea within minutes of baling out by the destroyer *Wheatland*, acting as close escort for *Avenger*.

With the Sea Hurricanes so depleted, it was left to the CAM-ship *Empire Morn* to launch her Hurricane, flown by Flying Officer Burr. The launch was accompanied by friendly fire from other ships in the convoy until he was finally out of range. Despite problems with the barrage balloons flown by some of the merchantmen, he managed to break up a German attack, setting one aircraft on fire. Once out of ammunition, rather than ditch, he saved his precious aircraft by flying it to Keg Ostrov airfield near Archangel.

Clearly, even an escort carrier with a mix of fighters and Swordfish was hard pressed to provide adequate air cover. Indeed, such a convoy could have done with two or more escort carriers, or one of the larger ships such as *Nairana* or *Vindex*, with up to fourteen Swordfish and six Wildcat fighters, a much better aircraft than the Sea Hurricane. As the convoy approached its destination, there was no sign of the promised Red Air Force air support.

QP14's Troubled Course

Meanwhile, the homeward convoy QP14 took over the destroyer escort and several other ships from PQ18 on 17 September 1942. The convoy had left Archangel on 13 September, escorted by six British minesweepers, four of which then detached leaving the convoy with the remaining minesweepers, two destroyers, two AA ships, four corvettes and four anti-submarine trawlers. The escort was considerably enhanced by the escort carrier *Avenger*, the cruiser *Scylla*, AA ship *Alynbank*, two submarines and seventeen destroyers under Burnett's command.

Initially, there was little trouble from the Germans as the *Luftwaffe* was concentrating on PQ18, but the convoy was shadowed by reconnaissance aircraft that edged to within AA range before moving away again. A number of destroyers were detached to lay a false trail, while the convoy was joined by Force Q. Despite U-boat sightings, the first sign of trouble came at 05.20 on 20 September when *U-435* put two torpedoes into the ocean minesweeper *Leda*, a veteran of the convoys. Commander A. H. Wynn-Edwards and eighty-six of his crew were rescued, along with two Merchant Navy officers (survivors from PQ17). They were spread over three of the rescue ships, although six died from wounds or hypothermia later. That same day a Swordfish depth charged a U-boat, and the destroyer *Ashanti* went in pursuit of another U-boat, which it also depth charged, at the time believing it had succeeded in destroying it. An attempt by the submarine *P614* to torpedo *U-408*, caught on the surface, failed when one of the torpedoes blew up. The explosion set off the other, allowing the U-boat to dive and escape.

At 17.45, *U-255* torpedoed one of the PQ17 survivor's, *Silver Sword*, and the ship burst into flames, her ship's company making their escape with some difficulty. The destroyer *Worcester* later sunk her with gunfire.

As the U-boat threat developed, Colthurst aboard *Avenger* had to signal Burnett, informing him that his Swordfish crews were at the limits of their physical endurance. Realizing the problem, and that both *Avenger* and the cruiser *Scylla* were fast becoming liabilities rather than assets, Burnett transferred his flag to the destroyer *Milne*. Three destroyers were detailed to provide an anti-submarine screen for the two ships, which were then sent home. Burnett's decision was logical as the German air threat had diminished, leaving little for the

Sea Hurricanes to do. In addition, if the Swordfish crews were beyond the limits of their physical and mental endurance, they were more likely to be a danger to themselves and the convoy than additional protection. A Swordfish crash-landing could have inflicted considerable damage on the carrier, as at this time unused depth charges were retained during landing.

Somali, one of the Tribal-class destroyers, was torpedoed by *U-703* later that day. The destroyer's commanding officer tried to comb the torpedo, and while two destroyers attempted to hunt down the culprit, another destroyer and a trawler came alongside to take off survivors. Five men were killed and four wounded in the ship's engine room. The stricken destroyer's commanding officer signalled that he thought his ship could be towed with just a skeleton crew aboard, and her sister ship, *Ashanti*, was ordered to her assistance.

The following morning, 21 September, saw a Catalina flying boat from the RAF's No. 330 Squadron based in Shetland, over the convoy. The aircraft was just in time to spot *U-378* on the surface, but was itself spotted and came under accurate AA fire that ripped into the fuel tanks. Despite his aircraft being crippled, the pilot dived towards the submarine. As it crash-dived it dropped four depth charges, before having to make a forced landing. The crew of the Catalina were picked up by the destroyer *Marne*, which then destroyed the aircraft.

Despite renewed air cover, at 06.30 on the morning of 22 September, after Burnett had left the convoy (which still had eleven destroyers, plus corvettes and trawlers supporting it), *U-435* managed to get within the screen. In one of the most successful actions by a U-boat, within minutes three ships were sunk – two merchantmen and the fleet oiler *Grey Ranger* – although without loss of life. Among those aboard the *Bellingham* was the convoy commodore, Captain J. C. K. Dowding, RNR, who joined the other survivors aboard the minesweeper *Seagull*. He handed over to his vice commodore, Captain Walker, aboard the *Ocean Freedom* – another survivor from PQ17.

On 23 September the rescue ships and some of the destroyers headed for Seidisfjord to refuel, while the rest of the convoy continued towards Cape Wrath on the north-western tip of Scotland as the weather deteriorated and a gale approached. The remaining ships of the convoy were to make a safe landfall, but on 24 September, the gale that had proved to be a nuisance for the surviving ships was putting paid to any hope of salvaging *Somali*. The ship had already slipped her tow once, and her condition was perilous. Most of her port side was holed, although most of the other compartments apart from the engine room and a boiler room were dry. Nevertheless, as the rising sea tortured the stricken ship further, the inevitable happened and her back was broken, splitting the ship in two. Bow and stern sections quickly went vertical and sank beneath the feet of the men as they scrambled into life-rafts and Carley floats. Out of eighty-two men aboard, just thirty-five survived, with many being swept under the bows of *Ashanti* as she returned to their rescue with the trawler *Lord Middleton*. Some who were rescued died from hypothermia.

The U-boat menace had not gone completely, however, and a Catalina from No. 210 Squadron spotted *U-253* less than a mile from the rear of the convoy. The U-boat crash-dived but the Catalina dropped six depth charges as the submarine went down. As the depth charges exploded, the U-boat was blasted back to the surface, before submerging for a second time. Suddenly she reappeared on her beam ends, before her bows dived and her stern lifted to the vertical, hanging there for a moment, then disappearing for good.

The efforts of the destroyer escort seemed to be disappointing at the time, but unknown to those aboard, they did inflict damage to five U-boats. The problem was that while the escort carrier had proved itself beyond any doubt, they did not become more generally available until 1943, so there were to be many more convoys without any real attempt at air cover.

Chapter 15

Hiatus

The relative success of convoys PQ16 and PQ18 had finally brought about an understanding of the necessities for survival required by the Arctic convoys. Most of all a convoy needed its own air cover, and for much of the time that could only come from the presence of an escort carrier, which needed both fighters and anti-submarine aircraft. Next on the wish list was a strong 'fighting destroyer escort', free to roam in the knowledge that the much slower and sturdier corvettes would stick with the convoy. The presence of rescue ships also meant that the escorts would not be distracted from their work, and that those rescued would find aboard the basic clothing items and other comforts that they needed. Survivors from a sinking ship rarely had time to collect their possessions, and on the few occasions that this was done it became clear that it had to be discouraged both because of the delay in conducting a rescue (during which the rescue ship was a sitting duck target), and because of the clutter brought into over-crowded accommodation. Nevertheless, only those working on deck or on the bridge would have adequate clothing for the Arctic conditions.

The AA ships were also welcome as they provided the intense AA fire that was so necessary to discourage the *Luftwaffe*. The presence of a cruiser was a morale booster for those aboard the merchantmen and the smaller escorts, but while the cruiser would be a reasonable defence against a German opposite number, it was vulnerable if out-gunned and was yet another ship in need of protection from the U-boats. The true value of a cruiser was that it contributed further to the volume of AA fire and also provided the command and control communications facilities and personnel that such a substantial number of ships operating together needed.

Scant sympathy came from the Soviet Union for the plight of PQ17, and Stalin was moved to comment with considerable disdain about the effectiveness of the Royal Navy. It was not just that Stalin had little or no grasp of maritime matters himself and did not appreciate the sacrifices being made, but even if the Soviet dictator had bothered to listen to his own naval staff, they would also have failed to appreciate the difficulties. The Soviet Union, and indeed Tsarist Russia before it, had no experience of continuous and intensive fleet operations, or of the demands made by convoys that had to face the certainty of near continuous aerial and submarine attack, and the strong possibility of attack by heavy surface units.

The unavoidable delays between PQ17 and PQ18 simply added to Stalin's irritation and frustration. The UK was seen as the main culprit. This was partly because of the overwhelming role of the Royal Navy. During the first year of convoys, the majority of the aircraft and tanks supplied had been built in the UK, which was hard-pressed to equip its own armed forces. Better aircraft were sent to the Soviet Union than were available for the defence of Malaya and Singapore when the Japanese invaded in 1942.

Despite its earlier rejection by the Russians, the hospital unit remained close to the hearts of the British, and after protracted negotiations it was eventually accepted. It was sent to the Soviet Union aboard the cruiser *Argonaut* in October 1942, escorted by the destroyers *Intrepid* and *Obdurate*. These ships also collected the air and ground crews for the Hampden bombers and Spitfire reconnaissance aircraft, which were handed over to the Red Air Force.

Operation FB

One factor that Stalin could not understand and would not accept was that of the few Soviet merchant ships available for convoy duty, inevitably a number were stuck at British or American ports waiting for a convoy to form. It was because of his insistence that these ships had to be returned to the Soviet Union that a plan, Operation FB, was formulated to send through single ships during the interval between convoys PQ17 and PQ18. The idea earnt for the British the contempt of senior Russian officers of all three services, who regarded the level of supplies as pitifully insufficient for their needs and, of course, were either ignorant of or overlooked Stalin's role.

The idea of running single ships had few supporters in the Admiralty, although the idea did appeal to some, possibly believing that single ships might scrape through unnoticed. In fact, the only argument for single ship operations was that, given a suitable ship, it could be much faster than a convoy, whose speed was dictated to some extent by that of the slowest ship. Another factor was that a single ship could expect to berth and be unloaded quickly, rather than having to wait her turn as in the case of a large convoy arriving at a congested port.

Desperate to try anything, a number did allow themselves to be swayed by the arguments. One British shipowner reputedly offered a bonus of £100 for an officer and £50 for a rating, payable in cash and in advance, for those willing to volunteer for single ship operations. These were considerable sums for the day, bearing in mind that the standard pay for a rating in the British Merchant Navy in 1939 had been just £8 per month, although this trebled when in a war zone.

At first it looked as if the single ship argument was right. On 11 August, the Soviet merchantman *Freidrich Engels* sailed from Iceland, followed the next day by the *Belomorcanal*, and both arrived safely.

Nevertheless, while many regarded this as clear evidence of success, there was a further delay before any more ships were sent through. During this time PQ18 was fought through, admittedly with considerable losses but nevertheless on a far lower scale than PQ17. Then, between 20 October and 2 November, alternating British and American merchant vessels departed for Russia alone at roughly twelve hour intervals, with one Soviet vessel inserted between them. The ships left from different ports and were, as far as possible, individually routed, given the nature of the gap between the north of Norway or the Russian Murman coast and the polar ice. Protection consisted of submarines patrolling north of Bear Island, while further south along the route anti-submarine trawlers provided a patrol line, with four each from Iceland and from Murmansk. For the Germans this was akin to looking for a needle in a haystack, as one advantage of the convoys was that U-boats were attracted to the sheer number of ships, which were hence easier to find. In fact, when one trawler attacked a U-boat without success, the Germans finally realized that something unusual was going on.

The results were predictably grim. On 2 November the *Empire Gilbert* was sunk by *U-586* while still close to Iceland, and on 4 November KG30's Ju88s found and sank the Russian merchantman *Dekabrist*. The American *William Clark* was first damaged by a bomb, and then torpedoed by *U-354*. On 6 November *U-625* torpedoed the *Empire*

Sky, who went down with her entire crew of forty-one. Later, on 7 November, the *Donbass* was sunk by the German destroyer *Z27*. Three ships, the British *Briarwood* and *Daldorch*, were recalled because of the losses, as was the American *John H. B. Latrobe*. Five ships, the *Empire Galliard* and *Empire Scott*, plus the American *Richard H. Alvey*, *John Walker* and *Hugh Williamson* got through northbound. The five 'balancing' Soviet ships also reached Iceland without incident, and a further twenty-two were sent between November 1942 and 24 January 1943.

By this time, there was another reason for delaying the convoys. Operation Torch, the Allied landings in North Africa began on 8 November 1942, and drew away both naval vessels and merchant ships. It was also to draw away *Luftwaffe* units from Norway as Vichy French forces crumbled and Axis forces in North Africa came under heavy pressure from the Allies.

Typically, the Germans were not the only hazard on the Arctic route, the weather played a part, as did the difficulty of navigating in latitudes so high that magnetic compasses were inaccurate and days of constant cloud cover made obtaining a fix from the sun or the stars impossible. One ship that fell victim to this combination was the British cargo ship *Chulmleigh*, which was waiting at Hvalfjord to join PQ19, but instead was sent on alone. Heavily armed, she had eighteen gunners drawn from the DEMS organization and the Maritime Regiment of Artillery (MRA), and the ship had a 4-in gun aft, plus for AA defence a Bofors and four Oerlikons as well as two machine-guns. Nevertheless, there had been no opportunity to take a sighting for several days when, while she was only 20 miles off course, she ran aground off Spitzbergen during the early hours of 6 November. She had hit the reef so fast in a rising sea that her stern was stuck fast on rocks while her bows were in the clear water beyond. The ship had four lifeboats, but the first of these was launched so badly that the two men handling it were thrown overboard, and while one was rescued by a lifeboat handled by the master, Captain D. M. Williams, the other was found dead in the cold sea.

Williams returned to his ship exhausted. He had ordered the first mate and second engineer to remain aboard while the other three lifeboats had been lowered. At 02.30 he ordered some of the firemen to return aboard to raise steam, but while they attempted to get the ship off the reef, it soon became clear that the situation was hopeless and at 04.00 a signal was sent to the Admiralty advising them that the ship was being abandoned. The ship's company waited near the wreck until daylight enabled them to find a way out from the reef, and as they did so a formation of five Ju88s bombed the ship, setting her on fire. Later, she was to be bombed a second time and finally blown apart by torpedoes from *U-625*. They set course under sail in the lifeboats for the mining settlement of Barentsburg, but when the smallest of the boats fell behind, her occupants were shared out between the other two, giving twenty-nine men in one and twenty-eight in the other. The boats were soon separated and suffered alternating flat calm and heavy gales, but came together again on 8 November. Williams had kept a small supply of fuel for his boat's engine and tried to reach the coast, but a further storm blew up and on 10 November, the chief steward died. With Williams by this time unconscious, his boat was taken over by the third mate, just twenty years old. The crew were now suffering from a lack of food, water, sleep and, most of all, from the extreme cold. Most had hands that were frostbitten and found handling the halliards all but impossible. They sighted land, but their first attempts to get ashore were thwarted by reefs. They got the sails down and shipped the oars, and at 03.00 on 12 November, in the dark and in a storm, the boat was deposited on the shore of Spitzbergen within sight of the lights of Barentsburg. Three died as they scrambled ashore, but by a stroke of good fortune, further up the beach stood a line of wooden huts used by seal hunters during the summer, which provided welcome shelter.

Daylight enabled them to find a stove and supplies of tinned food and coffee, which raised morale until the agony of thawing flesh intervened. With the onset of gangrene, thirteen men died from gangrenous septicaemia during the next four days. The third mate and one of the MRA gunners set out to reach Barentsburg, but were forced back twice by harsh terrain and severe weather. By Christmas, despite finding further stores, their food had run out, and they were forced to drink the oil in which some whale blubber had been preserved. Williams made an attempt with another gunner, but they were also beaten back. On Christmas Eve another man died. By 2 January just nine men were left alive. Then, one of the men who had left the hut looking for fuel returned babbling. At first they thought that he had either gone mad or that polar bears were heading for them. Instead, two Norwegian soldiers on routine ski patrol appeared.

The survivors were rescued by sledge early the following day and taken to hospital, although the third mate, on whom so much responsibility had devolved at such an early age, died. The survivors remained at Barentsburg for four months until they were picked up by the cruisers *Bermuda* and *Cumberland*, which had come to replenish the garrison, and they eventually reached Thurso in the north of Scotland on 15 June 1943. No trace of the other boat was found. Just eight men had survived out of a ship's company of fifty-eight. Their bonuses were more than outweighed by the loss of pay which stopped once the ship had been abandoned.

QP15

Allied landings in North Africa contributed still further to the shortage of merchant shipping capacity, while there were a number of ships left at Archangel that would be stuck there for the winter once the White Sea froze. The answer was for a further convoy to be run westwards before the year end. Convoy QP15 departed on 17 November, with fourteen American ships providing the largest contingent, although two of these were to turn back. In addition there were also eight British ships, seven from the Soviet Union and a Panamanian vessel, thirty altogether and about half as many again as Tovey thought wise given the escorts available. The one advantage that the Allies now had in the Arctic was that the *Luftwaffe* had been forced to pull out squadrons from Banak and Bardufoss because of the increasingly critical Axis position in the Mediterranean.

The convoy commodore, Captain W. C. Meek, flew his pennant in *Temple Arch*. There was just one rescue ship, the *Copeland*, as the other, *Rathlin*, needed repairs to her rudder.

As usual, the convoy was escorted out of the White Sea by four of the resident minesweepers stationed by the Royal Navy in northern Russia, while a fifth joined the ocean close escort to return to the UK. Two Russian destroyers accompanied the convoy until 20 November, when they turned back as previously arranged, but with terrible results. The close escort comprised the AA ship *Ulster Queen*, four corvettes and four destroyers, with Captain Scott-Montcrieff in the destroyer *Faulknor* as senior officer of the escort until his ships had to detach on the 26th to refuel. Other destroyers should have taken over at this stage, but failed to make contact with the convoy because of the severe weather. Additional cover west of Bear Island was provided by Rear Admiral Louis 'Turtle' Hamilton in the cruiser *London*, accompanied by another cruiser, *Suffolk*, and three destroyers.

175

Four submarines, two British, one Free French and one Norwegian, were to keep watch for heavy units of the *Kriegsmarine*.

QP15 was struck by a severe gale on 20 November, scattering the ships and putting the close escort under pressure. Fuel became a problem as the ships struggled to maintain contact in poor visibility. On 24 November the *Ulster Queen* and two corvettes were forced to leave the convoy to refuel. While the convoy was to steer a course north of Bear Island, Ultra intelligence warned of a wolf-pack of eight U-boats east of Bear Island and ordered Captain Meek to take the convoy to the south of the island. Not all of the merchantmen received the signal, and in the poor visibility and scattered state, the change of course by those who did receive it could not be seen by the others.

A day earlier, on 23 November, despite the appalling weather and poor visibility, *U-625* torpedoed and sank the British cargo vessel *Goolistan*, and *U-601* torpedoed and sank the Russian vessel *Kuznetz Lesov*, both of which went down with all hands. Both ships had changed course to the south.

Despite the problems with the weather and the close escort, the ships of the convoy eventually reached Iceland where they were rounded up and sent as two convoys to Loch Ewe, the first arriving on 30 November and the second on 3 December. The weather that had proved such a strain for those aboard the ships had in fact been their saviour, keeping German aerial reconnaissance grounded and the cruiser *Admiral Hipper* in port, largely because the Germans considered the weather too bad for destroyers to put to sea!

While British ships far smaller than a destroyer had coped with the weather, the fact that the *Kriegsmarine* was not being wholly over-protective can be judged by the fate of the two Soviet destroyers that had been part of the initial escort. On 20 November one of them, *Baku*, suffered serious cracks in her hull while the heavy seas swept away part of her superstructure, and shipping water, she limped back to the Kola Inlet. At the same time as *Baku* was struggling for her own survival, the other, *Sokrushitelni* was pooped by a heavy sea, which crashed down on her deck and forced its way into the engine and boiler rooms, so that all power was soon lost. The ship wallowed without any hope of assistance from *Baku* as that ship struggled to save herself. The distress signal was picked up, however, and Admiral Golovko sent three more destroyers to her aid. Meanwhile, the ship was buckling under the continuous beating of the sea and on

22 November, she broke her back. It was little short of a miracle that in such heavy seas the three rescuing destroyers managed to save 187 men.

It was clear by this time that a convoy was the only rational means of sending supplies to the Soviet Union, especially when the larger escort carriers could be deployed with a reasonable number of both fighters and anti-submarine aircraft. Unfortunately, as the attacks on the *Tirpitz* showed, no sooner were adequate numbers of escort carriers available than fresh tasks were found for them. Indeed, the British classification of auxiliary carrier for these ships was more than justified, as they provided fighter cover for landings at Salerno and in the South of France, and their aircraft complemented those of the fleet carriers off Norway and in the East, indeed taking over from the fleet carriers off Malaya and Singapore.

Chapter 16

The Arctic Sea Battles

While the British priority was to get supplies through to the Soviet Union, there can be little doubt that the admirals on both sides relished the prospect of a major naval engagement. Indeed, the feeling emerged throughout the naval war that many senior officers resented the place of the big gun battleship being taken by carrier-borne aircraft. Yet, in the Arctic, the prospect of bringing the enemy to battle was made more difficult both by the weather and by growing nervousness on the part of Hitler that prestigious big ships should not be hazarded.

The irony is that it was the need to protect the convoys that brought surface ships of both sides to engagement in the Arctic.

Battle of the Barents Sea

While the German armies in the Soviet Union were forced to stop their advances during the winter months, the Red Army saw this as the most opportune time to attack, and indeed during the winter of 1942–43, the Red Army regained ground lost the previous summer and lifted the siege on Stalingrad. While Stalin still persisted in demanding a second front, he had in fact been given just that by the Allied successes in North Africa. In Germany, the Nazi leadership had to decide whether the priority was AA or anti-tank defence as the Anglo-American bombing campaign got into its stride.

In the meantime a large convoy, which would have been designated PQ19, had been assembling but going nowhere, while the Soviet Union continued to demand more from the United States and UK. Given the poor weather and short hours of daylight, as well as the *Luftwaffe*'s preoccupation elsewhere, Admiral Sir John Tovey felt that smaller, lightly escorted convoys were the way ahead, but he was overruled by the Admiralty, which believed in larger convoys with cruiser protection staying close to the convoys until Bear Island had been passed. In the end a compromise was reached, with PQ19 being divided into two smaller convoys, JW51A and JW51B.

JW51A departed from Loch Ewe on 15 December with a retired naval officer, Rear Admiral C. E. Turle, as commodore in the merchantman *Briarwood*. The sixteen ships included the oiler *Oligarch*, which had the duel role of refuelling the escorts and then taking what remained of her cargo to the Soviet Union. Surprisingly, the convoy was without a rescue ship, but its close escort included two corvettes, an ocean minesweeper and two anti-submarine trawlers. Three destroyers left as the convoy passed Iceland, to be replaced by a fighting destroyer escort, once again under Captain Scott-Montcrieff in *Faulknor*, and five other destroyers. Rear Admiral Robert Burnett commanded the cruiser escort, Force R, flying his flag in *Sheffield* accompanied by *Jamaica*, with three destroyers providing an anti-submarine screen. Despite the improved strategic situation, the Home Fleet with Tovey at sea again in *King George V* also included the cruiser *Berwick* and just three destroyers, but still no aircraft carrier, the warship feared most by the German Navy. Once again, there was no escort carrier either, as these were still in short supply and would not become more commonplace until well into 1943.

Force R was to remain to the west of the convoy until Bear Island, then refuel its destroyers and hand them over to the fighting destroyer escort before the cruisers headed direct for the Kola Inlet, which they reached on Christmas Eve 1942, a day before the convoy.

Despite the presence of *Tirpitz*, *Lutzow*, *Hipper*, *Koln* and *Nurnberg* in northern Norway, the convoy was not attacked.

JW51B's fourteen ships sailed from Loch Ewe on 22 December, under the command of Commodore Melhuish who flew his pennant in the *Empire Archer*. The close escort was commanded by Commander H. T. Rust in the minesweeper *Bramble*, with two corvettes and two trawlers, as well as three destroyers, which were to continue beyond Iceland to join the Home Fleet's distant cover. Once again, a fighting destroyer escort was to be provided, this time by the 17th Flotilla under the command of Captain R. St Vincent Sherbrooke in *Onslow*. While his own ships headed for Seidisfjord, Sherbrooke stayed behind to attend the pre-sailing briefing of the convoy masters, then took *Onslow* and two older destroyers, *Achates* and *Bulldog*, on what was meant to be a fast passage to Iceland ahead of the convoy. The weather was so severe that the elderly *Bulldog* was badly damaged and had to turn back, and *Achates* needed repairs on reaching Iceland. Additional support was to be provided by Burnett's two cruisers, which constituted Force R and had a screen of just two destroyers, all of which left Kola on 27 December. The Home Fleet would be at sea, this time with Vice Admiral Sir Bruce Fraser in the battleship *Anson*, accompanied by the heavy cruiser *Cumberland*, with five destroyers.

Bad weather and a strong southerly gale accompanied the convoy to Iceland, while JW51B was soon spotted, despite the weather, by German aerial reconnaissance on 24 December and then followed by *U-354*, unknown to the convoy escort. The six destroyers of the fighting destroyer escort joined the convoy on Christmas Day while it was 150 miles east of Iceland and Sherbrooke took over command of the escort. The weather soon closed in with heavy, freezing rain and snow, while ice accumulated on decks. The ships had difficulty keeping station in the high winds and seas, and in poor visibility. The destroyer *Oribi* lost her gyro compass and was forced to head for land. She then took the risk of following the Norwegian coastlines and then the Murman coast before finally arriving safely in the Kola Inlet on the last day of the year.

Life aboard the merchantmen was no better. Two ships had to hove to, so that deck cargoes of bombers could be secured after breaking loose, and one of them in turn misled the two ships and an armed trawler following. When the weather improved, Commander Rust in the minesweeper *Bramble* was sent to gather up the stragglers as his ship had the best radar. After darkness on 28 December two destroyers nearly collided, but the following day three of the missing merchantmen rejoined the convoy while another was secure with an armed trawler to the north.

Burnett's Force R came close to what he believed was the location of the convoy at noon on 29 December, and prepared to get into position to the north of the convoy, to avoid shadowing aircraft, and astern, to avoid any shadowing U-boats. *U-354* had in fact radioed that the convoy was lightly escorted, although he mistook one of the destroyers for a light cruiser. The U-boat then made its way ahead of the convoy and was preparing to attack when one of the destroyers picked her up on asdic, then spotted *U-354* on the surface in the dark and attempted to ram her, although the U-boat dived and avoided the collision. A second destroyer then joined the hunt for the U-boat for which on this occasion two hours were allowed, but the time passed without success. *U-354* returned to its previous station and its commander, *Kapitänleutnant* (equivalent to lieutenant commander) Herbschleb, radioed his headquarters again with his position.

The Germans had a plan for attacking JW51B – Operation *Regenbogen,* 'Rainbow'. The *panzerschiff Lutzow,* officially now a heavy cruiser, and the heavy cruiser *Hipper* were to attack the convoy provided that superior forces were not present, and ideally capture some British officers and if possible a ship, but not to waste time on rescuing men from sunken ships. At 18.00 on 30 December, *Vizeadmiral* Kummetz took *Hipper,* accompanied by *Lutzow* out of the Altenfjord with an escort of six destroyers, managed to evade the patrol line of Allied submarines, and headed north-east. As before, no sooner was this powerful force at sea than Kummetz received a signal from *Vizeadmiral* Kluber at Narvik, reminding him that he was not to engage a comparable force as this would expose his heavy cruisers to unacceptable risk. Later, at midnight, Kummetz was informed by *U-354* that she had been joined by *U-626,* and was given an update on the convoy position. He also learnt that two British cruisers had left the Kola Inlet on 27 December.

Kummetz intended to attack within the few hours of twilight that formed the middle of the Arctic winter day, with his forces divided and striking from both sides of the convoy. *Hipper* would attack from the north, *Lutzow* to the south, with the two heavy ships some 75 miles apart and the six destroyers strung between them in line abreast, until the convoy was sighted and then they would close to screen the two cruisers. At 02.30 on 31 January, the force deployed to these positions, and at 07.15, a lookout aboard *Hipper* spotted the convoy. The heavy cruiser slowed so as not to come within sight of the convoy until the light was good enough for gunnery using optical sighting.

The British dispositions at this time were that *Bramble* was far away still searching for a missing merchantman, while an anti-submarine trawler and another merchantman were some way north of the convoy, with Force R between them and the convoy itself. None of these groups was in touch and all were outside radar range. The corvette *Hyderabad* picked up a vessel astern at 08.20, but those aboard initially assumed it was one of the missing merchantmen, then

181

thought that it was one of the Soviet destroyers come to reinforce the escort, so made no report. It was not until lookouts aboard the destroyer *Obdurate* saw first two and then three German destroyers that the alarm was raised. Sherbrooke sent *Obdurate* to investigate and at 09.30 the German destroyers, falling back to rejoin *Hipper*, opened fire, beginning the Battle of the Barents Sea. Sherbrooke took his own ship and two others to help *Obdurate*, while the rest of the escort was ordered to make smoke across the rear of the convoy.

At 09.40, *Hipper* opened fire on the destroyer *Achates*, busy making smoke, and missed. Sherbrooke broke radio silence to warn Force R that the convoy was under attack, having correctly identified *Hipper*. *Onslow* and *Obedient* started to return radar-controlled fire. Twenty minutes later, Commodore Melhuish turned JW51B south-west to increase the distance between it and *Hipper*. Meanwhile, Sherbrooke took *Onslow* and *Obedient* to the north and sent the other two destroyers back to cover the convoy. At about the same time, having initially been confused about the true position of the convoy by radar traces of the trawler and straggler, Force R raced south to the sound of gunfire, just as *Hipper* headed north, before turning back to engage the two destroyers. Quickly finding *Onslow*'s range, *Hipper* soon sent four 8-in shells into the destroyer, knocking out 'A' and 'B' guns, wrecking the bridge, the main aerials and radar scanners, splitting the funnel in two and holing the engine room, leaving forty men dead or wounded. Among the wounded was Sherbrooke, temporarily blinded in his left eye, which had been dislodged, but he remained on the bridge after handing over control of the operation to Lieutenant Commander Kinloch in *Obedient*.

Hipper and Force R were by this time coming within range of one another, while *Lutzow* had been spotted by the escorts. Meanwhile, as she headed north, *Hipper* spotted *Bramble* and opened fire, crippling the minesweeper. Then the destroyer *Friedrich Eckholdt* went in to torpedo the stricken ship. After this, *Hipper* turned south again, in a further attempt to reach the convoy, but ended up on the same side of the convoy as *Lutzow*, losing all of the advantages of a pincer attack. Next, *Hipper* turned her heavy guns on the *Achates*, hitting 'B' turret and setting the ship on fire forward as ready-use ammunition lockers exploded. Forty members of the crew of *Achates* were killed, including her commanding officer. Further hits and shrapnel from exploding shells inflicted further damage on *Achates* as Kinloch raced back towards her with his three destroyers, but he was too late. Even as the trawler *Northern Gem* came to offer a tow, *Achates* rolled over on to her port side and then overturned, her torpedo mounting simply dropping off as she rolled. As she pulled men out of the water, *Northern Gem* was shaken by a series of explosions as the depth charges on the sinking destroyer found their pre-set depth and exploded.

As *Lutzow* raced around the convoy, *Hipper* was finally discovered by Force R, and both *Sheffield* and *Jamaica* opened fire, firing four salvoes before *Hipper* responded, doubtless because British guns by this time used flashless cordite and so it would have taken longer to appreciate that the ship was under fire. She then turned, making smoke, and headed off at 28 knots, badly damaged. The German destroyer *Friedrich Eckholdt* raced towards *Hipper* to offer assistance, but found that she was approaching *Sheffield* instead. After considering ramming the smaller ship, *Sheffield* raced past her, guns fully depressed and all firing, reducing her to a blazing sinking wreck within minutes. Gunfire from *Jamaica* drove off another destroyer, *Richard Beitzen*. It was not until 11.42 that *Lutzow* eventually opened fire on the convoy, with shell splinters from a near miss hitting an American cargo ship without wounding anyone. At 11.48, Kummetz signalled that his force was to withdraw, but *Lutzow* fired again, only managing to score a near miss on *Obdurate*. Nevertheless, the British destroyers being mindful of their responsibility to the convoy, now called off the action, leaving the German ships to withdraw with Force R in hot pursuit. A brief exchange of gunnery occurred at 12.23 but the action ended at 12.36, even though the radar operators aboard *Sheffield* continued to track the Germans until 14.00.

Burnett kept Force R on station, looking for the cruiser *Nurnberg*, believing that she might also be at sea. Convoy JW51B was able to continue on its way without further trouble.

The British tactics had saved the day, but partly because of a lack of determination on the part of the Germans, who feared the effect of torpedo attack by the British destroyers. When he heard the account of the action, Hitler demanded that the German surface fleet be scrapped. This was not done, but from this time on all available shipbuilding capacity was given over to the U-boats. The German Navy's Commander-in-Chief, Raeder, was forced to resign. For this action, Sherbrooke received the Victoria Cross and eventually attained flag rank before he retired.

Battle of the North Cape

Just as Convoy JW51B had led to the Battle of the Barents Sea, JW55B and its homeward counterpart, RA55A, were to lead to an even greater battle, and further humiliation for Germany.

In late December 1943, the Admiralty heard from Ultra intelligence that the battle-cruiser *Scharnhorst* was on short notice for steam. The *Scharnhorst* was reputed to be Hitler's favourite ship, but to the Royal Navy and Royal Air Force she had been the subject of a humiliating episode when in company with her sister, *Gneisenau*, and the heavy cruiser *Prinz Eugen*, she had raced through the Straits of Dover in the celebrated Channel Dash. This had taken place right under the noses of the British, who despite having well laid plans, partly because of excessive secrecy and partly through poor communication and cooperation between the Admiralty and the Air Ministry, failed to stop the three ships. Earlier, with *Gneisenau*, the *Scharnhorst* had sunk the aircraft carrier *Glorious* during the withdrawal from Norway.

On 21 December 1943 Sir Bruce Fraser, now a full admiral and Commander-in-Chief Home Fleet, was aboard his flagship the battleship *Duke of York* as she entered Akureyri fjord in Iceland, escorted by the cruiser *Jamaica* and four destroyers. He had received the news about the *Scharnhorst* and the following day assembled his captains for a conference. His plan was that once refuelled, his squadron, now to be known as Force Two, should head north at 15 knots to conserve fuel, and if they did encounter the *Scharnhorst*, *Jamaica* was to remain with the flagship while the destroyers were to divide into two divisions and mount a torpedo attack. *Duke of York* would open fire at a range of 7 miles, initially using star shells.

This was the same day that the most easterly portion of Convoy JW55A arrived in the White Sea bound for Archangel, while homebound RA55A was leaving Kola with an escort consisting of eight destroyers, three corvettes and a minesweeper. The balancing convoy for RA55A was JW55B, and the two convoys were due to cross off Bear Island on Christmas Day. JW55B had a mixed Royal Navy and Royal Canadian Navy escort, while once again Rear Admiral Burnett was providing the cruiser support with *Belfast*, *Norfolk* and *Sheffield*, which Fraser had code-named Force One.

Having topped up his ships' fuel tanks again on 23 December to ensure that they had the maximum possible amount of fuel, Fraser took Force Two to sea at 23.00 that night. Ultra decrypts had warned him that U-boats had been ordered to attack JW55B, while the *Scharnhorst* was on three hours' notice to sail. The Germans had discovered JW55B almost by accident, as the aircraft that spotted them was on weather reconnaissance. Two U-boats, *U-601* and *U-716* had made contact with the convoy on 24 December, but were driven off by the escorts. As this was being done, Fraser was having a dummy attack mounted on his flagship by one of his destroyers, even though the weather was bad and the whole operation had to be conducted by radar. He had earlier also exercised his force while on passage to Iceland.

Due to sickness, *Vizeadmiral* Kummetz had been temporarily replaced by *Konteradmiral* (Rear Admiral) 'Achmed' Bey – not a big ship man, but an experienced destroyer commander. Bey was flying his flag in the *Tirpitz*, but on Christmas Day was ordered to transfer to the *Scharnhorst*. Bey objected to plans to send the battle-cruiser to sea, preferring instead to make the maximum use of destroyers, his weapon of choice. As it happened, his orders were not to hazard the *Scharnhorst*, and he was also free to use destroyers only if he felt that the conditions were right. Later he was to be told directly by the head of the German Navy, *Grossadmiral* (equivalent to Admiral of the Fleet) Karl Dönitz, who had taken over from Raeder, that he must 'disengage if a superior enemy force is encountered'. Like Bey, Dönitz was not a battleship man, but had risen to prominence leading Germany's successful U-boat fleet.

That same day, the two convoys passed, but both had their courses altered by Fraser, so that they were heading away from the Norwegian coast and towards the ice. Four of RA55A's destroyers were ordered to reinforce the escort for JW55B. RA55A later ran into foul weather, but reached Loch Ewe on 1 January 1944 without trouble. JW55B was becoming increasingly spread out in the bad weather, and on Christmas Day had difficulty complying with an order to turn west, so instead reduced speed to allow the stragglers to regain the convoy and was later joined by the destroyers from RA55A.

While *U-601* continued to track the progress of the convoy, the Germans remained unaware of the presence of Force Two. Signals between Fraser and the two convoys had been intercepted, but had been misunderstood, while the Germans expected the heavy units to be kept well to the west of the convoy.

Just before 19.00 on Christmas Day, Bey had his flag captain, *Kapitän* Hintze, prepare to sail, and the German 4th Destroyer Flotilla had the order passed on to it. The five destroyers preceded the battle-cruiser as the force steamed out of the Altenfjord, and set off west at 25 knots. In an exchange of communications, Bey was assured that no significant surface was within 50 miles of JW55B, although the intelligence was out of date, and he informed naval HQ at Kiel that the weather would inhibit the operational efficiency of his destroyers, rolling wildly in the severe weather and high sea state.

Even aboard the *Duke of York*, slightly larger than the *Scharnhorst*, at 35,000 tons to 31,800 tons, the motion of the ship was uncomfortable. Despite having the heaviest armour plating of any contemporary battleship, the ship was not completely proof to the weather that it was now facing because of her low hull lines, which were intended to allow her 'A' turret to fire forwards. Oerlikon AA cannon were swept off the foredeck by the crashing waves coming over the bows, despite the slow speed being made, and cold sea water poured through the rivet holes into the messdeck below. The most forward of the gun turrets, 'A' turret, also suffered water ingression, some of it finding its way to the shell room below. Once again, it was the destroyers that suffered the most, and as with the German ships, they too would find high speed action impossible unless the sea conditions eased.

Both ships were a compromise. The *Duke of York* had been limited to 35,000 tons by the Washington Naval Treaty of 1922. Originally intended to have 16-in guns, a further treaty limited the calibre to 14-in. The *Scharnhorst* was originally intended to have 15-in guns, but had to make do with 11-in, and although it was always the intention to upgrade her weaponry at a refit, the opportunity never arose.

Very early on 26 December, at 01.30, a signal from the Admiralty based on an Ultra decrypt informed Fraser that a code-word had been flashed to the commanding officer of a battlegroup, suggesting that an operation was about to begin. The intelligence was ten hours old. Confirmation was not long in coming, for at 02.17 the signal came: 'Emergency SCHARNHORST probably sailed 1800/25 December.' A further signal followed almost immediately advising that a German patrol vessel had been warned at 17.15 that the battle-cruiser would soon pass outward bound. Then at 04.00, Fraser was told that the 'Admiralty appreciate that SCHARNHORST is now at sea'.

Fraser was less inclined to keep radio silence than his contemporaries in the Royal Navy, believing that knowledge of the disposition of other fleet units and warning of impending events was far more important. The risk was that signals traffic betrayed both position and intention. Nevertheless, on balance he was almost certainly right bearing in mind the number of occasions when the absence of communication had resulted in failure. Now, unaware that the convoy had been unable to turn west, he was concerned that he was still too far away from the convoy to help. He ordered speed to be increased to 24 knots, then signalled Force One and the convoy to report their positions, even though this meant revealing his own. There was no risk as the Germans either did not intercept the signals or they ignored them.

It was as well that Fraser had made the signal. He discovered that the convoy was 50 miles south of Bear Island, with Force One 150 miles from the convoy, but planning to be within 30 miles of it by 08.17. Force One was 350 miles from the convoy and too far away to save it, although it would be able to stop the Germans from returning to their base. Now understanding that the convoy had not turned round, Fraser ordered it to turn north. While the order was received, it took some time to retransmit this to all of the ships in the convoy, and it was not until around 06.00 that the change of course could be made. Bey, meanwhile, was heading due north 100 miles from the convoy, but just 90 miles from Force One. His plan was to attack the convoy as it cleared the North Cape.

The relatively narrow stretch of water between the edge of the Polar ice cap and the enemy-held shoreline that had so seriously compromised the order to scatter given to PQ17, now forced a further compromise. At 06.28, Fraser ordered JW55B to take a revised course, heading north-east to avoid being caught between the ice and the Germans.

Bey, meanwhile, who had informed Dönitz of the difficulties suffered by his destroyers, was surprised to receive a signal from the *Grossadmiral* telling him to leave the destroyers behind if they could not keep station, and attack the convoy with the battle-cruiser alone. This was contrary to the *Konteradmiral*'s own instincts and experience.

The U-boats, *U-601* and *U-716* were tailing the convoy, but had failed to notice the turn to the north. Thus it happened that as the *Scharnhorst* approached the expected position of the convoy, and *Kapitän* Hintze broadcast the message from Dönitz that a successful attack would relieve the situation on the Eastern Front before sending the men to action stations, there was a massive anti-climax as nothing was found. Frustrated, Bey turned his force south-west and spread his destroyers at 5 mile intervals. At around 09.40, the northernmost destroyer passed the southernmost escort of the convoy at a distance of around 15 miles, both completely unaware of the other's presence in the poor visibility. As the weather worsened, and the destroyers suffered as ice built up on their decks and superstructure, with frost and snow covering the optical gunnery control instruments, Bey was forced to order speed reduced first to 12 knots and then to 10 knots. This put the battle-cruiser at risk of attack by Allied submarines, so he took the ship on a zigzag course astern of the destroyers.

Force One had gone to action stations shortly before dawn, at around 08.30, and shortly afterwards, *Norfolk* picked up radar echoes of a single ship 17 miles to the west-north-west. *Belfast*, Burnett's flagship, then picked up the same echoes. At 09.21 the lookouts on the third cruiser, *Sheffield*, spotted a large ship on the horizon 7 miles to port. Immediately, *Belfast* opened fire with star shell, but these fell short. At 09.29, Burnett ordered the three ships to open fire with their main armament, 6-in for *Belfast* and *Sheffield*, 8-in for *Norfolk*. Force One turned to port to close the range, but this created difficulties and prevented all three cruisers from bringing their guns to bear fully on the German ship. Using radar control, however, *Norfolk* succeeded in sending six broadsides towards the *Scharnhorst*, with three 8-in shells exploding on the battle-cruiser, destroying her main radar scanner and her port high-angle (AA) gunnery director, while a fourth shell went through the upper deck but failed to explode.

One of the German destroyers was off course, and the others assumed this meant that the enemy was approaching. Their leader signalled the *Scharnhorst*, only to receive a reply that she was being engaged by British cruisers.

As the shells exploded aboard the *Scharnhorst*, Bey had her turn south-east and make smoke while speed increased to 30 knots. At 09.40 Force One ceased fire and gave chase, but as the distance between the hunters and the hunted widened, Burnett realized that they had no chance of catching the battle-cruiser in such weather as her greater size meant that she could cope with a heavier sea than any of the cruisers. Force One turned back towards the convoy.

This time, the Germans were not running away, but simply playing for time. Bey intended to attack the convoy from the north, with the destroyers attacking from the south. The destroyers' 5.9-in guns were almost a match for those of two of the cruisers, while torpedo attack would also threaten the cruisers, leaving the *Scharnhorst* free to savage the convoy.

Fraser again ordered the convoy onto a northerly course and had the four destroyers from RA55A diverted to reinforce the screen around Force One's cruisers. McCoy, the senior officer of the escort, was already offering assistance to Burnett. Shortly afterwards Fraser ordered the convoy back onto a north-easterly course, again concerned about it becoming trapped between the ice and the Germans, and then later left the entire matter to Captain McCoy, who decided at noon to change course to the south-east. At the same time, *Belfast* found the *Scharnhorst* on her radar again. Burnett's concern for the convoy was well-founded, as the battle-cruiser had steamed in an arc and reappeared 40 miles to the north. At 12.20 the battle-cruiser came into sight and Burnett ordered his cruisers to open fire and his destroyers to mount a torpedo attack.

Fearing a torpedo attack, *Kapitän* Hintze opened fire and started to take evasive action to avoid the destroyers. The range shortened to 4.5 miles, while his gunnery direction officers concentrated fire on *Norfolk*, whose 8-in guns were not using flashless cordite and so allowed her range to be established easily. The heavy cruiser was soon taking fire, with an 11-in shell knocking out 'X' turret aft, and her radio sets were also disabled. *Sheffield* was showered in shell splinters. In return just one shell from the British cruisers hit the German ship, landing on the quarterdeck, but failed to explode. Then, disappearing at 12.41 almost as quickly as she had appeared, the *Scharnhorst* raced off to the south-east. The high seas meant that the destroyers had been unable to get into position for a torpedo attack before the battle-cruiser disappeared from sight. This time the cruisers gave chase at 28 knots, using radar to maintain contact, while the destroyers did their best to keep up. By 14.00 the battle-cruiser, instead of homing in on the convoy, was some 30 miles ahead of it, desperately seeking to return to the Altenfjord. Force One was now in the happy position of driving the German ship towards the 14-in guns of *Duke of York*.

Those aboard the British battleship had been through moments of despair, feeling at first that their prey had evaded the cruisers. Then Force Two was spotted by a Blohm und Voss Bv138 flying boat, which could not have failed to notice the significance of the ships. They were not to know that the aircraft simply reported 'one big and

189

several smaller ships', which aroused no suspicions at all. Fraser signalled that unless contact could be regained by Force One, he had no chance of finding the *Scharnhorst*. At the back of Fraser's mind was the real possibility that the battle-cruiser was not in fact interested in the convoy, but instead was seeking to break out into the wider Atlantic, packed with convoys and the large fast passenger liners now acting as troopships bringing American and Canadian troops for the forthcoming invasion of Europe. He turned Force Two to west-south-west. His change of course caused a ripple of disappointment to run through his squadron, as it was clear that their high hopes of catching the German ship were going to come to nothing. The mood changed almost as abruptly as Fraser received news of a fresh contact, and ordered Force Two to turn back to its previous course.

Meanwhile, the German destroyers found that the convoy was not where they had expected it to be, thanks to the changes of course taken and misleading reports from the U-boats. At 14.18, when he had finally decided to return to the Altenfjord, Bey also signalled to his destroyers to return.

Aboard the ships of Force Two, at 15.30 everyone went to action stations and they closed up for combat, closing all armoured hatches and watertight doors. They had not too long to wait. At 16.18, the trace of the *Scharnhorst* appeared on the *Duke of York*'s radar, and soon afterwards a cluster of smaller traces showed Force One still on the chase. At 16.32 the battle-cruiser appeared on the fire control radar at a distance of 11 miles, but Fraser decided to hold fire until the distance closed further. He ordered his destroyers to prepare for a torpedo attack, but to await the go-ahead.

Force Two and the *Scharnhorst* were less than 7 miles apart at 16.50, when Fraser changed course to allow all of his guns and those of the cruiser *Jamaica* to come to bear on the battle-cruiser. The secondary armament of 5.25-in guns aboard the *Duke of York* fired four star-shells which exploded above and behind the *Scharnhorst*, illuminating her against the dark night and showing that she was completely unprepared for action with her guns aligned fore and aft. Fraser ordered a full broadside, with all ten 14-in guns firing at once, with the 6-in guns of *Jamaica* following. The radar-controlled guns were spot on target, and the green glows of shell hits could be seen, having taken just fifteen seconds to travel the 6.8 miles separating the opposing ships. The German's 'A' turret forward was wrecked. *Kapitän* Hintze swung his ship away to the north, only to find

190

himself facing the pursuing cruisers of Force One, although *Sheffield* was dropping back with a technical difficulty. The other two cruisers opened fire, causing Bey to order a turn eastwards.

The *Scharnhorst* was now outpacing Force One, although her actual progress was reduced by Hintze swinging the ship from time to time to allow her 'B' turret to return fire. At 17.00 Force Two's destroyers were still attempting to overhaul the Germans so that they could mount a torpedo attack, a penalty for Fraser's refusal to allow them to start earlier. Two shells from the battle-cruiser passed harmlessly through the battleship's tripod mast. At 17.13 the destroyers were ordered to launch their torpedoes, but while they could still hang on to the battleship, they were in no position to launch as they pitched and rolled in the heavy seas. *Jamaica* was also falling behind, and it looked as if the faster German battle-cruiser would also outrun the British battleship. The prospect now was for a gunnery duel between the two ships, with the 14-in guns of *Duke of York* capable of hitting a target at 18 miles. Unfortunately, the massive broadsides had wrecked the gunnery radar, and visual gunnery was being made difficult by smoke coming from the *Scharnhorst*.

Once again, events on the German side at first unknown to the British were to change the position. One of the 14-in shells had penetrated the starboard boiler room and the battle-cruiser's speed fell to 10 knots, although fast work in appalling conditions by her engine room personnel saw the steam supply reconnected and speed increased again to 22 knots, with the range opened up to 11 miles. While this was happening, the British destroyers had closed on the battle-cruiser, and while two on the *Scharnhorst*'s port quarter attracted the fire of her secondary armament, the star-shell from the destroyers also hid the approach of two more on the starboard side until they were 2 miles away. The *Scharnhorst* turned abruptly to starboard to comb the tracks of any torpedoes, but the two destroyers *Scorpion* and *Stord* fired sixteen torpedoes at 18.52, and one of them struck home. The change of course gave *Saumarez* and *Savage* their chance, and a dozen torpedoes were fired at the battle-cruiser, with one of them wrecking a second boiler room and another distorting a propeller shaft. The speed of the wounded ship fell to 10 knots.

While the four destroyers withdrew, having attacked under fire and taken damage and casualties, the *Duke of York*'s gunnery radar had been repaired. *Jamaica* was fast catching up as the German ship had changed course. Force Two now opened fire, with both ships quickly finding their range, steaming past the battle-cruiser and repeatedly hitting her with armour-piercing shells. The *Jamaica* detached to give the *Scharnhorst* another torpedo attack as she slowed and her guns fell silent. Then Force One appeared, with *Belfast* and *Norfolk* ready for torpedo attack, which came at 19.18. Force One's destroyers were also sent into action, with two of them on the port side where the bilges were already exposed. Damaged voice pipes meant that the torpedo crews aboard *Matchless* missed the order to fire, but *Musketeer*'s torpedoes struck home. The German ship was now listing heavily to port, with her crew mustered on deck ready to abandon ship. *Kapitän* Hintze ordered them to slide into the water on the port side and not to forget to inflate their life-jackets.

No one on the British side saw the end of this great ship, as smoke hanging over the scene obscured their view, and even when a radar operator reported that the blip was fading, he was told to retune it. More than half an hour passed before *Belfast* was able to confirm that the *Scharnhorst* had indeed been sunk. A single raft contained frozen survivors. The destroyer *Scorpion* picked up thirty of them, while *Matchless* picked up a further six, but 1,767 officers and men had lost their lives, including the *Konteradmiral* and the *Kapitän*. The loss of so many suggests that her final moments must have seen a traumatic capsizing that trapped many of those on the port side as she rolled over. The freezing seas would have accounted for many within minutes, especially the lightly clad men from below decks.

While all this was going on, convoy JW55B sailed on, unmolested, with its ships reaching Murmansk on 27 December, while the Archangel portion reached that port safely on 29 December. The shadowing U-boats that were hoping to attack were sent on a fruitless search for survivors from the *Scharnhorst*.

Chapter 17

Stalin Prepares to Dominate Europe

The convoys to northern Russia continued until the end of the war. The hazards remained the same, especially the weather, but never again would the Germans have the opportunity to catch convoys unawares, and as elsewhere, the balance started to swing in favour of the Allies. Attacks on German bases in Norway became increasingly frequent by both the Royal Air Force and carrier-borne naval aircraft, while the German coastal convoys supplying bases or carrying iron ore for German industry became prey to British air strikes.

Paradoxically, the Normandy landings in June 1944 resulted in a further interruption to the convoys. If the Allied bombing campaign, then the invasion of Sicily, and later, mainland Italy, were not the second front that Stalin demanded, then Operation Overlord was a second front beyond all doubt. Yet such were the demands on Allied shipping that the Arctic convoys had to be suspended between April and August 1944, with the exception of a dash by three destroyers, with supplies for Allied vessels stranded and awaiting a return convoy. Stalin bitterly resented the interruption to his supplies, but his armies were on the advance, and his aim was to occupy as much of Eastern Europe as possible before his wartime allies could overrun Germany.

There were many indications of Stalin's true intentions once the war ended. It was not simply a question of a battle for the Soviet Union against invasion by Nazi Germany, and it was certainly not a desire to simply clear the Germans out of Europe. The massacre of Polish Army officers in the Katyn Forest in May 1940 was one early indication that post-war Poland would not be allowed its freedom. The irony was that the first indications that something was amiss did not come until after the beginning of Operation Barbarossa and the re-establishment of diplomatic relations between the Free Poles and the Soviet Union, when an attempt was made to find officers for a Polish Army raised from Poles in the Soviet Union.

The Winter War with Finland (covered earlier) was another earlier indication, as was the occupation and then incorporation within the Soviet Union of the Baltic States. This, of course, assumes that the Soviet Union was only really concerned about gaining a buffer zone when it occupied eastern Poland in September 1939. Nevertheless, it was Poland that suffered most and soonest from Soviet duplicity.

The Warsaw Rising

There were two Warsaw risings. The first started on 19 April 1943, when the Jewish inhabitants of the Warsaw ghetto rose to fight for their freedom. This was an act of desperation by people who had come to realize that they had nothing to lose as they were bound to die anyway. The operation took the Germans by surprise, and it took until 16 May before the leader of the German forces, SS *Brigadeführer* Stroop was able to announce that the ghetto had been cleared successfully, although pockets of armed resistance remained until mid-July.

The second Warsaw rising was far more serious and could have been strategically significant. The rising was intended not just as a means of seizing the city and expelling the Germans, it was also a political gesture of independence against the Soviet Union, whose forces were advancing on the city.

The Polish Home Army planned an uprising against the Germans under the code-name Operation Tempest. In January 1944 an olive branch was held out to the Soviet Union by the Polish Home Army, which promised full cooperation with the Red Army in the liberation of Poland and against the retreating German forces, as long as Polish independence was respected. This order came from General Kazimierz Sosnkowski, who had taken over from General Sikorski as Commander-in-Chief of Polish forces under the control of the Polish government-in-exile after the latter had been killed in an air crash in July 1943.

Initially, Operation Tempest set out to liberate a number of important Polish centres, with the Polish Home Army inflicting heavy defeats on the retreating Germans, capturing equipment and liberating cities such as Lublin and Lvov. In some areas, the Polish Home Army and

Red Army units did cooperate successfully at first, including the province of Volhynia, but at Wilno (Vilna to the Russians, Vilnius to Lithuanians) the Red Army simply arrested the Poles. Regardless of success, once the mission had been completed and the Red Army had moved on, being replaced by internal security units, the Polish Home Army commanders were arrested and executed. The men were disarmed and ordered to join the Soviet-sponsored Polish Army in the Soviet Union, also known as Berling's Army – until April 1944 part of the Thirty-third Soviet Army. Those who failed to do so were deported with some 50,000 eventually imprisoned in the Gulag prison camp system.

In Lublin, however, Soviet troops had been accompanied by the 'Polish Committee of National Liberation', which had arisen out of the National Council for the Homeland, a Communist organization. A few days earlier in Chelm, the committee had published its Manifesto to the Polish People, which clearly reflected Soviet thinking. In Lublin, the committee signed an agreement with the Soviet government giving it the power to administer those areas liberated by the Red Army and which the Soviet Union accepted as being Polish, although this also entailed allowing the Soviet Union to annex the Polish provinces east of the River Bug.

The original intention was that Warsaw would not form part of Operation Tempest, but Lieutenant General Count Tadeusz Komorowski, the Commander-in-Chief of the Polish Home Army, ordered that Warsaw be taken, believing that for Poles to have liberated their own capital city was vital if the political objectives inherent in the operation were to be achieved.

On 1 August 1944, the second Warsaw rising started. It was scheduled to last just ten days, but in the event it lasted for sixty-three. Under the command of General Antoni Chrusciel, 36,500 Polish Home Army members started the rising, aided by some 900 other insurgents. The task that faced them was enormous, as no more than 14 per cent of the men were armed, while there were only 1,386 rifles and 2,665 revolvers or pistols, 844 sub-machine-guns and less than a hundred light machine-guns, with just twenty heavy machine-guns. At the beginning, given this inauspicious armoury, the fighting mainly involved hand-grenades and home-made Molotov cocktails. Nevertheless, the situation improved as weapons were captured from the Germans and both the Western Allies and the Soviet Union air-dropped arms and ammunition.

To maintain an element of surprise, the rising broke out at the most unlikely hour of 17.00. The Germans knew it was imminent, which was hardly surprising given their experience in Poland over the previous few months, however, it does seem that the Germans also knew the hour it would commence, but lacked insufficient forces within the city to respond immediately. A substantial part of Warsaw, a city of around a million inhabitants at the time, was soon 'liberated' with universal popular support, but in subsequent fighting the area was broken up into separate districts, often unconnected. Where the rising failed in its initial objectives was to capture the railway stations and other major lines of communication. Nevertheless, a radio station was organized and newspapers published.

Despite being hard-pressed on several fronts, the Germans eventually reacted, and by 20 August more than 20,000 well-equipped German troops arrived in the area, including a brigade of convicted criminals and units comprised of Russian exiles. In a brutal response ordered directly by Himmler, all Poles were to be shot whether or not they were part of the insurgency. In just five days, more than 40,000 Poles were slaughtered until the order was countermanded by the local commander, just before the Germans counter-attacked.

The German counter-attack between troops who were well-equipped, including armoured units, and supported by aircraft, inevitably meant that the struggle was unequal. The Poles established their own fire-fighting and AA squads as well as hospitals, despite their shortage of equipment. The Western Allies were still too far away to help, but now, just when a Soviet advance could have resolved the situation and relieved Warsaw and its hard-pressed inhabitants, the Red Army did nothing. Certainly, a German counter-attack had checked the Soviet advance, but the Red Army could have renewed the offensive while the Germans were under pressure. Between 16 and 21 September, Berling's Polish troops landed on the western bank of the Vistula, but heavy casualties forced them back. Stalin dismissed the Warsaw rising as an 'adventurous affair', which was harsh, but possibly excusable from a man concerned with overall strategy and with large armies at his disposal. What was not acceptable was Stalin's refusal to allow the Western Allies to use Soviet airfields so that they could render assistance. Heavy losses saw just a few relief flights from British bases in Italy. On the one occasion that USAAF aircraft were allowed to use Soviet airfields, the supplies dropped on 18 September mainly ended up in German hands as the Polish controlled area of Warsaw had shrunk so much.

The civilian population remained remarkably loyal to the Polish Home Army. Even when, at the beginning of September, the Red Cross arranged an evacuation, less than 10 per cent of the surviving population left. By 30 September only the central district remained under Polish control, and on 1 October, Komorowski decided to surrender. The Germans insisted that the capital be completely evacuated, but agreed to treat the insurgents as combatants, almost certainly a unique concession on their part.

In all, the uprising saw at least 15,000 members of the Polish Home Army killed, along with between 200,000 and 250,000 Polish civilians. German losses were at least as heavy as those of the Polish Home Army. In the short period between the uprising ending and the Red Army taking the city, the Germans razed 83 per cent of the city.

Giving Stalin Eastern Europe

By the time of the Allied conference at Yalta, code-named Argonaut, between 4 and 11 February 1945, German defeat was inevitable. The main topics were political rather than strategic, and included the division of post-war Germany. In return for gaining Soviet agreement to declare war on Japan, without the knowledge of the British wartime Prime Minister, Winston Churchill, the United States agreed to Soviet demands that gave it territory in the Far East. Although this affected the Chinese nationalist leader, Chiang Kai-shek, he was not informed.

Yalta saw a declaration on Liberated Europe issued, calling for free elections and democratic governments in all of the territories liberated by the Allied forces, but this was immediately flouted by Stalin the following month, when the Soviet Union established a minority Communist government in Romania.

Nevertheless, the pass had been sold even earlier, at a meeting between Churchill and Stalin in Moscow between 9 and 19 October 1944, at which the United States was only represented at ambassadorial level. Code-named Tolstoy, this conference had also been primarily aimed at encouraging the Soviet Union to declare war on Japan, which it did not do until 8 August 1945, when Japanese defeat was inevitable. Stalin, no doubt sensing weakness, pressed for assurances over the degree of influence that the Soviet Union should have in the post-war Balkans. Churchill wrote on a piece of paper:

Romania – Soviet Union 90%, others 10%
Greece – UK (in accord with the USA), 90%, Soviet Union 10%
Yugoslavia – 50–50%
Hungary – 50–50%
Bulgaria – Soviet Union 75%, others 25%

Stalin ticked the piece of paper, which enabled Churchill to send a British expedition to Greece at the end of October. Further negotiations between Anthony Eden and Molotov, the foreign ministers, saw the figures for both Bulgaria and Hungary changed to 80 per cent Soviet Union, 20 per cent others. Significantly, attempts to discuss the future of Poland, over which the war had actually started, came to nothing.

General Marshall, in overall command of the United States Army, not only allowed the Red Army the chance to be first to reach Berlin, he also rejected a plea by Churchill that a force be sent to occupy Prague. To some extent Marshall was supporting his man in Europe, General Dwight Eisenhower, Supreme Commander, Allied Powers Europe, who believed in an advance on a broad front, although his deputy, the British General Bernard Montgomery, favoured a sharp thrust to take Berlin. At this time the Russians were allies who were greatly admired by many in the West for the sacrifices that they had made during the war.

The Allied conference at Potsdam in Germany from 17 July to 2 August 1945, not only prepared surrender terms for Japan, but also drew up the boundaries and peace terms for Europe. At the previous conferences at Teheran and Yalta, the Allied powers had agreed in principle to effectively moving Poland westwards, with the country ceding territory east of the River Bug to the Soviet Union and in return gaining some of Germany's eastern territories. The resulting westward boundary became known as the Oder-Neisse Line, and ran south from the Baltic Sea along the line of the two rivers to the border with Czechoslovakia. The Soviet Union pressed for the Western Neisse to become the border, giving the Poles the maximum westwards extension, despite Western misgivings.

In fact, the Soviet Union had been rigging the shape of post-war Europe as its influence spread westwards with the German retreat.

198

Bulgaria had hoped to remain neutral at the outset of the war, and the Nazi–Soviet Pact gave hope that this would be achieved. Yet, even before Operation Barbarossa, German pressure for Bulgaria to join the Axis increased, and fears that further talks between von Ribbentrop and Molotov put Bulgaria inside the Soviet sphere of influence finally swung the decision that Bulgaria should join, but left the date uncertain. Bulgaria eventually joined the Axis on 1 March 1941, enabling German troops to use her territory to enter Greece. Strangely, while declaring war on both the UK and the United States, Bulgaria never declared war on the Soviet Union, and did not send forces to join the invasion. Heavy bombing of Bulgarian targets did not start until 19 November 1943, but during 1944, the activities of various left wing groups became more organized. The Fatherland Front, originally formed in 1941 and including Communists among its members, gained support due to the bombing. Soviet forces entered Bulgaria on 8 September 1944, and the following day a *coup d'état* was mounted by the Fatherland Front, which secured important ministries while in rural areas local committees were established that purged their political opponents. Bulgaria then declared war on Germany and the army was quickly remodelled on the Soviet pattern, and as early as 20 September 1944, political commissars were appointed. This was followed by the removal of 800 officers for political reasons. Bulgaria was well on the way to becoming a Communist state by VE-Day.

Czechoslovakia had come close to being the *casus belli* for the UK going to war with Germany in 1938. A Czech provisional government-in-exile had been established in London by mid-1941, and after Operation Barbarossa was launched, a Czech–Soviet Treaty of Alliance was signed. As with so many of the Eastern European nations, whatever free forces might be raised in the UK, there were also equivalent forces in the Soviet Union. Edvard Benes, who had been Czech president at the time of the Munich Agreement, naturally enough distrusted the Western Allies, but soon came to understand that he could only return to Czechoslovakia after the war through cooperation with Stalin. He helped to organize the Slovak uprising in 1944, and the Prague uprising the following year accelerated the Red Army's advance. At the time, General Patton's US Third Army was approaching from the west and Marshal Konev's First Ukrainian Front from the east, but Eisenhower refused to allow Patton to go to the aid of the Czechs.

Hungary in 1939 was a shadow of its former self as the result of the failure of the Austro-Hungarian Empire in the First World War and the consequent Treaty of Trianon which led to the loss of some two-thirds of its territory to neighbouring states. As a result, there was considerable temptation to side with the Axis when they promised to revise the Treaty. The Hungarians had also experienced Communist rule in 1919, albeit briefly, and as a consequence there was a persistent fear of its return. On 27 June 1941 Hungary finally supported Operation Barbarossa after an incident in which the town of Kassa in the north of the country was bombed by 'Soviet' aircraft, widely believed today to have been disguised German aircraft. By December, the country was also at war with the UK and the United States.

Poorly equipped at the outset of the war, Hungarian forces suffered badly at Stalingrad. Another problem was the fear of invasion by Romania, which led to plans to create a 220,000 strong Home Army, but Hitler, while replacing Hungarian equipment losses at the front, refused to help equip the Home Army. Hungary's tentative negotiations with the Western Allies, to withdraw from the war-fuelled German suspicions about the country's reliability as an ally and as a source of food and increasingly vital raw materials and fuel, resulted in German occupation starting on 19 March 1944. Like Czechoslovakia, it soon became clear that Hungary would have to conclude an armistice not with the Western Allies but with the Soviet Union. After the Hungarian–Soviet preliminary armistice on 11 October 1944 was announced, the Germans moved quickly to install a puppet regime. The Soviet Union in turn created a puppet Soviet-backed provisional government on 22 December 1944.

Romania was another country that owed its size and shape to Versailles. The country struggled between the wars and disillusionment with democratic government led to the sovereign establishing an absolute monarchy in 1938, the same year that Romania entered into an economic agreement with Germany, under which the country's natural resources could be developed by German companies. Germany also became Romania's main market for its agricultural produce and oil.

Initially Romania was neutral, and found herself forced to cede territory to the Soviet Union as a result of the Nazi–Soviet Pact of August 1939, losing Bessarabia and Northern Bukovina. Further agreements resulted in territory being handed over to both Bulgaria and Hungary, but in return King Carol II received German assurances of protection. The loss of territory and 3 million ethnic Romanians created such an outcry that Carol II was forced to abdicate and handed over the monarchy to his son Michael. Nevertheless, the Germans then took over control of the economy and the army, and later a military dictatorship was established under General Ion Antonescu. On 22 June 1941, the country supported Operation Barbarossa, but the support evaporated after the Dniester was crossed and there were demands for Romania to return to neutrality. The UK had not declared war on Romania while its forces were in its former territories, and also recognized the pressure applied to the Romanians by Germany, but under pressure from Stalin they issued an ultimatum and officially declared war on the country on 7 December 1941.

The German hold on the country was largely behind Antonescu's refusal to withdraw from the Soviet Union during the Stalingrad siege, but discussions were held with Italy over a joint approach to the Allies. When this idea was rejected, direct contact was attempted with the Allies through neutral countries. All attempts to withdraw from the conflict floundered on Allied insistence for unconditional surrender, which Romania feared would place the country under Soviet influence. With the Red Army advancing rapidly towards Romania, King Michael had Antonescu arrested on 23 August 1944 and then the Romanian forces surrendered to the Red Army. A Soviet–Romanian armistice was signed on 12 September, but this gave the Soviet Union the dominant political and economic interest in the country. A puppet government was installed on 6 March 1945.

The Balkans

Yugoslavia was founded on 1 December 1918, following the collapse of the Austro-Hungarian Empire, but its foundation preceded Versailles. In addition to the former Austro-Hungarian provinces, it included the previously independent kingdoms of Montenegro and Serbia. Fault lines emerged almost immediately as Orthodox Serbs tried to create a Yugoslavia possessing 'national oneness', but this only served to emphasize the differences between the constituent parts of the country. The country veered between ineffectual democracy and an absolute monarchy after 1929.

In September 1939, Yugoslavia declared itself neutral, although both sides pressed for its support. The Serbs were inclined to support the Allies, as had happened during the First World War, and the regent, Prince Paul, was also known to be an Anglophile. Nevertheless, economically and strategically, the country was vulnerable to the Axis, mainly because Italy, a First World War ally, had changed sides. The Croats were tempted by Italian promises of independence, while other minorities looked to Bulgaria or Hungary as possible saviours. No less important, German interests dominated much of the economy, including the output of non-ferrous metals, and provided the main market for the country's agricultural production. The picture emerges of a country surrounded by nations with claims on parts of its territory, riven by internal dissension, and increasingly reliant, almost to satellite status, on Germany.

After pressing Yugoslavia to join the Axis from November 1940 onwards, the regent played for time, hoping that the outbreak of hostilities between Germany and the Soviet Union would save the country. When eventually he was forced to sign in March 1941, civil unrest followed in Yugoslavia, despite the fact that the country was not committed to full membership of the Tripartite Pact. Germany and Italy eventually invaded Yugoslavia on 6 April 1941, although it was to prove to be one of the most difficult territories over which to maintain control, as away from the coast the mountainous interior aided partisan activity. Communications were so difficult that coastal shipping was necessary to supply many Axis units.

King Peter, having been projected into the role of national leader immediately before the invasion, eventually arrived with his ministers in London in June 1941 to find that they were regarded as heroes by the Allies. They established a government-in-exile and set about supporting partisan activity in Yugoslavia. A pro-royalist partisan leader seemed to be less active than the Communist partisan Tito, and so it was to the latter that British support went. While Tito expected to control most of the country when the Germans went, the pro-royalist faction, the Cetniks, controlled Serbia. As a result, in July 1944, Tito appealed to Stalin for assistance. Stalin diverted part of the Red Army from its thrust towards Germany, and the Cetniks faced a combined Communist partisan and Soviet assault. When the Red Army moved on to take Hungary, Tito was left in charge, forming a Communist dominated coalition government with his opponents in March 1945. After German surrender, Tito consolidated his power.

Adjoining Yugoslavia, Albania was a small kingdom subjected to influence by both Italy and Yugoslavia, although tending to look to the UK for support. On 7 April 1939 Italy invaded, finding little resistance in a poor country with just a million inhabitants, although Colonel Abas Kupi handled two battalions so well that he delayed the Italian advance by thirty-six hours and allowed King Zog to escape to London. Kupi continued to fight as a partisan during the occupation, but following the Axis defeats in North Africa, Communists became more prominent with encouragement from Tito. As in Yugoslavia, the Communists, led by Enver Hoxha, received the greater part of British aid. Even though Kupi and his allies put the greatest pressure on the retreating Germans, it had been decided that British support should be concentrated on the partisans who controlled the southern part of the country. Eventually, the Communists took control of the country with Yugoslav support.

Oddly, in the post-war world, Yugoslavia eventually took a more independent line than most other Communist states, leaving the Warsaw Pact and dealing with the West, while Albania went in the opposite direction and allied with Communist China, becoming one of the most austere states in Eastern Europe.

The one country that did escape the Communist takeover was Greece, but at the cost of civil war as German forces pulled out. Greece had originally planned to remain neutral, although it did provide some support for Britain and France. It had also received assurances from the British government that it could expect British assistance in the event of an Axis invasion. The UK had been one of the original 'protecting powers' when Greek independence had been gained in the 1830s, along with France and Tsarist Russia. Italy invaded Greece on 28 October 1940, using Albania as a springboard. Fierce Greek resistance, aided by terrain that favoured defence, stalled the Italian advance, then drove them back into Albania. A German invasion was necessary, starting in April 1941, by which time British, Australian and New Zealand troops were present to fight alongside the Greeks. The country was plundered to support the Axis war effort and the puppet government required to cover the full costs of the occupation, which resulted in hyperinflation worse than that suffered in Weimar Germany. The winter of 1941–42 resulted in a famine that killed around 100,000, and the government-in-exile, led by the Greek King George II, persuaded the Western Allies to allow a partial lifting of the blockade so that in subsequent winters Red Cross aid could reach the Greeks.

While official British policy favoured the restoration of the Greek monarchy after the war, both the main partisan groups were republican, although only one of them was Communist. During the winter of 1942–43, fighting actually broke out between the two main partisan groups, and a truce had to be negotiated between them. Nevertheless, by February 1944, the Communists had established a Political Committee of National Liberation to administer the substantial part of rural Greece under its control. While this was not supposed to be a government-in-waiting, it clearly represented a threat to the government-in-exile, and within days a mutiny broke out among Greek soldiers stationed in the Middle East, with the leaders demanding a government based on the committee. After a conference held in the Lebanon in May 1944, to which all political groups were invited, the committee demanded the control of key ministries from the new government of national unity.

The situation was resolved over the heads of the Greek leaders by Churchill and Stalin. The British Prime Minister feared that the Red Army's advance through Europe would be used to extend Communism, and was concerned that should Greece follow the same route, it would pose a threat to British communications with the Empire. This was the start of accepting Soviet domination in Romania, followed by Bulgaria and Yugoslavia.

Nevertheless, simply agreeing that Greece should come under the Anglo-American sphere of influence was not of itself enough, and the British had to mount Operation Manna, to ensure that the Communists did not take over and to allow the government-in-exile to return. British warships, known as Force 120, were sent to the Aegean, to prevent any Axis evacuation by sea, while a military force, Force 140, landed on the Peloponnese, and eventually entered Athens on 14 October 1944, followed by the full British Expeditionary Force on 16 October. The Greek Prime Minister arrived on 18 October.

Greece was saved, but only at the cost of a protracted civil war. This was another case of Churchill overruling his own military advisers who were more concerned with the advance on Germany. It remains a moot point whether more would have been achieved by strengthening the British contribution to the advance on Germany, possibly reducing the influence of the Red Army elsewhere, or whether the threat to Greece was so real that it deserved the priority Churchill accorded it. Given Eisenhower's attitude, there was no guarantee that any of the Eastern European states could have been saved, but at least Churchill's action did keep Greece in the Western democratic fold. Further, a Communist regime in Greece could have destabilized neighbouring Turkey and would have added a further unwelcome edge to the crisis that started in Cyprus during the 1950s.

If the United States had any doubts about the nature of the Soviet Union post-war, they should have been dispelled at the height of the air offensive against Japan. Three Boeing B-29 Superfortress bombers ran short of fuel and made an emergency landing at a Soviet airfield near Vladivostok. The aircraft were immediately impounded by the Russians, hardly the action of an ally, and copied, later appearing as the Tupolov Tu-4 heavy bomber, which was given the NATO reporting name of 'Bull'. The B-29 was the aircraft that dropped the atomic bombs on Hiroshima and Nagasaki. The Soviet Union had an aircraft post-war that gave it a strategic bombing capability for the first time.

Appendix I

The Convoys

Taking Convoy PQ18 as an example, the volume of war material that could be shipped to the Soviet Union in a typical convoy was considerable:

	Vehs	Tanks	Aircraft	Explosives	Other Cargo*
Ships from UK	312	230	271	1,601 tons	37,799 tons
Ships from USA	2,588	384	175	7,297 tons	72,288 tons
Lost UK ships 4		123	89	38	134 tons	10,862 tons
Lost US ships 8		1,385	132	82	2,249 tons	36,554 tons

The loss of the tanker *Atheltemplar* also meant the loss of 9,541 tons of fuel oil.

* Other cargo included more than 11,000 tons of TNT.

The Convoys

Operation Dervish left Liverpool 12 August 1941, then Hvalfjord on 21 August.

This was followed by **Operation Gauntlet** on 19 August, which picked up Russian miners and took them to Spitzbergen, while the Norwegian residents were evacuated.

Royal Air Force personnel were taken to the Soviet Union as **Operation Strength**, which departed on 30 August 1941.

A British and American government mission to the Soviet Union left the UK on 22 September, sailing aboard the cruiser *London*.

This was followed by a mission from the Trades Union Congress (TUC) on 6 October, sailing to Seidisfjord aboard the destroyer *Antelope*, and there they transferred to the destroyer *Norman* for passage to Archangel. The mission returned from the Soviet Union on 27 October, arriving in the UK on 2 November.

Convoy QP1: The first convoy from Russia, it returned the ships used in **Operation Dervish** as well as Soviet vessels, and left Archangel on 28 September 1941.

Convoy PQ1: The first eastbound convoy, it assembled in Iceland and left the Hvalfjord on 29 September 1941.
Convoy PQ2: Left Scapa Flow in Orkney on 17 October 1941.
Convoy QP2: Left Archangel on 3 November 1941.
Convoy PQ3: Left Hvalfjord on 9 November 1941.
Convoy PQ4: Left Hvalfjord on 17 November 1941.
Convoy QP3: Left Archangel on 27 November 1941, returning the ships of PQ2.
Convoy PQ5: Left Hvalfjord on 27 November 1941.

The Foreign Secretary visited the Soviet Union in December, sailing from the UK on 8 December to arrive in the Soviet Union on 12 December, leaving for the return voyage on Christmas Day and arriving back in the UK on 29 December.

Convoy PQ6: Left Hvalfjord on 8 December 1941.
Convoy QP4: Left Archangel on 29 December 1941.
Convoy PQ7A: Left Hvalfjord on 26 December 1941.
Convoy PQ7B: Left Hvalfjord on 31 December 1941.
Convoy PQ8: Left Hvalfjord on 8 January 1942.
Convoy QP5: Left Murmansk on 13 January 1942.
Convoy QP6: Left Murmansk on 24 January 1942.
Convoys PQ9/10: Left Reykjavik on 1 February 1942.

Between 9 and 15 February, the British ran warships through to transfer a number of sailors.

Convoy QP7: Left Murmansk on 12 February 1942.
Convoy PQ11: Left Loch Ewe on 6 February and sailed via Kirkwall in Orkney, leaving there on 14 February.
Convoy QP8: Left Murmansk on 1 March 1942.
Convoy PQ12: Left Loch Ewe and sailed via Reykjavik, which it left on 1 March 1942.
Convoy PQ13: Left Loch Ewe on 10 March and again sailed via Reykjavik, which it left on 20 March 1942.
Convoy QP9: Left the Kola Inlet on 21 March 1942.
Convoy PQ14: Left Oban on 26 March and Reykjavik on 8 April 1942.
Convoy QP10: Left the Kola Inlet on 10 April 1942.
Convoy PQ15: Left Oban on 10 April 1942 and Reykjavik on 26 April.
Convoy QP11: Left Murmansk on 28 April 1942.

HMS *Trinidad* left Murmansk on 13 May.

Convoy PQ16: Sailed from Reykjavik on 21 May 1942.
Convoy QP12: Sailed from Kola on 21 May 1942.
Convoy PQ17: Sailed from Reykjavik on 27 June 1942, but was ordered to disperse on 4 July.
Convoy QP13: Sailed from Archangel on 26 June 1942, and was joined by ships from Murmansk on 28 June.

These were followed by **Operation Gearbox**, a code used repeatedly for relief of the Spitzbergen garrison, and in this case operated between 25 June and 3 July.

Ammunition and stores for the ships of the **PQ17** escort were sent from Scapa Flow on 20 July.

Followed by an independent passage by the *Friedrich Engels* sailing from Reykjavik on 11 August, and another by the *Belomorcanal* the following day.

RAF personnel and stores were sent from Greenock on 13 August. Later, on 24 August, an anti-submarine operation sailed from North Russia.

Convoy PQ18: Left Loch Ewe 2 September 1942, left Hvalfjord on 8 September.
Convoy QP14: Left Archangel on 13 September 1942.

Between 13 and 28 October, RAF medical personnel, previously rejected by the Soviets, were moved to Russia and on the return the air and ground crew of two Hampden squadrons, transferred to the Red Air Force, were brought home.

Operation FB: Operation Torch then interfered with the operation of convoys, and **PQ19** had to be cancelled. As a sop to Soviet anxieties, it was decided to run a number of independent sailings east and westbound, with the former known as **Operation FB**. The idea was to run merchant ships lying in Iceland at twelve hour intervals, with British and American ships alternating, between 29 October and 2 November. A thirteenth ship – Russian – was added at the last moment. The demands of the invasion of North Africa meant that escorts could not be provided, but seven armed trawlers were stationed at intervals along the route, while additional reconnaissance flights were made by RAF Catalina flying boats. An attack on a U-boat by one of the trawlers, *Northern Spray*, and the recce flights may well have alerted the Germans. The result was that only five of the ships completed their voyages, with another five sunk and three more turned back. The ships waiting to leave the Soviet Union fared much better, with twenty-two out of twenty-three arriving safely in Iceland. Unusually, the lost merchant ship was attacked by a German destroyer, *Z27*. The westbound operation was not given an official code-name.

Convoy QP15: The last convoy of the PQ/QP series, left Archangel on 17 November.

Convoy JW51A: Sailed from Loch Ewe avoiding a call at Iceland on 15 December 1942. NB: This one remained undiscovered!
Convoy JW51B: Sailed from Loch Ewe on 22 December.
Convoy RA51: Sailed from the Kola Inlet on 30 December.

After the Battle of the Barents Sea, two destroyers made an independent passage from Kola to Scapa Flow between 11 and 15 January 1943, carrying seriously wounded personnel.

Convoy JW52: Sailed from Loch Ewe on 17 January 1943.

The Russians sent four merchantmen on independent sailings westwards during January 1943, of which two were lost on 26 January to *U-255*, while the two that reached Iceland safely were damaged in air raids.

Convoy RA52: Sailed from Kola on 29 January 1943.

Convoy JW53: Sailed from Loch Ewe on 15 February, with **Convoy JW53A** (just three ships) sailing the following day to catch up and combine with the main convoy. In bad weather the cruiser *Sheffield* had to turn back after a wave peeled the roof off 'A' turret, while the escort carrier *Dasher* also had to turn back after the forward end of her flight-deck was damaged.

Convoy RA53: Sailed from Kola on 1 March 1943.

Convoys were suspended in mid-March 1943 as the battleship *Tirpitz*, battle-cruiser *Scharnhorst* and heavy cruiser *Lutzow* were all based in northern Norway. The Allies were concerned that this powerful striking force would break out, and the United States Navy hastily assembled Task Force 22 at Portland, Maine, to reinforce the Royal Navy's Home Fleet and protect the Atlantic convoys in case of a break-out. Heavy losses in the North Atlantic, problems in cooperating with the Soviets and the longer hours of daylight all meant that convoys to the Soviet Union would have to be suspended until the darker days of winter.

At the end of the autumn, in **Operation FQ**, the Norwegian garrison at Spitzbergen was relieved by an American cruiser and destroyer assisted by two British destroyers.

Operation Holder saw British and Canadian destroyers sail to Russia with supplies for the escort vessels that had spent the summer there waiting for the convoys to resume. This was between 1 and 11 October 1943.

Operation FR saw additional escorts sent to the Soviet Union to bring back merchant ships stranded there during the summer suspension of sailings.

Convoy RA54A: First convoy of the 1943–44 winter sailed westward from the Kola Inlet on 1 November.

Convoy JW54A: Sailed from Loch Ewe on 15 November 1943.

Convoy JW54B: Sailed from Loch Ewe on 22 November.

Convoy RA54B: Sailed from Archangel on 26 November.

Convoy JW55A: Sailed from Loch Ewe on 12 December.

Convoy JW55B: Sailed from Loch Ewe on 20 December. This led to the Battle of the North Cape on 26 December 1943, which saw the loss of the *Scharnhorst* with just thirty-six survivors – all ratings.

Convoy RA55A: Sailed from the Kola Inlet on 22 December.

Convoy RA55B: Small convoy of eight ships sailed from the Kola Inlet on 31 January 1943.

Convoy JW56A: Sailed from Loch Ewe on 12 January 1944.

Convoy JW56B: Sailed from Loch Ewe on 22 January 1944.

Convoy RA56: Sailed on 3 February 1944 with the ships of the two preceding convoys, as well as their escorts plus three additions.

Convoy JW57: Sailed on 20 February 1944. The growing problems of detecting U-boats in Arctic waters meant that greater attention was paid to the anti-submarine escort, with an escort carrier, *Chaser*, with experienced anti-submarine airmen aboard, as well as a radar-equipped cruiser dedicated to directing aerial operations.

Convoy RA57: Sailed from the Kola Inlet on 2 March, supported by *Chaser* and *Black Prince*.

Convoy JW58: Sailed from Loch Ewe on 27 March and was joined at sea by three ships from Iceland. Two escort carriers.

Convoy RA58: Sailed from the Kola Inlet on 7 April 1944, with the same two escort carriers as **JW58**, *Activity* and *Tracker*.

As a number of empty merchantmen remained in Russian ports, a number of escort vessels were sent to Kola arriving on 23 April. Unfortunately, they were also supposed to escort a large transport to collect 1,430 Russian crew for British warships awaiting transfer to the Soviet Navy, but this ship had to turn back with mechanical defects.

Convoy RA59: Sailing on 28 April, this carried the Soviet sailors in many of the merchant ships of this large convoy, while United States Navy personnel returning to the West were accommodated in Royal Navy vessels, as were the Russian admiral and his staff, with their first close-up of carrier operations aboard *Fencer*.

The Normandy landings, **Operation Overlord,** then took up the available escort and heavy units of the Royal and United States

212

navies, suspending convoys to the Soviet Union for the time-being. **Operation DC** saw three destroyers sail on 29 June with supplies for the escorts stranded in Soviet ports, starting their return on 4 July.

Convoy JW59: Sailed from Loch Ewe on 15 August, and was joined on 17 August by the ex-British warships now with the Red Navy, giving the escort an extra battleship as well as twelve patrol boats.
Convoy RA59A: Sailed from Kola on 28 August.
Convoy JW60: Sailed from Loch Ewe on 15 September.
Convoy RA60: Sailed from Kola on 28 September.
Convoy JW61: Sailed from Loch Ewe on 20 October.
Convoy JW61A: Sailed from Liverpool for Murmansk on 31 October, consisting of just two large troopships carrying 11,000 Soviet nationals captured in Normandy while serving with the *Wehrmacht*. No one from the British ships, merchant or naval, was allowed ashore! The cruiser *Berwick* also carried a Norwegian contingent destined to serve alongside Soviet forces poised to invade the north of occupied Norway and intended to ensure the continued sovereignty of Norwegian territory. Additional Norwegian troops that should have been flown in, but were prevented from doing so by bad weather, were embarked in two destroyers in **Operation Freeman,** making an independent passage sailing on 3 November and catching up with **JW61A.**

Convoy RA61: Sailed from the Kola Inlet on 2 November, although some ships had started their passage from the White Sea as early as 30 October.
Convoy RA61A: Sailed from the Kola Inlet on 11 November with two ships of **JW61A,** and no doubt their guards, probably around 1,100 British troops.
Convoy JW62: Sailed from Loch Ewe on 29 November.
Convoy RA62: Sailed from the Kola Inlet on 10 December.
Convoy JW63: Sailed from Loch Ewe on 30 December 1944.
Convoy RA63: Sailed from the Kola Inlet on 11 January 1945.
Convoy JW64: Sailed from the Clyde on 3 February, after Loch Ewe anchorage ended.
Convoy RA64: Sailed from the Kola Inlet on 17 February.
Convoy JW65: Sailed from the Clyde on 11 March 1945.
Convoy RA65: Sailed from the Kola Inlet on 23 March.
Convoy JW66: Sailed from the Clyde on 16 April 1945.

This was a major operation to stop U-boats blocking the Kola Inlet, where thermal layering made asdic detection more difficult. Despite the problem, the Soviets delayed authorizing the laying of deep level mines, too deep to harm passing surface vessels but well placed to catch a passing U-boat, and permission was not given until 16 April. The ships for **Operation Trammel** sailed from Scapa Flow at 22.00 on 17 April, arriving at Kola at noon on 21 April, planning to begin the deep lay that night, but a further day was lost due to chaotic refuelling arrangements. Nevertheless, the deep lay was completed before the arrival of **JW66**.

Convoy RA66: Sailed from the Kola Inlet on 29 April, but was joined by a second fleet oiler on 5 May.

Convoy JW67: Sailed from the Clyde on 12 May, four days after German surrender and well before the Soviet Union declared war on Japan, but as all U-boats had not been accounted for, the Royal Navy maintained that convoys should continue for some weeks.

Convoy RA67: Final sailing from the Kola Inlet on 23 May 1945. Between June and August 1945, thirteen merchant ships sailed independently from the Soviet Union westbound, while another five were retained in the Soviet Union.

Appendix II

The Merchant Navy and Shipping

Many British shipping companies employed Indian, Goanese, Chinese, Sudanese and Somali seamen, as deck and engine room hands, stewards and waiters. The gap between the Royal Navy and the Merchant Navy was immense, even at officer level, but at rating level the gap became a yawning chasm. Shipping companies could dismiss a man at forty-eight hours' notice, and he could leave his ship at the same period of notice. Few ratings had the benefit of a longer-term contract, although there were instances of the better companies awarding long-serving senior ratings a pension on retirement. There were also vast differences between companies, with the owners of often elderly tramp steamers usually paying little more than the Board of Trade minimum plus free food and accommodation. Conditions were much better with the smarter passenger liner operators. Much has been made of the poor treatment of the ordinary merchant seaman in the past, but the cost of improving his lot has been the 'flagging out' of tonnage and the loss of jobs. No longer is the idea of 'running away to sea' really an option for restless British youngsters.

At the outset of war, ratings in the Merchant Navy received pay of just £8 per month, which was stopped once their ship was lost even though they might spend a considerable amount of time adrift in the open sea before being rescued, and yet more time after being rescued before finally signing on to another ship. One benefit of the war was that almost all of them suddenly became due danger money, which raised their monthly pay to £24. Merchant Navy ratings did not, as a rule, wear uniform – something that was to diminish their status in the eyes of the Russians – and did not generally receive what would now be described as 'work wear' from their employers. It was all the more of a revelation for many on the Arctic convoys to find that the shipowners had provided them with a basic set of Arctic clothing, including a fur-lined duffle coat, two pairs of heavy woollen long johns, a white submariner's polo-necked thick sweater and heavy sea boot stockings.

For the single unescorted sailings to and from northern Russia, large cash bonuses were offered in advance of £50 for ratings and £100 for officers. The offer of bonuses was not entirely a success on other occasions. Faced with a desperate shortage of seamen, on one occasion bonuses of £100 were offered to prisoners in Glasgow's notorious Barlinnie Gaol to act as firemen on the *Empire Archer*, the commodore's ship on JW51B. The men broached a consignment of rum intended for the Russian-based minesweeper flotilla and a disturbance ensued.

Aboard merchant ships of the day, at night the deck watch consisted of three, a helmsman and two lookouts, as well as an officer, but in wartime this was increased to four, with a helmsman, lookout and two men manning AA guns.

To cope with the shortage of crews, men were effectively conscripted into the Merchant Navy under the wartime direction of labour schemes. Many who might not have considered a career at sea found themselves hastily trained, while others were brought back from retirement. Youngsters of sixteen were too young for service at sea in the Royal Navy, but found themselves employed at sea in the Merchant Navy.

Shipping

The popular belief is that the Liberty ship was a completely American concept, but in fact there were also wartime utility British vessels. The recession between the wars had affected British shipbuilding almost as much as the shipowners. In contrast to American and German practice, British industry was in any case notoriously slow to modernize – keeping equipment long after it had been superseded by more modern and productive machinery, just so long as it did the job. One of the rare exceptions to this rule was the Thompson Yard in Sunderland, in the north-east of England, which had not only modernized during the recession, but had also planned for expansion. In 1935 it built the first of what it conceived as a standard cargo vessel, a coal-fired ship of 9,300 tons, for Hall Brothers of Newcastle, which was put into service as the SS *Embassage*. It was followed by the construction of no less than twenty-four further vessels for a number of owners. As shipping losses mounted in the North Atlantic, the Ministry of War Transport (MOWT) started to purchase ships, which entered service under the management of private sector shipping companies. The MOWT selected the Thompson design as its standard vessel, with the first purchased by it being the SS *Empire Liberty*, operated by Chapman, another Newcastle owner. Thompson's in fact sent the chairman's son, Cyril Thompson, to assist the Kaiser Yard in the United States with the development of the Liberty ship concept, while Kaiser also became a prominent constructor of the much-needed escort carriers. Afterwards, Cyril Thompson also helped to develop shipbuilding in Canada – before the war a much under-industrialized nation.

The naming of ships gave much away to the interested observer. The British standard ships purchased by the MOWT had names prefixed with *Empire*, and included not just cargo ships but also tankers and grain carriers, which were especially suitable for conversion into merchant aircraft carriers. Some confusion was possible with the British naming policy as captured enemy ships and ships built for special roles were also allotted the *Empire* prefix. It says much for tradition that ships were given names rather than numbers, especially since it was not until Churchill became the first wartime First Lord of the Admiralty that British submarines began to have names as a matter of course. The American built and manned Liberty ships were named after prominent American citizens, which meant that they were easily identified, while the 200 or so built in the United States but manned by British crews had names prefixed with Sam, meaning 'superstructure aft of midships'. The British operated ships were oil-fired and had accommodation amidships. Canadian-built ships had the accommodation divided and a cargo hold between the bridge and the funnel – a design feature that was intended to confuse attacking U-boats! Again the names gave away the arrangements under which the ships were built and operated, with those named after *Parks* being Canadian-built and Canadian-crewed, with those Canadian-built but British-crewed having names including *Fort*.

The Liberty ships took an average forty-two days from keel laying to launch, largely as a result of extensive prefabrication allowing much work to be completed away from the shipyard, even well away from the coast. Earlier American standard designs in the 'C' series had been abandoned by this time as being too complicated for rapid expansion of output. The fastest construction of a sea-going merchant vessel on record was that of the Liberty ship *Robert G. Peary*, which took just four days, fifteen-and-a-half hours from keel laying at the Permanente Metals Yard at Richmond, California, to launch on 12 November 1942, and was completed (that is fitted out) just three days later.

No one could describe the Liberty ships as attractive, a criticism that could be levelled at much wartime production, including utility buses, for example. Even Roosevelt described them as 'dreadful-looking objects'. Quality was not their forte either. Much had still to be learnt about prefabricated construction, welding was still in its infancy as a shipbuilding technique, and the shipyards were using much unskilled labour, partly because of expansion, partly because so many of the pre-war workers were in the armed forces. Early Liberty ships produced weld failures, but the later vessels survived and many were still working hard, often having had two or more owners, in the 1960s and into the early 1970s. These ships were also large for the day, with 10,500 deadweight tons of cargo, and were able to steam at 11 knots – far faster than most convoy speeds.

Built to a wartime specification, the Liberty ships were armed from the outset, with a 4-in low-angle gun for defence against surface attack by a submarine, and the AA weapons included a 12-pdr and either Oerlikon or Bofors cannon. Some were fitted with AA rockets, which trailed wires into the air to bring down an attacking aircraft.

Sources and Bibliography

Beevor, Antony, *Stalingrad*, Viking, London, 1998.

Dear, I. C. B., *The Oxford Companion to the Second World War*, OUP, Oxford, 1995.

Harrison, M., *Soviet Planning in Peace and War 1938–1945*, Cambridge, 1985.

Ireland, Bernard, *Jane's Naval History of World War II*, HarperCollins, London, 1998.

Keegan, John, *The Price of Admiralty*, Hutchinson, London, 1988.

Kennedy, Ludovic, *Menace: The Life and Death of the Tirpitz*, Sidgwick & Jackson, London, 1979.

Kilbracken, Lord, *Bring Back My Stringbag: A Stringbag Pilot at War*, Pan Books, London, 1980.

Laffin, John, *British VCs of World War 2*, Sutton, Stroud, 1997.

Mallman Showell, Jak P., *The German Navy Handbook 1939–1945*, Sutton, Stroud, 1999.

Moore, Capt. John, RN, *Escort Carrier*, London, 1944.

Poolman, Kenneth, *Armed Merchant Cruisers*, Leo Cooper in association with Secker & Warburg, London, 1985.

Poolman, Kenneth, *Escort Carrier: HMS Vindex at War*, Secker & Warburg, London, 1983.

Poolman, Kenneth, *The Sea Hunters: Escort Carriers v U-boats 1941–1945*, Arms & Armour Press, London, 1982.

Preston, Antony, *The History of the Royal Navy in the 20th Century*, Bison Books, London, 1987.

Roskill, Captain, S. W., *The Navy at War, 1939–45*, HMSO, London, 1960.

Roskill, Captain S. W., *The War at Sea, 1939–45, Vols I-III*, HMSO, London, 1976.

Thomas, David A., *Battles and Honours of the Royal Navy*, Leo Cooper, Barnsley, 1998.

Thompson, Julian, *Imperial War Museum Book of the War at Sea, 1939–45: The Royal Navy in the Second World War*, IWM/Sidgwick & Jackson, London, 1996.

Van der Vat, Dan, *Standard of Power – The Royal Navy in the Twentieth Century*, Hutchinson, London, 2000.

Various authors, *Istoria Velikoi Otechestvennoi Volny, Sovetskogo Sojuza 1941–1945/The History of the Great Patriotic War of the Soviet Union 1941–1945*, Moscow, 1960.

Winton, John, *The Victoria Cross At Sea*, Michael Joseph, London, 1978

Woodman, Richard, *Arctic Convoys*, John Murray, London, 1974.

Wragg, David, *Carrier Combat*, Sutton, Stroud, 1997.

Wragg, David, *Combustible, Vulnerable, Expendable – The Escort Carrier at War*, Pen & Sword, Barnsley, 2005.

Wragg, David, *Second World War Carrier Campaigns*, Pen & Sword, Barnsley, 2004.

Wragg, David, *Stringbag: The Fairey Swordfish at War*, Pen & Sword, Barnsley, 2004.

Wragg, David, *The Fleet Air Arm Handbook 1939–1945*, Sutton, Stroud, 2001 and 2003.

Wragg, David, *The Royal Navy Handbook 1939–1945*, Sutton, Stroud, 2005.

Index

Burnett, Rear Admiral Robert, RN, 163, 167, 179–80, 183–4, 188–9
Burr, Flying Officer, RAF, 166
Burrough, Rear Admiral, RN, 56, 62, 76, 108, 119, 123, 136
Bv138, Blohm und Voss, 84, 102, 120–2, 139–40, 144, 147, 149, 164–5, 189

C-47 Dakota, Douglas, 50
Cameron, Lieutenant Donald, RN, 95
Campbell, Lieutenant Commander C. H., RN, 84
Canada/Canadian, 12, 57
Canadian Pacific, 57
Cape Kanin, 153, 158
Cape Terberski, 68
Casey, Captain D. A., RNR, 82
Catalina, Consolidated, 131, 144, 146, 159, 162, 166, 168–9
catapult-armed merchant ships, CAM-ships, 31, 41, 119, 121–2, 125, 138, 153, 159, 163, 166
Chamberlain, Neville, 2
Channel Dash, 184
China Squadron, Soviet, 44
Churchill, Winston, 2, 9–10, 15, 34, 52–5, 59, 71, 76, 101, 108, 118, 131
Churchill tank, 34, 148
Ciliax, *Vizeadmiral* Otto, 77–9, 135
Civil War, Russian, 14, 20–1
Civil War, Spanish, 23
Cleveland-class, 90
Clyde, 32, 69
Coastal Command, RAF, 32, 131
Cochrane, Air Vice Marshal the Honourable Ralph, RAF, 97–8
Colthurst, Commander, RN, 165–7
combat air patrol, CAP, 164
Common Brothers, 65
Communism, 4, 22–3, 52, 59
Convoys, 30, 54–70 – a complete list of convoys to and from the Soviet Union using the Arctic route is given between pages 207 and 214, but in addition there are references in the narrative as follows:
  JW51A, 179; JW51B, 179–80, 183–4; JW55B, 184–8, 192; PQ1, 60–1; PQ4, 49; PQ5, 62; PQ6, 63; PQ7, 65; PQ7A, 65; PQ7B, 65; PQ8, 67–8; PQ9, 69–70; PQ10, 69–70; PQ11, 69–70; PQ12, 76–9, 102, 129; PQ13, 79, 82–3, 89, 101–2; PQ14, 101–4, 129; PQ15, 110–12, 119, 129;

PQ16, 33, 119–27, 131, 163, 170; PQ17, 41, 101, 127, 131-62, 167–8, 170–2, 187; PQ18, 101, 161, 163-72; PQ19, 173, 178–9; QP1, 60; QP2, 60–1; QP3, 62; QP4, 65–6; QP5, 68; QP6, 69; QP7, 70; QP8, 76, 78; QP9, 82, 89; QP10, 102–4; QP11, 110, 113–17; QP12, 120–1; QP13, 136–7, 139–40; QP14, 163, 166-9; QP15, 175–7; RA55A, 184–5, 189; SC60, 65
convoy commodores, 34, 76, 82, 102–3, 111, 119, 126, 136–7, 168, 175, 179
Copper, John, 73
Cork, Admiral Sir, 8
Corsair, Vought, 96
Crete, 26, 41
Cripps, Sir Stafford, 24
Crombie, Captain J. F. H., RN, 111, 126–7
Cubison, Commander, 137
Cunningham, Admiral Sir Andrew Browne 'ABC', RN, 132
Curteis, Vice Admiral, RN, 76–7, 82, 112
Czechoslovakia, 22, 38, 198–9

Dam Busters, 97–100;
Darkins, Captain H. S., 125;
defensively equipped merchant ship, DEMS, organization, 31, 83, 103, 125, 173
Denham, Captain Henry, RN, 134
Denmark, 6, 12, 52
Denmark Strait, 138
Denny, Captain, RN, 77
Dönitz, Admiral, later *Grossadmiral*, Karl, 43, 185, 187
Dowding, Captain, later Commodore, J. C. K., 57, 136, 156, 168
Downie, Captain, 103
Dvina, River, 127

E-boats, 62
Eden, Anthony, 62–4
Egerton, Rear Admiral J., RN, 128
Eisenhower, General Dwight, US Army, 198
escort carrier, 163–9;
Essex-class, 90
Estonia, 15
Ethiopia, 3
Ewing, Lieutenant Commander Alastair, RN, 83, 165

Far East, 40
Finland, 14–19, 25, 71;
First World War, 1, 3–5, 15, 20–1, 58, 200

222

225

227

229

230